CAGED WOMEN

The Netflix series *Orange is the New Black* has drawn widespread attention to many of the dysfunctions of prisons and the impact prisons have on those who live and work behind the prison gates. This anthology deepens this public awareness through scholarship on the television program and by exploring the real-world social, psychological, and legal issues female prisoners face. Each chapter references a particular connection to the Netflix series as its starting point of analysis.

This volume brings together scholars to consider both media representations as well as the social justice issues for female inmates alluded to in the Netflix series *Orange is the New Black*. The chapters address myriad issues including cultural representations of race, class, gender, and sexuality; social justice issues for trans-gender inmates; racial dynamics within female prisons; gender and female prison structures/policies; treatment of women in prison; re-incarcerated and previously incarcerated women; self and identity; gender, race, and sentencing; and repro-duction and parenting for female inmates – all with a particular focus on cases and experiences in the U.S.

In doing so, *Caged Women: Incarceration, Representation, & Media* highlights the many areas impacting incarcerated women, going beyond the events shown in the Netflix series to address the wide array of social issues related to women in prison and in women's prisons.

Shirley A. Jackson, is Professor and Chair of the Black Studies Department at Portland State University. She is the editor of *The Handbook of Race, Class, and Gender* (Routledge/Taylor & Francis 2014). She is a sociologist whose research focuses on race/ethnicity, gender, social movements, and inequality.

Laurie L. Gordy, is the Dean of Academic Affairs and Professor of Sociology at Newbury College. Her research interests include gender, class, race in media, gender and sports, and the scholarship of teaching and learning.

SOCIOLOGY RE-WIRED

Edited by **Jodi O'Brien**, Seattle University, and **Marcus Hunter**, University of California, Los Angeles

Sociology Re-Wired captures this combustible moment in American and global societies with new books that innovate and re-configure social and political issues. This hybrid series publishes timely, relevant, original research and textbooks that address significant social issues informed by critical race theory, Black feminism and Queer Studies traditions. Series books are written in a publicly accessible, multi-vocal style broadening the reach and impact of significant scholarly contributions beyond traditional academic audiences.

Some titles published in this series were published under an earlier series name and a different editorship.

Published:

Social Theory Re-Wired: New Connections to Classical and Contemporary Perspectives, Second Edition
by Wesley Longhofer and Daniel Winchester

Social Statistics: Managing Data, Conducting Analyses, Presenting Results, Third Edition
by Thomas J. Linneman

Who Lives, Who Dies, Who Decides?: Abortion, Assisted Dying, Capital Punishment, and Torture, Third Edition
by Sheldon Ekland-Olson

Caged Women: Incarceration, Representation, & Media
edited by Shirley A. Jackson and Laurie L. Gordy

The New Black Sociologists: Historical and Contemporary Perspectives
edited by Marcus A. Hunter

Forthcoming:

All Media are Social
by Andrew Lindner

Note from the Series Editors

The United States incarcerates one third of the world's women prisoners, yet research and policy focus primarily on men and men's prisons. The Netflix original series *Orange is the New Black* (*OITNB*) is a compelling reminder that women, too, are entangled in the policies that send millions of Americans to prison. In addition to being a national hit, the show has captured the attention of scholars from multiple disciplines as a hard-edged, gritty contemporary rendering of the inter-sections of gender, race, class, age, and sexuality as played out in the machinations of the prison industrial complex. *Caged Women* provides a critical social science perspective on *OITNB* as America's mediated lens on women in prison. Editors Shirley Jackson and Laurie Gordy – sociologists specializing in criminology, gender, and race – have assembled a collection of richly engaging essays that examine pro-minent themes and information about women and prison as portrayed in *OITNB*. In addition to a much-needed analysis of women's incarceration, the authors highlight the tensions inherent in visibility rendered through the medium of entertainment television. This superb collection of essays is a must read for anyone interested in gender, race, and criminology, as well as the implications of popular media as form of addressing contemporary social issues. We are very excited to add *Caged Women* to our series.

Jodi O'Brien and Marcus Hunter
Sociology Re-Wired Series Editors

What Americans think of policing, crime and prisons strongly reflects what they have seen on television, and when *Orange is the New Black* began on Netflix in 2013, suddenly the incarceration of women became culturally visible, and the tremendous variety hidden in the single word "women" was exposed. This volume of essays brilliantly captures both the potential unleashed in that dramatic moment and reveals the distortions that existed in our media-based knowledge. The editors have shaped an engaging examination of how women's prisons have become something we viewers believe we now know something about, and so have created a fabulous tool for discussions on social dynamics depicted on screen that can connect to and enliven social analysis about the sweeping effects of mass incarceration on women, men and children today.

Myra Marx Ferree,
University of Wisconsin-Madison

Historically, incarcerated women have been an invisible population, and the important and timely work presented in *Caged Women: Incarceration, Representation, & Media* brings them into the spotlight. From pregnancy and mothering behind bars to more overlooked topics such as racial inequality and transgender prisoners, the chapters in this book offer comprehensive insight into a host of critical issues that combine to bridge the gap between the fictionalized imagery presented in *Orange is the New Black* and other popular media forms and the real lives of women in prison.

Dawn K. Cecil,
University of South Florida St. Petersburg

CAGED WOMEN

Incarceration, Representation, & Media

Edited by Shirley A. Jackson and Laurie L. Gordy

Routledge
Taylor & Francis Group

NEW YORK AND LONDON

First published 2018
by Routledge
711 Third Avenue, New York, NY 10017

and by Routledge
2 Park Square, Milton Park, Abingdon, Oxon OX14 4RN

Routledge is an imprint of the Taylor & Francis Group, an informa business

© 2018 Taylor & Francis

Library of Congress Cataloging in Publication Data
A catalog record for this book has been requested

ISBN: 978-1-138-29739-5 (hbk)
ISBN: 978-1-138-29740-1 (pbk)
ISBN: 978-1-315-09930-9 (ebk)

Typeset in Bembo
by Taylor & Francis Books

CONTENTS

CONTRIBUTORS

Hadar Aviram holds the Harry and Lillian Hastings Research Chair at UC Hastings College of the Law. Her work examines the criminal justice system at the intersection of law, criminology, and public policy. She is the author of *Cheap on Crime: Recession-Era Politics and the Transformation of American Punishment.*

Sabrina Boyer holds a Ph.D. in Educational Leadership and Cultural Foundations. Her research interests include media studies/media theory, Queer Theory, Feminist Theory, Critical Race Theory, Immigration studies, and popular culture. Currently, she is an Associate Professor at Guilford Technical Community College in English and Humanities.

Carrie L. Buist is an Assistant Professor of Criminal Justice at Grand Valley State University. Dr. Buist has published on white collar crime, the social construction of gender, and LGBTQ issues. Most recently, her award-winning book, *Queer Criminology* coauthored with Dr. Emily Lenning calls for a more inclusive criminology.

JaDee Carathers is a doctoral candidate in the Department of Sociology at Portland State University in Portland, Oregon. Her dissertation research is an ethnographic analysis of radical doulas and the reproductive justice movement. More broadly, her research interests include gender and sexualities, bodies and embodiment, and feminist epistemology.

Carolyn Chernoff is a cultural sociologist of everyday inequality. Her research and teaching examine intersectional identity and power in collaborative group settings as well as in media and pop culture.

Miltonette Olivia Craig, M.S., J.D., is a Ph.D. candidate in the College of Criminology and Criminal Justice at Florida State University, a McKnight Doctoral Fellow, and volunteer GED instructor at Federal Correctional Institution, Tallahassee. Her research interests include gender and crime, race/ethnicity and crime, and prisoner reentry and recidivism.

Diane M. Daane, M.S., J.D., is a Distinguished Professor Emeritus at the University of South Carolina Upstate. The criminal justice system as experienced by women has headed her research agenda for many years. Prior to entering academia she worked as a corrections caseworker and practiced law.

Kristin Nicole Dukes, Ph.D. is Professor of Psychology at Simmons College. She researches stereotyping, prejudice, and the application of social psychological research to social justice issues.

Janet Garcia-Hallett is an Assistant Professor at the University of Missouri – Kansas City's Department of Criminal Justice and Criminology, as of Fall 2017. Her research focuses on the impact of incarceration on families and communities of color, the obstacles women face post-incarceration, as well as the racial-ethnic differences in policing strategies.

Laurie L. Gordy, Ph.D., is the Dean of Academic Affairs and Professor of Sociology at Newbury College. Her research interests include: gender, class, race in media, gender and sports, and the scholarship of teaching and learning.

Edward L. W. Green is Assistant Professor of Criminal Justice at Roosevelt University, Chicago, specializing in corrections and criminological theory. He is currently engaged in prison ethnography and social justice.

Tracy L. Hawkins is an Assistant Professor of Philosophy and Religious Studies at the University of Wisconsin-Whitewater. Her research connects popular culture and technology with gender, sexuality, and social responsibility.

Jeanne Holcomb is an Assistant Professor at the University of Dayton. Her research interests lie at the intersection of family life experiences and public health recommendations, especially those relating to parenting and child well-being.

Shirley A. Jackson, Ph.D., is professor and chair of the Black Studies Department at Portland State University. She is the editor of *The Handbook of Race, Class, and Gender* (Routledge/Taylor & Francis, 2014. She is a sociologist whose research focuses on race/ethnicity, gender, social movements, and inequality.

Valerie Jenness is a Professor in the Department of Criminology, Law and Society at the University of California, Irvine. Her research focuses on the politics of crime control and transformations in corrections policy. She is the author of four books and many articles published in sociology, law, and criminology journals.

Edith Kinney, Ph.D., J.D., is an assistant professor in the Department of Justice Studies at San José State University. Her research interests focus on the role that social movement organizations play in criminal justice reform efforts around human trafficking, sexual violence, prison conditions, and reentry.

Sarah Lazzeroni earned an M.S. in Criminology & Criminal Justice and an M.S. in Educational Leadership & Policy from Portland State University. Her research interests include feminist criminology, white collar crime, legal studies, sports, culture, and sociology of the body. She works at Teachers College, Columbia University in New York City.

Emily Lenning is Professor of Criminal Justice at Fayetteville State University. Her publications range from state-sanctioned violence against women to pedagogy. She is co-author of *Queer Criminology* (with Carrie Buist). She is recipient of rewards from the North Carolina Criminal Justice Association and the American Society of Criminology.

Amber Lopez is a graduate student at the University of California Santa Barbara, currently pursuing an MA and ultimately a Ph.D. in sociology. Her current research extends her prior interest in film and society by focusing on the relationship between media, sexuality, gender, and the law.

Rebecca Rodriguez Carey is a doctoral candidate and a Ronald E. McNair fellow in the Department of Sociology at the University of Missouri. Her research interests include crime, deviance, and gender, specifically the social effects of mass incarceration on pregnant prisoners and their families.

Michael Royster is an adjunct faculty member at Prairie View A&M University in the Division of Social Work, Behavioral and Political Sciences and author of the forthcoming book entitled *African American Civil Religion: The Pendulum Guided by the Invisible Hand* by Ashgate Press.

Cheryl D. Snead-Greene holds a Ph.D. from the University of Texas at Austin and has over 15 years of experience in higher education to include administration and teaching. Her research interests include: sociology of education, studies in inequality, and studies in culture and consumerism.

Kimberly Tauches is Assistant Professor of Sociology at Centenary University, focusing on gender and sexuality in the media. Her recent ethnographic study is on how people do gender and understand their own gender performances and the role that sexuality plays in the context of everyday life in urban public spaces.

Terri Toles Patkin is Professor of Communication at Eastern Connecticut State University. She holds a Ph.D. and M.A. from Cornell University and a B.A. from Arcadia University.

Madhavi Venkatesan has a Ph.D., M.A. and B.A. in Economics from Vanderbilt University, a Masters in Sustainability and Environmental Management from Harvard University, and a Masters in Environmental Law and Policy from Vermont Law School. She is a faculty member in Northeastern University's Department of Economics.

Kimber Williams holds a J.D. from University of San Diego and Masters in Justice Studies from Arizona State University. She owns an attorney recruiting firm and is active with the anti-death penalty movement in California, domestic violence issues, and the California Innocence Project.

L. Susan Williams is Professor of sociology and criminology at Kansas State University, specializing in gender and the importance of place. She is currently engaged in prison ethnography and prison design.

Bonnie Zare is Professor of Gender and Women's Studies at the University of Wyoming. She has co-taught a memoir course at the Wyoming Women's Prison and is co-writing a book on the prison. Her research and publications focuses on discourses of identity and social justice in India.

FOREWORD

Valerie Jenness

Netflix has been heralded as a milestone in the production, distribution, and consumption of entertainment. With its modest subscription fee, absence of commercials, growing body of original work, boundary-pushing content, and over 100 million streaming subscribers (approximately 49 million domestic and 45 million international) who watch an average of 1 billion hours per week, Netflix is simply phenomenal. It stimulates talk – and hopefully understanding and critique – about politics (*House of Cards*), international drug cartels (*Narcos*), miscarriages of justice (*Making a Murderer*), dysfunctional families (*Bloodline*), and "older" women managing life's unforeseen challenges (*Grace & Frankie*), just to name a few of the topics that loom large on Netflix.

Orange is the New Black (*OITNB*), the dramedy based loosely on Piper Kerman's book by the same name, put Netflix on the digital, streaming entertainment map in 2013. It did so by focusing story-telling on women in prison, the fastest growing segment of the U.S. prison population; juxtaposing the main characters' lives in prison with their lives outside of prison (i.e., message-by-juxtaposition); capturing the public's imagination and desire to "binge watch." Consequently, the show has become a catalyst for discussions about race, gender, class, sexuality, age, reproductive health, inequality, justice, and the carceral state. It has been hailed by some as a humanizing portrait of a diverse group of female prisoners and condemned by others as yet another Hollywood production that plays fast and loose with the lives of women for the sake of profit. Debates about the show's merits aside, *OITNB* is credited as Netflix's most-watched original series and one of its main characters, Sophia Burset, a transgender prisoner played by Laverne Cox, was identified by *Time* magazine as the fourth most influential fictional character of 2013.

This volume is a testament to the transformative power of Netflix, the incredible visibility of *Orange is the New Black*, and, most importantly, the editors' recognition of the value of treating the series as a venue through which we can do what good education always does: stimulate curiosity and the desire to learn more; acquire, critique, and apply knowledge; understand and respond to the complexities of life by using information tools, research skills, creative thinking, reasoning and analysis; and engage in productive dialogue with people whose experiences differ from our own and who may be separated by time, space, culture, and station in life. Chapters in this volume address important questions about media portrayals of women, crime, and women in prison; the authors bring social science data to bear on assessments of the degree to which *OITNB* captures the empirical realities of women who are locked-up by the state in this era of mass incarceration and point to new ways of thinking about everyday acts of resistance and the disruption of taken-for-granted systems of oppression. For these reasons, this volume is as timely as it is important; likewise, it is as engaging as it is educational (in the truest sense of the word).

A decade ago Dawn Cecil (2007) anticipated the need for a volume like this when she published an article in *Feminist Criminology*, aptly titled "Looking Beyond Caged Heat: Media Images of Women in Prison." As she explains in the first sentence of this important article, "Women in prison are a vulnerable and invisible population; we rarely have the opportunity to hear their stories" (p. 304). This is particularly the case in an era in which, as Jonathan Simon (2000) rightly observed, the golden era of in-prison research – a type of research that was anchored in an up-close, ethnographic view of the interior of prisons – has long since passed. Cecil's "pre Netflix" empirical examination of Hollywood's depictions of female prisoners reveals that, in the absence of contemporary ethnographies on the interior of prisons, these shows depict critical issues facing incarcerated women. Unfortunately, "these programs still highlight factors that excite viewers, including sex and violence, thereby creating a sensationalized and damaging image of women behind bars" (p. 304).

Now, over a decade later, *Behind Prison Walls* follows in this tradition and goes well beyond in systematically interrogating the images promulgated by *OITNB*. The result is a multi-faceted and provocative view of the lives of the women in *OITNB*. Watching *OITNB* and reading this volume prompts me to confront "painful truths" about the carceral state, including, for example, the way race structures prison life, the use of shackles to control women during child birth, the privatization of prisons, the abuse inherent to solitary confinement, and the plight of those who struggle with aging, being infirm, mental illness, and/or being sexually assaulted in prison.

Even more, watching *OITNB* and reading this volume reminds me of the plethora of ways incarcerated women in prison embody and respond to the patriarchal, classist, racist, ageist, and heteronormative structures that create the context in which women live their lives both inside and outside of prison. The characters, identities, images and narratives that have made *OITNB* so wildly popular, bring these truths to life in both painful and humorous ways. The authors' analyses of these images and narratives make these truths infinitely more knowable and subject them to much-needed critique. The payoff is clear: a productive link between a high-profile product of the entertainment industry and the data driven, critical analyses that myth-debunking scholarship offers.

As I was reading this volume, I kept thinking about another important set of connections – the link between my understanding of the empirical realities of women's lives when they are in prison, my reading of Kerman's memoir *Orange is the New Black: My Year in a Women's Prison*, and my own viewing of the *OITNB* series. Reading this volume encouraged my thinking in terms of layers of complexity; it will do the same for others.

As an "in-prison researcher," I have learned we can never over-estimate the horrors of being locked-up or fully comprehend people's adaptations to those horrors. Gresham Sykes' (1958) classic study of a maximum security prison and decades of prison researchers following him have made it clear that "the pains of imprisonment" are born of the deprivation of liberty of all kinds, the scarcity of goods and services, the imposition of a rule-bound regime, and other universal characteristics of carceral environments. Criminologists James Bonta and Paul Gendreau (1990, p. 347) described prisons as "barren landscapes devoid of even the most basic elements of humanity."

The prison landscape is also racialized, gendered, classed and otherwise differentiated and experienced along well-known axes of social inequality. In the memoir that prompted *OITNB*, Piper Kerman speaks powerfully to problematic media images of incarcerated women when she recalls "the buzz" in the prison about the possibility of Martha Stewart doing her time there:

> A lot of nasty things had been written in the press about us. I wasn't the least bit surprised, but the women around me were upset, especially the middle-class ones. An article came out in *People* calling us "the scum of the earth" and speculating about the beat-downs and abuse Martha might suffer.
>
> Annette turned to me after mail call, anguished by her copy. "I have been subscribing to *People* magazine for over thirty-five years. And now I'm the scum of the earth? Are you the scum of the earth, Piper?"
>
> I said I don't think so. But the angst over *People* was nothing compared to the shock waves that rocked the Camp on September 20. I came from the track in the early evening to find a cluster of A-Dorm residents around Pop, cursing and shaking their heads over a newspaper. "What's up?" I asked.
>
> "You're not going to believe this, Piper," said Pop. "You remember that crazy French bitch?"
>
> On September 19 the Sunday Hartford Courant had published a front-page story – we always got newspapers a day behind, so the institution could "control the flow of information." Staff writer Lynne Tuohy had gotten an exclusive with a recently released Camper, "Barbara," whom Martha had

contacted for the inside scoop on life in Danbury Camp. And "Barbara" had some interesting things to say.

> "Once the shock of being in jail was over, it became a holiday," Barbara said in an interview after her talk with Stewart. "I didn't have to cook. I didn't have to clean. I didn't have to shop. I didn't have to drive. I didn't have to buy gas. They have an ice machine, ironing boards. It was a like a big hotel."

It was Levy, all right. After being whisked away to testify against her chiseler ex-boyfriend, she reappeared in the Camp for one short week in June, and then she was released, her six month sentence over. Apparently her stay had been far more enjoyable than she had let on when we had the pleasure of her company. She was singing the prisons praises in the paper...

> *(Kerman 2011, pp. 198–199)*

Barbara's praises included two libraries, the food, and getting her hair done every week. As she concluded, "This is a place that is so magnificent" (Kerman 2011, p. 199). This excessively positive portrayal of prison life left the other women still in prison furious, according to Kerman. As another prisoner reported to Kerman, "Why would she lie? You have the opportunity to get the truth out there about this place and instead she makes up these lies? We have nothing here, and she makes it sounds like a picnic..." (Kerman 2011, p. 11).

At the heart of this exchange anchored in realities, images, and positionality is a larger question that animates the work in *Caged Women*, whose experience prevails and whose experience is rendered invisible? Multiple perspectives are in play in this volume: the actual lived experiences of women in prison, as known through the lens of scholarly work; the best-selling memoir written by Piper Kerman; and the multiple award winning *OITNB* dramedy series.

The importance of a critical analysis of this nexus of perspectives and experience reminds me of a line one of my favorite *OITNB* characters, Suzanne Warren (aka "Crazy Eyes"), said in the most recent season of *OITNB* (a season not included for analysis in this volume). Injured and walking through a dark hallway in the middle of an ongoing prison riot that has left the prison without electricity, and thus without light, she tries to talk herself out of her fear:

> I am not afraid of the dark. The universe is dark all of the time. Stars are what make it light. So, it's always night, depending on how hard you look. Or, day, depending on how you see it. What's important is that ghosts are not real.

> *(Season 5, Episode #3)*

As I see it, this is a good synopsis for the entire series as well as how it is juxtaposed with social science analyses throughout this volume. The reality depends on how you look at it.

From my point of view, ghosts might not be real. And images are real insofar as they provide a reflective mirror for us to see and understand ourselves and our world, which in turn has demonstrable consequences – good and bad. What is undeniably real is the pain of imprisonment inflicted on women, and the role media images and narratives play in perpetuating beliefs that serve to aggravate or mitigate this state inflicted pain. *Caged Women* invites us to untangle these webs of meanings and realities, an important project for television watchers in the age of Netflix, as well as for those in the business of learning about prison, and for policymakers who play a key role in shaping our approach to state-directed punishment.

References

Bonta, J., & Gendreau, P. (1990). "Re-examining the Cruel and Unusual Punishment of Prison Life." *Law and Human Behavior*14, 347–366.

Dawn, C. K. (2007). "Looking Beyond Caged Heat: Media Images of Women in Prison." *Feminist Criminology* 2(4), 304–326.

Kerman, P. (2011). *Orange is the New Black: My Year in a Women's Prison*. New York: Spiegel & Grau.

Simon, J. (2000). "The 'Society of Captives' in the Era of Hyper-Incarceration." *Theoretical Criminology* 4(3), 285–308.

Sykes, G. (1958). *The Society of Captives: A Study of a Maximum Security Prison*. Princeton, NJ: Princeton University Press.

INTRODUCTION

Orange is the New Black (*OITNB*), created and produced by Jenji Kohan in 2013 on Netflix, takes the audience behind the prison gates to see the experiences, interactions, and backgrounds of fictitious female inmates and staff. It is based loosely on Piper Kerman's memoir of the same name. Kerman served 15 months in a federal prison for her minor role in an international drug dealing operation 10 years earlier. While the Netflix series follows the main character loosely based on Piper Kerman's memoir, it extends beyond that to present the "life stories" (through flashbacks) of several main characters of diverse races, ethnicities, gender identities, and sexualities. As with the memoir, the Netflix series is set in a fictitious Litchfield Penitentiary, a federal correctional facility, and covers many social issues such as sexual assault, prison privatization, relationships, religion, etc.

OITNB, while fictional, has drawn attention to many of the dysfunctions of prisons as well as the impact prisons have on those who live behind the prison gates. The benefits of shows such as *OITNB* is to raise awareness about issues that inmates face, yet often the seriousness of such issues gets lost in the humor. Many authors in this anthology explore the tension between the efforts of *OITNB* to shed light on serious issues that female inmates face while at the same time using them for entertainment purposes and thereby minimizing or dramatizing the issues. Given that the media representation and the scholarly research still remains centered on male crime and male inmates, the aim of our anthology is to highlight many areas impacting incarcerated women. The works in this volume explore the lives of incarcerated young women, trans women, and adult women. The contributors analyze the intricate nature of prison identity, factors that shape motherhood, hate crimes, and public policy. What are the characteristics of women in real prisons? How has the population of women in prison changed?

Characteristics of Female Inmates in the U.S.

The number of females in prison has grown tremendously despite the decline in recent years in the prison population overall. According to the U.S. Bureau of Justice Statistics, the percentage of females in prison increased 18.1% between 2010 and 2014 (Minton & Zeng, 2015). While males still make up the majority of inmates, females are now at the highest percentage of the prison population. The Sentencing Project is a non profit agency that works to inform the public about the U.S. prison population and inequities in the prison system and to advocate for prison reform. Their data highlights that the racial disparities in women's prisons have been declining since 2000 yet even still the rate of African American women is 2.5 times the rate of White women and the rate of Latinas is 1.4 times the rate of White women. With the number of African American and Latina women who are arrested, convicted, and sentenced to prison, women's prisons, like their male counterparts, are overwhelmingly filled with black and brown bodies.

One of the biggest changes, according to The Sentencing Project, in the women's prison population is the reasons women are being sent to prison. Women are increasingly serving time in prison for drug offenses. Specifically, the percentage of women in state prisons for drug offenses has increased from 12% to 24% between 1986 and 2014. In the early years of the War on Drugs, mandatory sentencing led to what The Sentencing Project refers to as "the girlfriend problem." This is when large numbers of women were incarcerated in large part due to their connections to a partner involved in the drug trade. Although the male partner, oftentimes a boyfriend, was able to give important information on other individuals who were higher up in the drug trade, they could offer up names in return for a shorter sentence. The women, less well-positioned in knowing who was involved in the higher echelons of the drug trade, tended to have less to offer and thus, served lengthy prison sentences.

Another major change in the demographics of women in prison, according to The Sentencing Project, is the increase in the number of mothers imprisoned. Specifically, the incarceration rates for mothers has increased between the years 1991 and 2007 by 122%. With many of those incarcerated being persons of color, this does not bode well for large numbers of children whose parents lose custody or contact with them during or after their release. Jason Baker and colleagues explored the relationships between incarcerated mothers, their children, and their children's grandmothers, finding that this type of intergenerational co-parenting is an important step in addressing concerns of incarcerated mothers regarding the care of their children and their children's potential future behavioral problems. Mothering, giving birth, and other parenting issues while in prison are matters that several contributors in this work address. Incarceration is unable to completely prevent women from engaging in roles or activities that were placed in motion prior to their imprisonment. For some imprisoned women, mothering is key to their identities and they try hard to maintain this status.

Intersectional Approach to Analyzing Women in Prison

Sociologists Candace West and Don H. Zimmerman coined the concept of "doing gender" to explain how gender is socially created, challenged, and re-created through our everyday interactions, behaviors, and experiences. What do you envision when you hear the term, prison? Most likely it is a very violent and physically aggressive place filled with males. Both the actual prisons and the cultural images of prisons are based on a male and masculine model. This is evidenced by the assumptions about both who should work within prisons and how to treat those housed within prisons. Sociologist Dana Britton, analyzes how broader cultural meanings and structural arrangements around gender, race, social class, and sexuality shape the historical and contemporary design and operation of prisons. As with any social institution, prisons reflect the broader historical, cultural, and social context. Given the association of masculinity with violence in the U.S. culture, crime is often associated with males. This is reinforced by the way the media often presents prisons as predominantly male. Female inmates and female criminals receive very little attention in U.S. culture given this gendering of prisons.

Taking this analysis further, sociologist Jill McCorkel includes the intersections of race and gender in shaping policies and practices within female prisons. She notes that approaches towards female inmates have shifted to a "responsibilization" approach in which individual inmates are held responsible for their own efforts to change. According to McCorkel, this shift to responsibilization is driven by the increasing privatization of prisons and racial inequality. Similar to Michelle Alexander and Loïc Wacquant, and others, McCorkel notes that the war on drugs has contributed to disproportionate numbers of African American men and women in prison. As the female prison demographics shifted to result in more African American females imprisoned, McCorkel argues in her work *Breaking Women: Gender, Race, and the New Politics of Imprisonment* that race is central to both distinguishing the "good" from the "bad" inmates and also central to the adoption of a more "get tough" policy in female prisons.

How Does Prison Affect Images of Prisoners?

According to sociologist Loïc Wacquant (2009), while incarceration largely impacts those who are poor, it is their formerly incarcerated status that works to keep them poor. They are not likely to be hired when compared to their never incarcerated peers as imprisonment is stigmatized. Stigma, according to Erving Goffman, is a way of characterizing those who are different as being abnormal. Furthermore, as Devah Pager explains in her research on men with a criminal record, race may account for lack of employment even when one does not have a record. Pager found this to be especially the case with African American men and White men, with the latter being preferred at a slightly higher rate as employees even when they had criminal records and the former did not.

Sociologists and communication scholars, such as Mira Sotirovic, have shown how the media has a powerful influence on people's attitudes about social issues and social groups. It is important to examine how various social groups are represented in the media particularly in this day and age given the amount of time people spend interacting with the media. Many of those who have studied how the media presents crime, including legal scholars Robert Entman and Kimberly Gross, conclude that the media often reinforces stereotypes of African American and Latinos as violent and as criminals. This is particularly the case for African American and Latino males. Similarly, sociologist Patricia Hill Collins notes that African American women are often represented in the media as physically aggressive and/or as sexually loose. In a study of the television show, *Desperate Housewives*, media expert Debra Merskin concludes that the Latina in the show is highly sexualized and presented as using her sexuality to get what she wants. Several authors in our book also examine how *OITNB* presents Latinas and African American females and the effects of such representations. Sociologists note how the media plays a large part in socializing people into seeing social groups in certain ways. If the media presents African Americans and Latinos as more deviant then societal members may begin to perceive African Americans and Latinos in this way and thus be more inclined to also view these groups as criminals.

Conclusion

Given the popularity of crime shows, it is important to examine the media portrayals of crime and criminals, as these images can shape cultural attitudes towards crime and criminals. *OITNB* is a successful show and it has sparked many discussions about female inmates while also raising concerns about their portrayals. As the number of females in prison has increased tremendously over the past 10 years, it is important to understand the experiences of incarcerated females and the kinds of issues that impact the women, their families, and the larger society. What are the opportunities for changing who enters or re-enters prison that might be addressed through changes in policy? Additionally, what are the kinds of barriers to recidivism that exist for these women?

This book is organized around several key themes: identity, inequality, mothering, prison policies, and culture. Consider the following questions as you read this book:

- How does prison affect how inmates see themselves and how others see them?
- What role does racial inequality play in the perceptions and experiences of inmates?
- How do female inmates manage pregnancy and parenting?

- How do societal perceptions of females shape their crime and their experiences with the criminal justice system? What impacts do prison rules and practices have on females in prison and also upon their release?
- How do cultural practices and cultural beliefs shape the experiences of female inmates?

We hope that through exploration of these issues the reader will gain a deeper understanding of how females end up in prison, how females experience prison, and how prison impacts females' abilities to maintain a sense of self in our society. While *OITNB* certainly raised awareness about the issues facing incarcerated females, we hope this book advances the conversation from awareness to action. Ideally, we hope this knowledge can lead to more informed social policies that avoid or prevent incarceration and that more adequately meet the needs of those females who are incarcerated.

We end each chapter with recommended readings. This will offer the reader additional information on key topics. Additionally, within each chapter, there are sources of information that serve to enhance readers' understanding of the breadth and depth of research that exists and the questions that remain unanswered. We encourage the reader to explore these and not only continue but actively participate in the dialogue.

References and Further Reading

Alexander, M. (2010). *The new Jim Crow: Mass incarceration in the age of colorblindness.* New York: New Press.

Baker, J.McHale, J.Strozier, A., & Cecil, D. (2010). Mother–grandmother coparenting relationships in families with incarcerated mothers: A pilot investigation. *Family Process,* 49(2), 165–184.

Entman, R.E., & Gross, K.A. (2008). Race to judgment: Stereotyping media and criminal defendants. *Law and Contemporary Problems,* 71, 93–133.

Goffman, E. (1963). *Stigma: Notes on the management of spoiled identity.* New York: Simon & Schuster.

Hall, S. (1981). The whites of their eyes: Racist ideologies and the media. In G. Bridges & R. Brunt (Eds.), *Silver linings: Some strategies for the Eighties* (pp. 28–52). London, UK: Lawrence & Wishart, Ltd.

hooks, b. (1995). *Killing rage: Ending racism.* New York: Henry, Holt & Company.

Kerman, P. (2011). *Orange is the new black: My year in a women's prison.* New York: Spiegel & Grau.

Lotze, G., Ravindran, N., & Myers, B. (2010). Moral emotions, emotion self-regulation, callous-unemotional traits, and problem behavior in children of incarcerated mothers. *Journal of Child and Family Studies,* 19(6), 702–713.

McCorkel, J.A. (2013). *Breaking women: Gender, race, and the new politics of imprisonment.* New York: New York University Press.

Minton, T.D., & Zeng, Z. (2015). Prison and jail inmates at midyear 2014 series. Retrieved fromhttps://www.bjs.gov/index.cfm?ty=pbdetail&iid=5299

Pager, D. (2003). The mark of a criminal record. *American Journal of Sociology*, 108(5), 937–975.

Wacquant, L. (2002). From slavery to mass incarceration: Rethinking the race question in the U.S. *New Left Review*, 13: 41–60.

Wacquant, L. (2009). *Punishing the poor: The neoliberal government of social insecurity*. Durham, NC: Duke University Press.

West, C., & Zimmerman, D. (1987). Doing gender. *Gender and Society*, 1, 125–151.

PART 1

Identity Construction and Prison

Shirley A. Jackson

Are identities in prison constructed the same as those outside of prison? Are prisoners able to maintain the outside prison walls identities with their inside prison walls identities? How does treatment of other prisoners and prison staff impact the ability of prisoners to maintain and challenge identities? These are important considerations as we enter the world of women in prison. The forces that shape their experiences are both internal and external. The past that was left on the outside must often be rebuilt or reshaped in ways that prevent disorder in the lives of imprisoned women, yet, these can also be at odds with prison life based on availability of resources, the acceptance of fellow inmates, responses of staff, and prison policies. In this chapter, these questions are addressed as authors aim to explore the ways in which identities are constructed and reconstructed, challenged, accepted, and maintained.

Erving Goffman's work on identity construction is especially instructive as we delve into the essays in this section (1959; 1967). Goffman's "dramaturgical approach" (1959) describes how we, as social actors, live our lives as though we are performing a role. We perform roles on a stage, so to speak. A case in point is the commonly held understanding of how one must act once entering prison – the persona of the prison tough. This individual rarely smiles, shares little eye contact with others, and most of all, does not take crap from anyone. This is understood to be a survival technique whereby those who adopt this role successfully will survive. Unfortunately, those less capable of adopting the role or maintaining it whereby others believe it, will find themselves victimized. Fictional prison life as depicted in the media often shows the weak prisoner – man or woman – who is considered bait by the stronger prisoners. They are shaped into something different as their sense of agency, well-being, and even safety, are oftentimes seriously compromised.

Within the walls of the prison, a total institution, are rules and expectations for behavior and treatment. For those who are veering from the path of normative social behavior, prisons can be especially difficult to navigate as the chapters in this section demonstrate. We first see this through the chapters that follow which discuss the lives of female prisoners in reality and those in the fictional Netflix series, *Orange is the New Black*. The "dramedy" series connects the poignant lives of prisoners in dramatic ways interspersed with humor. The viewer is introduced to myriad characters whose life histories and explanations of how they landed in prison are disclosed as the series unfolds. As women who are depicted wear the stigma of prisoner, they must conform in ways that contradict their lives beyond the prison walls.

Goffman's work *Stigma* (1963) argues that individuals may attempt to ward off the stigma attached to them. Attempts to normalize their appearance and inter-actions with others are important in maintaining a sense of agency and normality. For transgender female prisoners, this can include maintaining their appearance on the inside as they did outside the prison through the use of available beauty products – some purchased, others homemade. For mothers, this can be fomen-ted in their identification as mothers who reside within the prison without access to or contact with their children. Thus, motherhood as an identity may be adhered to even while others engage in the actual care of their children.

In "Who Are You Really? Identity, Authenticity, and Narrative in *Orange Is the New Black*" Carolyn Chernoff and Kimberly Tauches explore the ways in which authentic identities are challenged using an example not uncommon to transgender prisoners – that of having to not only explain but "validate" their identity. In drawing from an example in the series, *Orange is the New Black*, the desire to know of prisoners becomes a *need* to know who this interloper is who shares their space. As a result, well-liked character Sophia Burset becomes a victim of violence – in essence, a hate crime. Yet, her identity as a woman who has been beaten is not taken seriously by those who attack her and those who respond. When she attempts to clarify the situation to the prison staff, it is she, the victim, who is sent to solitary confinement for her own safety. Her identity is unaccepted, her authenticity challenged, and her narrative ignored.

The concepts of identity and representation of self are inextricably linked in the work of Chernoff and Tauches, particularly when they explore the ways in which prisoners must negotiate their day-to-day lives while also remaining safe. The matter of safety is foremost in the minds of those whose very lifestyles led to their imprisonment; but also for those for whom just "being" has made the target of other prisoners and staff. Although it is possible to escape some of the com-plexities while navigating through the system; not everyone does so easily. Impediments, whether, structural, personal, or situational, exist and one must find ways to maneuver through or manipulate them.

L. Sue Williams, Edward Green, and Kimberly Williams share their research on 32 women who poignantly tell their stories of how they have transitioned from civilian to felon. The authors connect their experiences to characters in the series *Orange is the New Black* providing insight into how women develop survival strategies and make sense of the world around them. The authors refer to the "identity vertigo" experienced by the series' main character Piper Chapman which is a suitable characterization of women who find that their lives as they knew them no longer exist.

While the authors discuss the physical and social changes incarcerated women experience, they broach the masculine structure of prisons. Prisons were made with men in mind, and thus, imprisonment is a gendered one for women who are otherized as women who are in prison. It is within these walls that women struggle to maintain their identities. In reflecting on several characters in the show, we see them impart beauty tips, focus on their looks even in the absence of the male partners they want to attract, and engage in gendered activities to which they have been socialized to accept as the rule. Williams, Green, and Williams contend that women find themselves emphasizing femininity. Their respondents recognize the importance of looking like you belong in prison or not looking like you belong. The latter receive far better treatment from the correctional officers compared to their counterparts who, by virtue of their less feminine appearance, look like they belong. For some of these women, acts of resistance can include challenging notions of gender by refusing to look feminine, choosing to continue to look feminine using products such as make-up or hair styling tools. Yet, for others, resistance comes in the form of behaving like women in men's prisons.

Emily Lenning and Carrie L. Buist focus on the stigmatized transgender woman prisoner. They shift the discussion forward as they discuss the severity of incarceration of transgender women prisoners in men's prisons. In the U.S., prison assignment is based on genitalia and not gender presentation. This can result in increased incidents of violence – sexual and physical – against transgender prisoners. As discussed in the work of Jenness & Fenstermaker (2013) and Sumner, Sexton, Jenness, and Maxson (2014), prison life can be problematic and traumatic if one is placed in a prison that contradicts one's gender presentation. With Lenning and Buist, they incorporate voices of those who often are unheard and the most victimized.

Lenning and Buist visit the attack on one of the most popular characters in *OITNB*, transgender prisoner, Sophia Burset. They underscore the vicious attack as a social justice issue because she is not only a victimized prisoner but the victim of a hate crime. Sophia's plight is not uncommon. She is victim in myriad ways due to being transgender. She is segregated from the other prisoners after they beat her mercilessly, for her own good, according to the correctional officers. She has to fight for the hormones to maintain her appearance as a woman; something that is a threat to not only how she identifies but how she presents to others. A transgender woman in a woman's prison has her safety and identity jeopardized in multiple ways.

Throughout this book, the reader will find several examples of socialization, deviance, and conformity. The selections in this first section of the book give readers an opportunity to gain understanding of the ways in which identities are malleable, while also remaining unvarying in important aspects. When prisoners attempt to maintain their outside personas they attempt to do so in settings that are designed to keep them from expressing themselves in ways that conflict with the prison as an institution that enforces conformity. All the while, in order to feel like "themselves" prisoners find it necessary to challenge concepts of not only who they are but who they should be.

References

Goffman, E. (1959). *The Presentation of Self in Everyday Life*. Garden City, NY: Doubleday.

Goffman, E. (1967). *Interaction Ritual*. New York: Pantheon.

Jenness, V., & Fenstermaker, S. (2013). Agnes goes to prison: Gender authenticity, transgender inmates in prisons for men, and pursuit of "the real deal". *Gender & Society, 28*(1), 5–31.

Sumner, J., Sexton, L., Jenness, V., & Maxson, C. (2014). The (pink) elephant in the room: The structure and experience of race and violence in the lives of transgender inmates in California Prison. In S. Jackson (Ed.), *Routledge International Handbook of Race, Class, and Gender* (pp. 128–143). London: Routledge.

1

WHO ARE YOU REALLY?

Identity, Authenticity, and Narrative in *Orange is the New Black*

Carolyn Chernoff and Kimberly Tauches

Introduction

While Season 3 of the Netflix series *Orange is the New Black* (*OITNB*) makes the question of *true* or *authentic identity* transparent, from its start this show has troubled the notion of who an incarcerated woman "really" is. In many ways, *OITNB* presents nuanced representations of women, some of whom may have committed heinous crimes, outside the standard script of *prison lesbian, victim,* or *sociopath*. At the same time, the narrative frame as well as the details of various stories reduce some character's identities to single stories. Focusing on the tension between prurience and empathy, this chapter will analyze the way *OITNB* simultaneously fixes individual identities at a single point while complexifying other aspects of the "woman in prison." We draw on feminist, postmodern, and queer theory to argue that identity is never single or simple, and yet the frameworks of the TV show necessarily limit and shape the audience's understandings of *who these women really are*. This framework disrupts conventional narratives, but not unproblematically. For women in Litchfield, the audience presumes that the moment of truth is whatever event led to their arrest – and yet *OITNB* as a show uses flashbacks, moments of redemption and revulsion, and other on-screen relationships to show the unstable narrative of the modern self. We argue that the way the show constructs authentic identity impacts viewers' understanding of women in the prison-industrial complex in three ways: (1) the "true" identity as criminal; (2) the "true" identity as human being; and (3) the way the show itself constructs "truth" through poignant and prurient uses of the flashback.

Identity and Authenticity in *OITNB*

Orange is the New Black (*OITNB*) produces a narrative of a group of women in Litchfield prison – one that complexifies issues of identity and authenticity, while also creating questions about representation and the blanket instability inherent in knowledge production around identity and identity politics. The questions around identity include who a person is, who a person was, and who a person will become. According to gender theorist Judith Butler, theories of identity from feminist, postmodern, and queer perspectives question the stability of identity, based on issues of definition, and well as social and contextual circumstances. Moving beyond the stereotypical women in prison sexploitation genre which reinforces criminal/authentic lesbian or queer identities with exploited/innocent sex objects as noted in the work of historian Estelle Freedman and several other scholars, *OITNB* allows for a multiplicity of identity narratives based on race, class, gender, and sexuality.

And yet the show does not (and perhaps cannot) escape the women in prison stereotypes. In the show, questions of representation and authenticity come to the forefront. Who is represented, in what ways, and to what effect are questions that might be asked about the characters, narratives, and identities portrayed onscreen. As a work of fiction, the series depicts a much more racially diverse group of women than the current US incarceration statistics suggest, or at least a whiter group, with more relative class privilege and education, and more multiracial interaction than most contemporary prisons and jails. On one hand, The Sentencing Project finds the show has been lauded for its efforts to educate the general viewing public about the impact of race and class inequality on US rates of incarceration, but again, the show certainly paints a rosier picture of the experience of incarceration than real life. The series both highlights and downplays the impact of racialized and class-based social inequality on incarcerated women.

The show is framed in a way that encourages the audience to see race and class as markers of authentic identity and belonging in complicated ways across the seasons. From the show's first season, its ostensible protagonist, Piper Chapman, is portrayed as someone who does not belong in Litchfield. Her whiteness and class privilege are a part of that sense of misfit – but her performance of identity also marks her as someone out of context, and perhaps inauthentic within the frame of the prison. We see this sense of misfit or inauthenticity in her earliest interactions with fellow inmate "Nicky" Nichols. Nichols is White and class-privileged, like Chapman, but her queer identity, rough edges, and swagger, whether ascribed to her lesbianism or the drug addiction that landed her behind bars, makes her an "authentic," if unlikely, inmate.

Nichols and Chapman may share the many identity markers, but Nichols immediately sizes Chapman up as inauthentic, as someone who does not, and perhaps cannot, belong:

NICHOLS: Look at you, blondie. What'd you do?
CHAPMAN: Aren't you not supposed to ask that question? I read that you're not supposed to ask that.
NICHOLS: You read that? What, you studied for prison?

The notion of authentic truth that underlies the question of identity – who are you really – is the primary question that is faced by the characters on this show. This particular question is answered in two ways: first through the behaviors of individuals while in prison, and second through the use of flashbacks. The use of flashback offers us a glimpse of not only how these characters landed in prison, but also the motivations of their behaviors while incarcerated. Ongoing behavior and flashbacks tell us, the viewers, who these women are and who they were, in ways that are not possible based solely on their daily lives within the walls of the prison. As viewers, we read authenticity and continuity into this mix of past and present. Occasionally, the difference between past and present disrupts who we think a character really is, most notably in the case of White characters Lorna Morello and Tiffany "Pennsatucky" Doggett, but usually the story told reinforces common narratives of what historian Estelle Freedman refers to as "real criminals" and "innocent victims."

In order to make sense of the layered representations of the women in Litchfield, we employ a queer, feminist, postmodern framework through which we analyze depictions of women in the prison–industrial complex: (1) the "true" identity as criminal; (2) the "true" identity as human being; and (3) the way the show itself constructs "truth" through poignant and prurient uses of the flashback.

Identity, Feminism, and the Queer Turn: Incarcerated Bodies That Matter

Identity politics became popular in the 1960s when marginalized groups came together to build a movement based on their marginalized identity. The ideology of one single marginalized identity quickly came under attack by those like the Combahee River Collective Statement, sociologist Patricia Hill Collins and critical race scholar Kimberlé Crenshaw who addressed oppression based on multiple target identities. The women's movement was no different, and the focus became one of women and women's issues. Identity as a woman became a focal point of the movement, and the narrative of who counts as a woman and the marginalization that was faced became a contentious issue within the movement, particularly in terms of the ways in which intersecting oppressions operate. This theoretical model allowed us to consider how multiple identities intersect to create particular subject positions based on race, class, gender, and sexuality – ones that differ greatly from the issues of straight middle-class, White feminists.

Postmodern, queer feminist theory adds to the ways in which identity can be questioned. In "Imitation and Insubordination" Butler (2004) questions identity politics and the problematics of stating a particular identity at any particular point in time. In particular, Judith Butler finds problematic the constant reification of identity, as continuously naming and stating an identity reifies its definition, includes some in the identity category and excludes others. Butler questions what the term lesbian means, and whether lesbian will mean the same thing over time, and has always meant the same thing. She bases her discussion on Michel Foucault's paradoxical argument regarding identity – while it regulates us, it also offers us a space in which we might come together and resist that very regulation. The very basis of engaging with an identity is to engage in resignification and allows the potential for resistance to that very identity category.

The ideology of identity politics stems from a narrative and the very definition of who counts as a woman and who does not. The narratives that seem to fit the more narrow definition of what it means to be a woman are often deemed most authentic. Complicating this issue is the notion of sexuality – at the heart of most of these storylines are the relationships between these characters as well as between the characters and the outside world. *OITNB* draws on the history of the visual representation of female masculinity and incarcerated women, both of which posit incarcerated women as more or less authentic or "real" based on racialized aspects of gender.

Gender studies scholar Jack Halberstam (1998) offers a useful and complicated discussion of the butch in cinema. Ranging from a discussion of identity, representation, gaze, and intersections, the author provides a convincing analysis of the multiple ways in which butchness might be read, and moves beyond the familiar tropes of positive or negative analyses of stereotypes. The author acknowledges that there are dangers in terms of reifying the stereotypes of "the mythic mannish lesbian" according to cultural anthropologist and women's studies scholar Esther Newton, but also notes that there is power in representation of historically marginalized gender and sexual identities.

Halberstam also provides us with a discussion of the complications that readings of butchness might produce. In an analysis of the kd lang/Cindy Crawford *Vanity Fair* cover, Halberstam notes the multiple access points of viewers, as well as the complications of the identificatory display of butch/femme noting,

> By posting a conventional pinup as the object of butch lesbian desire, the photo-fantasy makes an unholy alliance between the male gaze and a more queer butch gaze. …flaunts stereotypes and by doing so explores the tension between homophobic and queer representation [and] calls for many different identificatory strategies from viewers: a heterosexual male must access his desire for Crawford only through the masculinity of a lesbian; a straight woman might identify with Crawford and desire lang; a queer viewer finds that dyke desire is mobile here and may take up butch, femme, masculine, or feminine spectator positions.
>
> *(1998, p. 176)*

In this discussion we see that there are many different ways in which the viewer might read that particular image, and also many different understandings that might be gleaned from the image. The issue of femme visibility is one major concern, and as Halberstam notes, Crawford, positioned as femme, is only visible as such in relation to lang, the visible butch. Further aiding in our analysis, Halberstam discusses the ways in which butchness might also be read in terms of black and Latinx bodies. The Black and Latinx and also White forms of femininity, particularly in terms of how we might be able to understand whether these images are reifying racial stereotypes or the "modes of power", are being questioned and subverted through alternative images of masculinity.

Jack Halberstam's analysis of the butch/femme relationship within the prison context provides a useful understanding of the importance of class, gender, and sexuality. The dichotomy of the innocent, new-to-prison femme, and the older, predatory butch (whom the femme must eventually turn into to survive) in these movies, according to Halberstam (1998, p. 202), offer a critique: "by making femininity into a luxury and a privilege, the prison film makes clear links between poverty, female masculinity, and the predatory butch" while simultaneously providing a cautionary message about the erasure of femininity through female criminality.

While there seems to be a surfeit of research on men in prison films (particularly films like *The Shawshank Redemption, The Green Mile,* and *Dead Man Walking*), "men in prison" has not become a separate media genre in the way "women in prison" films and pulp novels have. This is partly because of norms around gender and incarceration, where men in prison are simply men in a carceral context, whereas for women, the act of incarceration, though numerically significant, is an act of deviance conflated with gender and sexuality. Estelle Freedman writes about "the prison lesbian" as a "menacing social type", as a type of master status where incarceration itself confirms gendered and sexual deviance. Freedman traces this to the period following World War II, and further comments on the racialized aspects of the prison lesbian: Black women were assumed to be aggressive, White women assumed to be passive (although not long after, as women and gender studies professor Ann Ciasullo writes, White women were also seen to occupy the "aggressive" or "masculine" prison lesbian category). One of the reasons that the aggressive, masculine, predatory prison lesbian remains a trope in mass media, says Ciasullo (2008, p. 196), is because she is "an ideal figure onto which the cultural imaginary can project anxiety and ardor, loathing and lust, all with the ultimate promise that that which is dangerous and thrilling will be contained."

Film theorist Laura Mulvey's seminal work on the camera as male gaze (1975) reinforces aspects of the carceral state as masculine, heteronormative, and punitive: punishing women's bodies and sexual expressions unless for the benefit of men in power. While represented as strong – indeed, as violent, amoral predators – the women in prison genre embody what Ann Ciasullo (2008, p. 195) calls "an enduring cultural erotic fantasy," where women are "trapped with one another in a criminal and sexual underworld." Yet again, this underscores the situational deviance and desperation of incarcerated women, most of whom, it was suggested by print and media examples of the genre, will eventually leave prison and be "redeemed" by heterosexuality. The one character who is beyond redemption is the butch lesbian, usually positioned as the "real criminal" to the "innocent victim" of the (often temporary) femme. In the prison lesbian, we see the idea of the true invert, cited first in the work of Havelock Ellis in the late 1800s. These are those who will die in prison, so serious is their breach of social norms. The seeming permanence of the prison lesbian, and of women in prison films and novels as erotic and ultimately heteronormative pulp matters, though, partly because these reductive and salacious images reinforce the marginalization and objectification of real live incarcerated women. As criminology professor Dawn K. Cecil argues, it is not only fiction that reinforces marginalization – nonfiction media also depicts incarcerated women in a warren of sensationalized and ultimately damaging images.

And yet there is tension among the analyses of the women in prison genre as something that necessarily pathologizes lesbian, queer, trans, and gender non-conforming women, while reasserting heteronormativity. As Suzanna Danuta Walters writes, the women in prison genre also presents "images of women and women's relationships rarely found in more mainstream genres. Women in this world live together, love together, fight each other, and most centrally, fight back against the largely male systems of brutal domination that keep them all down" (2001, p. 106). In their fight against largely male systems of domination, in fact, genderqueer and sexually queer women in prison occasionally win. The question of whose identity is seen as authentic, real, or true, however, impacts on empathy viewers might feel for different characters. In turn, empathy for fictional incarcerated women can legitimate structural oppression when "real criminals" are seen as those from backgrounds of economic, gender, sexual, and racial marginalization and "innocent victims" are White, have class privilege, or otherwise conform to hegemonic notions of "appropriate" gender and sexuality.

Real Criminals and Innocent Victims?

The show depicts the different crimes of the women through the use of flashbacks that show the reasons why the women ended up in prison. These allow us to see who these women actually are – we know their actions throughout the series within the prison but the reasons why they landed in prison are always shown in flashbacks, and these flashbacks allow us to see the women outside of the structures of the prison system. Although their actions in the flashback are almost always connected to the circumstances that led them to prison, we see the ways in which race, class, gender, and sexuality all play a role for each of these women in terms of how they landed where they are. The actual crimes range from murder and assault to drug trafficking, drug selling, and fraud.

Yet at the same time that the show notes the criminality of the women in Litchfield, we are also regularly reminded through the flashback itself that these are real women who have been constantly oppressed through the various structures in society. This oppression can be seen in the relationship between these women and their families, religious figures, and the economic and political structure that landed them in prison. This is further complicated by race and sexual orientation, as these intersecting oppressions are shown throughout the show as the different ways in which the multiple aspects of society have had an impact on different women.

The constraints of race, class and sexuality also seem to structure most of the flashbacks, consistent with older women in prison genre fiction that connects something about women's sexuality (which is raced and classed) to the fact of incarceration. The flashbacks often build empathy, as in Tasha "Taystee" Jefferson's case, or reveal more complexity and tenderness than meets the eye with characters like Gloria Mendoza and Tiffany Doggett – but for characters like Mendoza and Doggett, in particular, their collective lack of formal social safety net coupled with the abuse and sexual assault from men in their lives seems consistent with folk explanations for why women go to prison. It is always something about the men in their lives, or the men absent from their lives, even as Doggett actually murdered someone with a hunting rifle for mocking her serial abortions.

The flashbacks in *OITNB* are shadowy and partial. Again, they build on and expand what we see of the women in their prison families and conflicts, but while the cameras at Litchfield are sneaky. We peek over shoulders, see into drawers, get unexpected point of view shots; for the most part, the flashbacks feel more like surveillance than the cameras in the prison do. The camera angles and motion reinforce the instability of identity, seeking to establish and reestablish various competing frames: real criminal? Innocent victim? Good girl gone bad? Bad girl gone good? At its best, the show keeps the audience guessing. At its worst, it reinforces stereotypes that lead to real-life violence, as in the case of Sophia Burset.

Sophia Burset: A Case Study

Sophia Burset's representation in *Orange is the New Black* brings together specific notions of identity, authenticity, and the use of the flashback, particularly related to how these come together to produce further regulation on the bodies of trans women. While there are several moments that serve to question the authenticity of Burset as a woman (such as the transphobic use of the phrase "he/she"), there are four moments in particular in her storyline in particular that highlight the ways in which identity, criminality, and the flashback operate to question the authenticity of Burset as both a person and as a woman. First, in the naming of her crime as fraud puts her authenticity as a person in question. Second, her argument with Mendoza in the third season shows that her acceptance by other inmates is called into question, particularly as a woman. Third, the reaction by the prison staff by sending her to the secured housing unit (SHU) legitimizes the notion that she is not a real woman by cordoning her off into a specific space that keeps her separated from the other women in the prison. Fourth, in the flashback, the producers of the show use Laverne Cox's brother to represent Sophia prior to her transition, further delegitimizing her claim throughout the show that she is a woman.

The crime of fraud indicates a moment in which Burset's identity is called into question. In the current carceral state, crime often is not about a single incident or moment of doing wrong but is about the entire person. A person does not just commit a murder but becomes a murderer. We do not just punish the person for a crime, but we punish the criminal. As such, Burset does not just commit fraud (by stealing credit cards to pay for her surgical transition to a woman), she is a fraud. This calls into question many aspects of Burset's being and the ways in which her very identity can be understood. In certain aspects Burset's crime begins the moment when we call into question her legitimacy as a woman and whether she even belongs in Litchfield. Importantly, this is also the moment in which we see Sophia as an entirely different person – that is, physically, the role of Sophia Burset is not played by the same actor (Laverne Cox, like her character an out trans woman) prior to her incarceration. Most of the inmates, except when we see them as children, are portrayed by the same actors in their backstories. In Burset's flashbacks, an entirely different person – and a man – represents Burset in her earlier incarnation as Michael (played by Cox's real life twin brother). This allows us to imagine Sophia and Michael as two completely different people (because they are), but knowing that Michael and Sophia are both the same person, coupled with the understanding that Sophia's crime is fraud, brings us to another moment where Sophia is called into question as a woman.

Throughout her time in prison, it becomes clear that Sophia's identity as a woman is unstable. This instability is due to the perspective of the other inmates and guards. Her experiences within the prison, particularly her job as a hairdresser indicates her expertise with femininity, but the constant ways in which she is referred to as "other" comes to a head in her argument with another inmate, Mendoza. While the discussion is about the influence and behavior of their children on each other, the argument culminates in two acts of violence – one in which Burset pushes Mendoza, and another when three inmates attack Burset in her hair salon using transphobic language and rationale to justify their brutal attack. This attack, particularly in her hair salon, along with the commentary prior to it about genitalia, constitutes an attack on Burset's identity as a woman within Litchfield.

When Burset complains about the attack to the guards of Litchfield, they place her in Solitary Confinement (the SHU). By doing so the guards and the upper echelon of the prison staff are calling her identity as a woman into question, yet again. They use solitary confinement, not as punishment, but as a way to separate her from the inmates "for her protection", which allows others to see her as outside of the norm for women – as "other" yet again. While Laverne Cox's performance as Burset has won rave reviews from fans and critics and provides a platform from which to discuss trans visibility, the real-life Bursets, many of whom have not undergone bottom surgery, often wind up, like CeCe McDonald, incarcerated in men's prisons for crimes of self-defense and self-preservation.

Discussion

OITNB moves past the existing "women in prison" exploitation genre to explore a complex range of stories and identities revolving around women's lives in the carceral state. At the same time, while LBTQ bodies and sexualities are framed as potentially predatory and hostile (most notably in the "bang contest" story arc of Season 2), *OITNB* challenges the race- and class-privileged femme representation of lesbian women that dominates mainstream porn and is reproduced on shows like *The L Word*. The women-in-prison genre is a staple of pulp literature and pulp media, dating back to the mid-20th century, presenting sex between incarcerated women as titillating, deviant, yet ultimately heteronormative. While the audience is nominally aware we are watching a fictional drama, the slow tease of the show's pacing helps construct the sense that we learn who the characters *really* are by integrating their backstories and details of the circumstances that led them to Litchfield. In all of this, the camera acts as omniscient eye and voyeur, presenting life details beyond the cells of Litchfield as both objective truth and counterfactual.

Critical response to the show, particularly in the first two seasons, focused on the complexity and humanity of the incarcerated women. This is a rare, humane representation of what have long been stock characters. Audiences also responded strongly, particularly on online sites like Autostraddle.com, a queer women's website devoted to pop culture and politics, which recapped every episode of the series and continues to post news of the show and of its many LBTQ actors and writers. The "realness" of an out trans actor (Laverne Cox) playing an out trans character (Sophia Burset) was lauded as groundbreaking, and audiences also responded strongly to the unusual demographics of the cast and crew, the majority of whom are women, many of whom are LBQ women, some of whom are women of color. This too is rare for television, and some of the resonance between characters and actors (particularly in terms of LBQ sexualities) also shapes how audiences perceive who's really "real."

But the show is a fiction. The reality of life at Litchfield? Even the country club prisons are brutal places of state control. Life in *OITNB* is not life for most incarcerated women. Much has been made of Kohan's strategy of using Chapman as a "Trojan Horse" to tell the stories of characters of color, even as Latinx characters are routinely flattened into single-dimensions, and Black characters exist as foils for and counters to the sexual escapades of normatively bodied White women. There is certainly something transgressive and fresh about *OITNB*, but like the characters, the audience is never entirely sure whether we are getting a glimpse at something real and new, or at cleverly produced genre fiction.

References and Further Reading

Butler, J. (2004). Imitation and Gender Insubordination. In S. Salih and J. Butler (Eds.), *The Judith Butler Reader* (pp. 119–137). Malden, MA: Blackwell Publishing.

Cecil, D. K. (2007). Looking beyond caged heat. *Feminist Criminology*, 2(4), 304–326.

Ciasullo, A. (2008). Containing "deviant" desire: Lesbianism, heterosexuality, and the women-in-prison narrative. *The Journal of Popular Culture*, 41(2), 195–223.

Clowers, M. (2001). Dykes, gangs, and danger: Debunking popular myths about maximum-security life. *Journal of Criminal Justice and Popular Culture*, 9(1), 22–30.

Freedman, E. B. (1996). The prison lesbian: Race, class, and the construction of the aggressive female homosexual, 1915–1965. *Feminist Studies*, 22(2), 397–423.

Halberstam, J. (1998). *Female Masculinity*. Durham, NC: Duke University Press.

Mulvey, L. (1975). Visual pleasure and narrative cinema. *Screen*, 16(4), 6–18.

Walters, S. D. (2001). Caged heat: The (r)evolution of women-in-prison films. In M. McCaughey and N. King (Eds.), *Reel Knockouts: Violent Women in the Movies* (pp. 106–123). Austin: University of Texas Press.

2

TRYING ON GENDER IS THE NEW BLACK

From Female to Felon

L. Susan Williams, Edward L.W. Green and Kimber R. Williams

The seasoned inmate, Morello, and the newby Chapman sat in the facility's white transport van, at the threshold of Chapman's passage into prison. Each seemed unaware of the poignancy of the moment for the other:

> "That's it? That's all you got?" Morello, voice ringing with a thick Bronx brogue, flips through the wedding magazine and had asked Chapman which dress would best accentuate her boobs and ass. Chapman replied cautiously, "They both look nice." Morello grabs the magazine back, retorting, "That's all you got to say?"

While Morello impatiently awaits Chapman's fresh sense of couture, the newly processed protagonist commences an identity vertigo, one in which everything seems topsy-turvy. The scene just described comes from Netflix's groundbreaking television series *Orange Is the New Black* (*OITNB*), the widely lauded and sharply critiqued story of life in a women's prison. The series is based on Piper's Kerman's 2011 memoir by the same name, which describes her 13-month stint in a minimum-security prison. While the series obviously exercises artistic liberty, it affords a glimpse into a world almost totally invisible from public eye – a women's correctional facility, packed with a diversity of women's bodies, cultures, and experiences. While we use *OITNB* as illustration, the chapter focuses on critical transitions of "lifers" in our four-year study at a women's correctional facility. As one of our participants, Benita (pseudonym), conveyed, "My life had died, and I was reborn a prisoner." We explore that journey.

Making it Work

This chapter delves into how women inmates navigate the gender order and, in turn, how gendering shapes what Benita refers to as "rebirth." Trying on gender – a concept capturing an experimental component of gendering – becomes a mechanism, a performance, to navigate situations within the hyper-masculine conditions of the contemporary prison. This is what we refer to as "trying on gender as the new black" – a form of impression management that takes on configurations enlisted for women in prison. Sociologist Erving Goffman referred to this kind of interaction as *presentation of self*, one in which performance meets reality. The imagery of performance underscores the agency, or initiative, of actors while also accounting for social structures (in this case, a prison and all its facets) that curtail agency. Each form – both agency and structure – limits the other, but in the case of carceral regimes, containment is extreme and coercive. Our question is, how do incarcerated women navigate transitions into an oppressive and distinctly masculine penal environment, and how do they define "making it work?"

Understanding women's adjustment to prison life matters because, as confirmed in a 2015 report of the U.S. Department of Justice, women are the fastest growing demographic in contemporary U.S. prisons, increasing from 15,118 in 1980 to 113,000 by year end 2014 – an increase of over 800% in the past three decades, a rate of increase double that of males. Still, incarcerated women remain least understood by policymakers and practitioners. For example, Mary Ellen Mastrorilli, assistant professor of criminal justice at Boston University, found that 75% of women in prison have been victims of violence and trauma, yet many security measures continue to re-traumatize those women. Increasingly, gender-sensitive training stands as a buzzword in the corrections world, but considerable problems persist, including a dearth of empirical research on a *gendered* prison environment. Understanding this conundrum is key to designing positive programming for the next transition – reentry into larger society.

We focus on micro-interactions as women experiment, resist, and explore options within the prison environment, assessing those experiences through prototypes offered in *OITNB*, and through actual interviews with women inmates. Data are drawn from a larger study of five state prisons, which included more than 100 interviews plus a plethora of observations, focus groups, and field notes. Thirty-two individual interviews and four focus groups from a women's facility constitute the bulk of data presented here; most participants were White, while three identified as Hispanic, six as Black, and one as Native American. The median age was 42, and the median length of sentence was 21 years. Names were altered for confidentiality, and ethnic pseudonyms were given to express diversity in the sample. This chapter focuses on gender, but we acknowledge that race, ethnicity, and other points of difference are critical markers of identity, and we include intersectional outcomes and discussion where possible.

We do not excuse harm-causing behavior that may have brought these women to prison. We do hope that a close inquiry into women prisoners' transitional "self" offers insight into the human cost of mass incarceration.

Body and Soul

As the late jazz performer Billie Holiday sang, "I spend my days in longin', I'm wondering why it's me you're wronging, I tell you I mean it...I'm all for you, body and soul." As Holiday croons, the lyrics imply a wholeness between the physical entity (body) and the metaphysical part of being (soul). In conventional studies of society, unfortunately, there is too often a sharp disjuncture between the physical body and our inquiry of events, encounters, experiences.

Gendered bodies hold particularized significance in the cases we present. Consider, for example, the protagonist in *OITNB*. In an early processing scene, Chapman, the White, upper middle-class young woman, is going through her first strip search when the officer orders, "Squat...spread your cheeks and cough."

Implicit in the scene just described is the involvement of the body, but not just the body; rather, the social context as experienced by the body. French philosopher Michel Foucault overtly addressed contemporary prison as a consequence of the need for public display of discipline over the prisoner's (now docile) body. However, his reference assumed gender-neutral bodies, and feminist scholars were quick to critique Foucault's neglect of gender-as-power – one that brings very different social meaning to an incarcerated female body. Angela King, writing in 2004 from the University of North London, argued that the presumed-docile female body exemplifies Foucault's theory of power, body, and spectacle – the "body politic," as feminist theorist, Susan Bordo, termed it in 1993. Body searches and the presumption of docility versus potential violence brings very different expectations (and treatment) for women's bodies than for men's. Yet, the significance of women's bodies as political has been largely ignored outside of feminist circles. In *OITNB*, the brief portrayal of Chapman's body search bears the history of women's bodies as chattel, the cultural penchant toward over-sexualization of women and girls, and the implications of gendered organizations where, overwhelmingly, men hold power over women.

In a rare reference to the import of body personification, sociologist Lonnie Athens speaks to the integration of physical and social space, claiming that body-less social experiences are as impossible to have as environment-less ones. Athens writes that the notion of social experience "integrates, rather than segregates the human body with its social environment, so that...their environments are not falsely separated" (p.151). In the current study, certain bodily manifestations are more conspicuous than others, but ample evidence demonstrates that the body represents a particularly salient slate upon which the prison experience is inscribed.

Australian sociologist Raewyn Connell (2014) asserts that "gender is about how bodies enter history." The analytical challenge within this rich concept centers on access, both intellectually (what theoretical tools are most instructive?) and practically (how can we understand real-life applications?). Because gender-as-process is most visible at boundaries and points of change, we argue that nowhere is Connell's pronouncement more evident than in women's prisons.

Prison strips inmates of all civil liberties, places them at the mercy of the Department of Justice, and confines both the physical and emotional well-being of the inmate.

While the justice system demands all that once was, is, and what may become of an inmate – both body and soul, male and female – criminologist Barbara Bloom and colleagues (2004) emphasize that justice is a deeply gendered structure, one in which bodies mark conjecture and inference. Cortney Franklin (2008) of Sam Houston State University contends that for women, the body symbolizes a) a history of oppression veiled in so-called "natural" demands, b) an instrument of control built around men's pleasure and convenience, and c) a subject of institutionalized power that habitually advantages one sex (male) over the other (female). To fully analyze the import of this statement, we turn now to gender as a social construct.

Framing Gender

Contemporary studies of gender have advanced well beyond simple sex differences. Gender scholars now acknowledge that gender is not a physiological "thing," nor is it a category, nor is it simply a bundle of roles and expectations. Rather, gender is an active, ongoing practice. Gender is something we *do*. Drawing on the "doing gender" perspective as advanced in 1987 by sociologists Candace West and Don Zimmerman, gender is defined as a "routine, methodical, and recurring accomplishment" (126). While it is individuals who *do* gender, it is a situated "doing" that is both interactional (occurring in imagined or actual presence of others), and structural (a feature of social arrangements). We contend that prison, as a very specific gender regime, commands a certain compressed conduct.

Two additional concepts extend the doing gender perspective. The first is intersectionality. Sociologist Patricia Hill Collins (1990) underscored the importance of including historically marginalized voices, highlighting Black women's experiences and pointing out the need to focus on intersections of race, class, and gender as mechanisms of inequalities that must be considered when examining real-life experiences. Following Kimberle Crenshaw (1989), whose work is credited with the term intersectionality, Candace West and Sarah Fenstermaker extended the doing gender perspective to one of doing difference. Collins (1990) referred to this composite as a matrix of domination, in which axes of social difference (such as race, class, sexuality, ableness, and so forth) are not simply additive but interact in complex and interlocking ways. This human complexity means that while the common denominator may be a women's prison, other factors such as background, entry points, and transitions vary widely. We argue that in the extreme case of identity transition from woman to felon, gender becomes powerfully salient.

Second, the concept of trying on gender contributes a unique framework when dealing with life change. First, author L.S. Williams has described the transition from adolescence to womanhood as one more provisional than previously thought. The girls in her 2002 study, rather than following a pre-dictable straight-line gendering process, resisted, played, experimented, and dis-covered a range of strategies to navigate the exciting and sometimes traumatic course to "becoming a woman." These processes are heavily shaped by the local gender regime, which organizes gender relations in place- and time-specific locations, and which are usually portrayed as what U.K. scholar Robert Smith (2013) calls an "unashamedly masculine endeavor."

No study has examined the transition from citizen/woman to female felon and the multiple contingencies of doing gender in transition. The transition from citizen to felon calls into question one's core identity, and a "trying-on" process begins. That is, everyday practices are calculated on gender habits, but the prison milieu is dramatically unique; thus, these habits (which seem "natural" but are not) are either challenged or inaccessible, and gendering becomes a tentative everyday experiment. As gender monitors the prison threshold, this study examines intersections between women's physical bodies and social experiences. We borrow from Holiday's "body and soul" concept to capture the complex yet fractured identities of incarcerated women within the hyper-masculine prison environment, one designed with the assumption of masculinity and male bodies; one built, guided, and groomed by men in power.

Transitioning to Felon

Feminist scholars agree that prisons are organized around a "male model" that treats women with a blueprint developed for men, while ignoring stark differ-ences between the two groups – physiologically, psychologically, socially, and relationally. This body of literature is summed up in Joanne Belknap's 2014 book, *The Invisible Woman*. One glaring difference between men and women prisoners is the disproportionality in abuse; overwhelmingly, most incarcerated women have suffered significant abuse. Criminologist Emily Wright and colleagues (2012) emphasized that although most women in prison share a history of abuse, their circumstances, kinds of injury, and personal responses vary widely. Furthermore, the historically masculinized prison environment embodies an especially aggressive version of gendered ideology known as hegemonic masculinity. Hegemonic masculinity is not assumed to be "normal" in the statistical sense and is not embraced by all individual men. But, as Raewyn Connell and James Messersch-midt point out, a powerful and aggressive form of hegemonic masculinity is presented as normative and may especially thrive in certain distilled settings such as sports, risk-taking activities, and certain all-male gatherings. Prison, as a total institution, affords just such a structure for observing dynamics when women prisoners are cast into these spatial and emotional conditions.

Two studies of total institutions inform our work. First, former convict John Irwin's 1970 foundational study *The Felon* describes the self-in-transition: "In the

Kafkaesque world of the booking room, the jail cell, the interrogation room, and the visiting room, the boundaries of the self collapse" (39). Second, Erving Goffman's classic 1961 work *Asylums* addresses internal context and culture. Parallel to the asylum as an instrument of institutionalization, the prison conditions the individual as "good convict," one who faces the impasse of either *becoming* a captive or preserving one's self. Goffman refers to the early phase of this process as mortification of self, "a series of abasements, degradations, humiliations, and profanations of self [that are] fairly standard in total institutions" (14). For women in the rigidly masculinized environment, one's identity *as a woman* is interrogated, her very status as appropriate woman called into question.

Findings: Everyday transactions

"It's like the less time you got, the slower it goes," is the plaintive observation from Lorna Morello, the sweet, soft-hearted woman with the thick Bronx-like accent in *OITNB*. Then she's quickly back to writing a beauty column for the prison newsletter. Daily, Morello uses coffee as eye shadow, tampons to curl her hair into retro waves, and always wears (forbidden) ruby red lipstick. In short, she uses everyday transactions to make herself (and, by association, others) happy in the direst of circumstances.

Sociologist Dorothy Smith, in *The Everyday World as Problematic* (1989), proposes that power is rooted in everyday transactions – those moments of coercion (or agency) that are visible only in retrospect or upon close analysis. Smith refers to "ruling relations" as those practices embedded in everyday interactions that coordinate the lives of those subject to administrative rule. That is, the very mission of the total institution is to strip the recruit of support provided by mainstream establishments (e.g., family, work, education) to remake the self. Tear it down. Rebuild. For women in prison, we know little about this strip-down process and how women arbitrate daily micro-interactions. These small goings-on – or performances – are part of a trying-on process, ways in which women use gendering techniques to craft a prison-bound endurance as sufferable or even somehow transformative.

This section documents experiences of female inmates to demonstrate a) pains of imprisonment; and b) the trying-on-gender techniques they use to mitigate the devastation of their gender identities during imprisonment. We think this is what happens: A catastrophe occurs, and the self is ravaged; yet the humanity in us strives to survive. We begin with subjective experiences of incarcerated women, as told to us, representing accounts of those that Smith (1989) designated as "historically silenced." Storylines from *OITNB* provide context and analytical framing.

Catastrophe and the Ravage of Self: Pains of Imprisonment

When catastrophe hits – just like a train wreck or crash spectacle beside the road – the first gaze turns toward the most visible crisis, the snarl and turmoil that immediately constructs the felon. The body is the most conspicuous manifestation of prisoner: In handcuffs, shackled, dressed in bright searing orange (or stripes or whatever chosen fanfare of dishonor), the new captive is paraded before the judge (and others) in a ritual of shame. American philosopher and gender theorist Judith Butler, in *Bodies that Matter* (1993), argues that all gender expression begins from the material body and therefore embodiment must be incorporated into theories of understanding. For women prisoners, the process begins to tear down the woman-as-citizen *and* the citizen-as-woman. The system attempts to neutralize, de-feminize, and deem the body unworthy of society's feminine markers. Once stripped down, the "appropriate" female body is masked; what remains is easier to deal with, both physically (locked down) and symbolically (essentially, deemed non-woman).

Throughout history, women's bodies have been disciplined, objectified, and contained. The woman's imprisoned body symbolizes one of those moments, as Connell proclaims, when the [gendered] body meets history. Therein begins the "pains of imprisonment," a term advanced by sociologist Gresham Sykes in his classic 1958 study of a New Jersey prison, referring to the various frustrations and deprivations that "pose profound threats to the inmate's personality or sense of personal worth." The shackled body, once broken down, becomes home camp; the volley on one's soul-self follows.

The threshold moment of sentencing – when the gavel strikes the judicial bench and the female citizen becomes felon – marks a particularly pernicious point in what becomes a long line of indignities. When we talked face to face with women in prison, the word used most often to describe that moment was "devastating." "It's devastating. Totally devastating." "I was devastated." "I felt like an empty shell." "It was like being kicked in the gut." "Hopeless." Laura (White female) gives the following, representative account:

> That first moment, it's like, "just kill me." You just want to die, and I even took a "thinkin' about that moment", when you look at your family and realize it's over, it's done and you're like, "how did this happen?"

At this moment of devastation, networks are torn apart, regret and remorse peak, and, as Irwin (1970) chronicles, everything social *and* the self's internal directions of identity are dissolved. Ready or not, a metamorphosis begins. Benita (Hispanic female) from our interviews well represents this juncture:

> I felt like my life, a complete life, had died and I was *reborn a prisoner* and that's who I was, and I identified myself like that. Every part of my life died at that time. Everything. I mean, even my children. "*I*" like went away.

These moments of self-loss are accompanied by self-realization. Regardless of design or detail, all our participants expressed a change in themselves; some good, others regrettable but seemingly inevitable. All longed for lost connections with family, especially their "momma" and children. They voiced regret in whatever brought them to prison; for many it was the association with a man in their life. But they also accepted responsibility (as prison code requires), even while recognizing the oft-blurred line between victim and perpetrator. Georgia (Black female), convicted of murdering her abusive partner, explains:

> Regret? I regret that it led to here but I don't regret being a survivor in the situation. I regret the fact that it came to here – this is how it ended. That's the main regret is that it had to come to this.

And for others, the question itself was just too painful. From our interview with Evelyn (White female):

> A lot of things. A lot of things (crying). I don't think I want to answer that one.

Consistently, we witnessed the loss and ravages of self in the women we interviewed. But a feminist perspective also demands that we attest to agency – individual determination, strength, and deep-found power – of women who manage to survive despite destruction in their lives. We are particularly interested in understanding, conceptually, how gender as an action – the doing of gender – may be exploited as a means of survival in the institutional masculine-geographies of prison, and, according to Connell and Messerschmidt (2005), may potentially reformulate the agency of women. How do women inmates begin to pick themselves back up? What's a woman to do?

The Strive to Survive: Trying on Gender

There is little doubt that fictional character Morello was damaged. Some speculate that she suffers from a form of mental illness; she experiences delusions ("Christopher" as fiancé despite his rebuke), explosive frenzies, violent outbursts, and occasional irrational decision-making. Still, she functions as a trusted van driver, greets and befriends new recruits, dishes out daily beauty advice, and finds ways to brighten others' existence. One poignant example comes when she steals a lollipop to provide comfort to Rosa after her chemo treatment. Somehow, Morello exists, even if – and perhaps because – she continues to live in her fantasy, temporarily wrapped in certain familiarities, which perhaps amplify or overcompensate for her identity as a woman. It is this tenuous, experimental aspect of gendering that constitutes trying on gender. Perhaps the dizzying conditions of a total institution, combined with the commuting of certain gendered expectations, allow a greater fluidity of gender, a "structural hole" as author Williams (2002) asserts, that affords greater latitude in gender experimentation. We turn now to examples of the trying-on-gender process, first as emphasized femininity, and then as resistance.

Trying on as Emphasized Femininity

In the same way that an exaggerated but ruling ideology exists around masculine as powerful, tough, even violent, the magnified version of extreme "female-ness" is referred to by Raewyn Connell (1987) as emphasized femininity. This concept includes attractiveness (by prevailing cultural standards), attachment to men, and compliance or docility. These traits do not represent a total femininity but provide markers with which to assess gender normative behaviors, even though, as writer and activist Audre Lorde (1984) contends, normative may be "mythical."

For women in prison, the stripping down of everyday feminine markers takes on magnified meaning. As Piper Kerman describes: "Two hundred women, no phones, no washing machines, no hair dryers – it was like *Lord of the Flies* on estrogen" (p. 174). Familiar gender norms, even those not fully embraced by individuals, become coping mechanisms, providing common ground with other women and a routine that is, to some extent, comforting. In *OITNB*, Morello exemplifies emphasized femininity and projects it onto others. The following example comes when "Big Boo" – a stereotypical butch-type character – is getting a "makeover":

MORELLO: [screaming] I'm so sorry, I can't help it. I just love makeovers, and you look so pretty.
PENNSATUCKY: Boo, you look fucking weird. [others look at Pennsatucky in annoyance] What? She does.
BIG BOO: [her eyes filling with tears] No, um... I look like my mother.

One of our participants, Wilma (Black female), illustrates a similar "makeover" strategy:

> You know how like you get a plant and if you don't know how to take care of it, it dies. You don't know when to water it, but you take it home and wipe 'em off and you talk to 'em, you know, and make sure they get sun-light. I used to kill plants because I didn't know how to take care of 'em. Now, I do. So, now I have pretty plants in my window. *It's the same thing with myself.* Like, I wear make-up now.

To be sure, emphasized femininity may seem superficial, serving only a perfunctory role. But it also ministers a worthy purpose in prison – it gets you through the day. Further, it can serve as an apparatus for endurance, a mark of affinity *as a woman.* Rhonda (Black female), from our interviews, provides an example of how a feminine look works to negate, if only momentarily, the stigma of a prison identity:

> I notice that if you're like a lady and you're all made up and you look kind of dainty, *if you don't look like you belong in a prison*, they treat you different. This lady asked, "Can I have a towel?" And [the CO] pulled out the towel and said, "What are you gonna say? Ain't you gonna say please?" When there's women that doesn't look like they belong in prison... they get treated way better. [If not] then it becomes a way bigger issue.

Gendered expectations of staff offer another social geography of doing gender. Whether presentation of the feminine is makeshift or deep-seated, the result is the same: the body becomes a carrier of situational prison experiences, directly or indirectly. Rhonda was not the subject of the CO's interaction (above), but the impression was the same: doing gender matters.

Certainly, there is acknowledgement that the feminine markers, such as lipstick and hair curlers, are skin-deep. As Ruiz in *OITNB* points out, these daily mechanisms are like a band-aid, "Once you rip it off, all we are to each other is scars." Still, the band-aid serves a purpose. Women in our study understood the value, both socially and instrumentally, in looking like "they didn't belong in prison." But not everyone has the same resources or desire to do so, finding value or allegiances another way. Tig (Black), a transgender inmate, explains:

> In the women's prison, most people might get a relationship or somethin', and they're lookin' for what they call studs. I would be considered a stud. Even though I don't like the word. They lookin' for whether it's a girly-girl or a stud girl, you know what I'm sayin'? That make their boo, and if you look good then you might could pick up a girl that got some money and she'll take care of you. If you don't look good then you better have some money to get companionship. That's what it's about. *If it ain't your looks, it's your books.*

Markers of emphasized femininity were predominant on our trips to the prison. On several occasions, we were on hand for "commissary day." Administrators had authorized the purchase of various [approved] toiletries from a local big-box store. After a three-van shopping spree, prison staff piled goods into a large conference room while inmate volunteers filled "orders" placed the previous week. Among a colorful array of shampoo, body wash, moisturizers, styling gel, lotions, tampons, and other personal care items, the excitement (and competition) was like mall shopping time for teenage girls. These accoutrements of femininity were highly sought after and supported the emphasized femininity practices we witnessed.

Trying on as Resistance

In her study of teenage girls, L.S. Williams defined trying on gender as resistance to include "ways in which girls refuse gender-typical demands" (2002, p.35). Here, we extend that concept to accommodate gendered practices that incarcerated women can and do appropriate as defiance and/or challenges against attempts to subjugate them. These tools of resistance incorporate something as subtle as Morello's forbidden ruby red lipstick to Big Boo's contempt for conventional femininity or Red's underground markets.

Everyday acts of resistance are usually not as extreme as a hunger strike or prison riot. Challenging power is generally more subtle. Note, for example, the use of sarcasm in an exchange between the *OITNB* character Chapman and the shop supervisor:

CHAPMAN: The thermal fuse blew.
JACK PEARSON: And you can fix that by yourself, honey?
CHAPMAN: Well, I sure can if I concentrate extra hard with my lady brain.

While these everyday resistances are plentiful in the savvy script of *OITNB*, instances of resistance in our interviews were not as apparent, but they were there – we clearly glimpsed quiet but poignant measures of everyday resistance, like this one from Edna (Black female):

> I keep a soap dish with broken pieces to remind me, "Look how blessed you are, you have a whole bar of soap," you know? And, if I see somebody need soap, ma'am, I give it to 'em and I'm not supposed to but I do, 'cause that's just who I am. If they need somethin', then I will give it to 'em, but I always tell 'em, "Don't pay me back. That's not why I gave it to you." *That's who I am for real.*

While several such poignant markers are evident in our data, others hinted at underlying aggression. Georgia suggested that when COs start "treatin' me like we're beneath them, then we start havin' a little issue"; and Rhonda (imprisoned since 1992) deftly uses her age (and gender) to chide young COs: "When I look 'em in the eye and says, 'I'm old enough to be your momma,' that kind of sets the mood."

By design, overt resistance in prison is extremely difficult and bears great cost. Laura (White female) told of a bloodletting fight between two inmates in which she called for officers. Consequently, there was a confrontation between her and the instigator of the fight. Though Laura vows to "break the silence," others find that act too dangerous and/or alienating. Georgia (Black female) explains:

> It's just not right, you guys tackle a girl and beat her, and then put gas on her…But, what I learned is you can't speak up here. So, you learn over a

period of time, after wearin' myself down and after hearin' the yells and the screams at night, you got to suppress it. That voice becomes a little bit non-human. *You gonna become the environment.* You gotta become a little bit more callous. You gonna become a little bit more non-understanding, a little bit more non-sympathetic.

The decisions to resist (and not) are as varied as the stories that bring them to prison. Every deed, every action, every non-action brings consequences. Such are the institutional conditions designed to not only strip an inmate of her civil liberties, but consistently to remind her of her status. Chapman, in OITNB, once said, "I just didn't expect to be punished while I was being punished."

Though precise techniques may change, these everyday transactions of resistance – ways in which the trying-on process moves them to challenge power – is not new to these women. Most have been through years of threats and turmoil and pain. As Lina explained, "A woman waits for death by the hand of her abuser. Then when she decides to live and stand up and fight back, she faces a different kind of death – life in prison. So, yeah, sometimes you just gotta challenge." For the female inmate, the transition involves not only demotion from everyday citizen to felon, but also the stripping of her identity as an "appropriate" woman.

Conclusion

Early on a Thursday morning, January 17, 2013, we entered the facility portrayed in this study, transported to another place (and, in some ways, time). Exactly 25 weeks later, on Thursday, July 11, 2013, Netflix premiered its groundbreaking series, *Orange is the New Black*. Little did we know the impact it would exert on our research. A prison study like this is rare due to a host of complexities such as access, time, and willingness of participants to share their stories. The most urgent hope of this chapter is to humanize the silenced and forgotten – women prisoners as the fastest growing population of incarcerated US citizens.

While *OITNB* represents a media sensation and has sparked this very dialogue, it has not divulged some rare anomaly. As one of the *OITNB* actors (we'll call her Diana) expressed to us recently, "these stories have been around for a long time; but now we get to tell them." Critics have argued about whether the show "gets it right." What the series *has* done is create an environment ripe for a long overdue discussion about women in an unprecedented age of mass incarceration. It made their issues relevant. Mainstream. Hollywood. In short, the show and the issues raised in this volume have been blessed, or cursed, with the Hollywood effect; it has garnered everyday conversation, public scrutiny, and a listening device for voices heretofore obscured or forgotten. And those voices tell us that women in prison are resilient, adaptive, and fiercely creative in navigating a parti-cularly oppressive hyper-masculine environment. Serendipitously, they often discover strength as a core piece of who they are: their multi-faceted, fully gendered selves.

The focus on provisional gendering in prison highlights two theoretical implications: It loosens outdated canons about gendering to reveal a broad array of situation-dependent approaches; and it underscores the diversity of gender-design and creativity among women. At a deeper level, women portrayed here demonstrate the power and viability of a gender system that can be ferociously oppressive but also, as UK criminologists Bosworth and Kaufman argue, a "potential site of – and resource for – resistance."

Reconsidering navigations of identity through the concept of trying on gender allows us to organize data between gender as emphasized femininity and as resistance; both represent attempts for self-empowerment. However, they are not equally potent in challenging hegemonic masculinity, which resides in social structures and cultural practices and appears even more robust within the spatial and emotional confines of prison. While emphasized femininity is primarily individual-level, collective resistance provides promise for real social change. To do so wholesale demands a group consciousness among women *as women*. This kind of awareness – common experiences among women without pitting all women against all men – is critical for creating actionable social movement. It has been said that the prison gate must be opened from the outside. As actor Diana expressed in our conversation, "We've seen a big energetic shift among women. Still, there's fear on both sides, for women and men. We've found the largeness of our own voice, but have not yet fully embraced it."

Considering incarcerated women as a new phenomenon via *OITNB* exerts a fundamental disservice to women who have always been subject to masculine hegemony. As Bosworth notes (and as *OITNB* actor Diane underscores), there is nothing "new" about confining femininity. However, what the series and this chapter attempts to do is shine a bright light on the outrages of current incarceration practices as well as daring attempts at change. University of Houston professor Brene Brown (of TED fame) contends, "you can't get to courage without walking through vulnerability" (2015). The women who shared their experiences, who braved trying-on-gender channels, exhibited this kind of courage. The spunk of Morello, the endurance of Red, the grit of Big Boo inspired us to dig deeper into our interviews. There we discovered the introspection of Wilma, who learned to nourish herself; the savvy of Rhonda, who discovered currency in "looking like you don't belong in prison"; the acumen of Tig ("if it's not your looks, it's your books"). These trying-on mechanisms highlight the agency, the tenacity and endurance of these women who, for a multitude of reasons, found themselves in prison – a position none of them expected. Here, we witness how women inmates employ gender techniques that were "knowable" from the outside, then test, experiment, craft "what works" on the inside. Paradoxically, both locations of power (outside and inside) are ordered through a masculine hegemonic institutional framework; women's bodies become the battlefield.

References and Further Reading

Belknap, J. (2014). *The invisible woman: Gender, crime and justice* (4th ed.) Belmont, CA: Wadsworth Publishing.

Bloom, B., Owen, B., & Covington, S. (2004). Women offenders and the gendered effects of public policy. *The Review of Policy Research*, 21(1), 31–48.

Bosworth, M. (2000). Confining femininity: A history of gender power and imprisonment. *Theoretical Criminology*4, 265–284.

Brown, B. (2015). *Daring greatly: How the courage to be vulnerable transforms the way we live, love, parent, and lead.* Garden City, NY: Avery Publishers.

Butler, J. (1993). *Bodies that matter.* New York: Routledge.

Collins, P.H. (1990). *Black feminist thought: Knowledge consciousness, and the politics of empowerment.* New York, NY: Routledge Publishers.

Connell, R. (1987). *Gender and power: Society, the person and sexual politics.* Stanford, CA: Stanford University Press.

Connell, R. (2014). Raewyn Connell. Retrieved from http://www.raewynconnell.net/p/theory.html

Connell, R., & Messerschmidt, J.W. (2005). Hegemonic masculinity: Rethinking the concept. *Gender & Society*, 19(6), 829–859.

Crenshaw, K. (1989). Demarginalizing the intersection of race and sex: A black feminist critique of antidiscrimination doctrine, feminist theory and antifascist politics. *The University of Chicago Legal Forum*, 140, 139–167.

Franklin, C.A. (2008). Women offenders, disparate treatment, and criminal justice: A theoretical, historical, and contemporary overview. *Criminal Justice Studies: A Critical Journal of Crime, Law and Society*, 21(4), 341–360.

Goffman, E. (1961). *Asylum: Essays on the condition of the social situation of mental patients and other inmates.* New York: Random House.

Irwin, J. (1970). *The Felon.* Berkeley, CA: University of California Press.

Kerman, P. (2011). *Orange is the new black: My year in a women's prison.* New York, NY: Spiegel & Grau.

Lorde, A. (1984). *Sister outsider: Essays and speeches.* Berkeley, CA: Crossing Press.

Lucas, A. & Lawston, J.M. (Eds.) (2011). *Razor wire women: Prisoners, activists, scholars, and artists.* New York: SUNY Press. Also see blog Razor Wire Women at https://razorwirewomen.wordpress.com/about/

Smith, D. (1989). *The everyday world as problematic: A feminist sociology.* Boston, MA: Northeastern University Press.

Smith, R. (2013). Documenting Essex-Boy as a local gendered regime. *International Journal of Gender and Entrepreneurship*, 5(2), 174–197.

West, C., & Zimmerman, D.H. (1987). Doing gender. *Gender & Society*, 1(2), 125–151.

Williams, L.S. (2002). Trying on gender, gender regimes, and the process of becoming women. *Gender & Society*, 16(1), 29–52.

Williams, L.S. & Green, E.L.W. (2017). When women are captive: Penal culture within women's prisons. In Griffin, H. & Woodward, V. (Eds.) (Forthcoming), *Handbook of corrections in the United States.* New York: Routledge Publishers.

Wright, E.M., Voorhis, P.V., Salisbury, E.J., & Bauman, A. (2012). Gender-responsive lessons learned and policy implications for women in prison: A review. *Criminal Justice and Behavior*, 39(12), 1612–1632.

3

A CRISIS BEHIND BARS

Transgender Inmates, Visibility and Social Justice

Emily Lenning and Carrie L. Buist

This chapter will highlight some of the injustices that face transgender inmates in the United States and highlight the positive contributions of Laverne Cox to the broader movement towards transgender visibility as victims, offenders and inmates by focusing on her portrayal of the character Sophia Burset on the Netflix original drama *Orange is the New Black* (*OITNB*). In the criminal legal field, specifically in corrections, there has been little focus on the experiences of incarcerated transgender inmates. Instead, most of the knowledge that the general public has acquired regarding the inequity that trans inmates experience has come from outside of the discipline and via popular media outlets including television, film, and social networks such as Facebook and Twitter. Thus, it is important to consider the impact that Cox's fictional character Sophia has had on revealing the transgender experience behind bars to the larger public, and how Cox herself has catapulted a social movement focused on the humane treatment of transgender inmates.

Indeed, even beyond the character of Sophia Burset, Laverne Cox's activism has become wide-reaching, as she regularly tours college campuses throughout the United States and frequently speaks at events such as *The National Conference of LGBT Equality*, has been interviewed by dozens of news outlets, and is currently the executive producer of a forthcoming documentary on CeCe McDonald, a Black transwoman who pleaded guilty to second-degree manslaughter after being threatened and assaulted on a public street in Minnesota. On her relationship with McDonald, Cox (2013) notes:

> In *Orange is the New Black*, which is set in a federal women's prison, I play Sophia, an African-American trans woman who is incarcerated. Sophia's story is very different from CeCe's, but when I auditioned for this role,

CeCe was in my heart. Every day I shoot, I think of CeCe and the many trans women of color who are incarcerated across this country. It is my hope that my performance will be guided, at least in part, by CeCe's courage, vision and fortitude…

In this chapter we will discuss the trans experience in prison, the media portrayal of trans inmates, and the impact of *Orange is the New Black*'s portrayal in particular, as well as Laverne Cox's broader influence. First, we turn to the transgender experience in corrections, namely in jails and prisons in the United States.

Trans Inmates in Prison: An Invisible Crisis

It is difficult, if not impossible, to know the exact number of inmates who identify as transgender within our jails and prisons, but psychiatrist George Brown (2009) indicates that the number could be as low as two to as high as 400 trans-identified persons in individual prisons and jails throughout the United States. So, while it is completely feasible that one prison will have zero trans inmates, another prison may have hundreds. Certainly these numbers would reflect the size of the jail or prison.

However, even with little concrete information regarding the exact percentage of transgender inmates throughout the United States, we have seen new jail policies implemented for transgender inmates in Cook County jails in Illinois, at Rikers Island jail in New York, in San Francisco county jails, in Men's Central Jail in Los Angeles, and even the United States Immigration and Customs Enforcement. According to journalist Christopher Mathias (2014), Rikers Island has recognized that their trans inmates "face disproportionate rates of violence, rape and harassment by both staff and other inmates – or choose to go into protective custody, which is essentially solitary confinement" and has decided to address this risk by opening a 30-bed wing specifically for trans inmates.

Regardless of the number of trans inmates in a given facility, the transgender inmate should be understood not just as an offender, but in all likelihood a victim as well. While transgender inmates serving time in jail and prison have committed criminal offenses and are subsequently being punished, it cannot be denied that many transgender inmates have also experienced victimization in their lives, often based solely on their non-conforming transgender identity, or as we explain in findings from our own research, their "expressions, and presentations [that] differ from [one's] biological sex." (Buist & Lenning, 2015, p. xviii)

In our book *Queer Criminology*, we explain that non-conforming or non-binary gender expressions have a long history of being policed and punished both in the United States and abroad, often couched within laws prohibiting the "imperso-nation of the opposite sex" and "masquerading" (Buist & Lenning, 2015, p. 35). Individuals have been arrested for wearing clothing seen as in opposition to their biological sex, especially when coupled with behavior that is not in line with the mannerisms that are commonly associated with "acceptable" gender expression. While these antiquated laws may be rarely enforced today, the policing of gender non-conformity is still informally practiced and so widespread that the phenomenon of trans folks being singled out by authorities who assume they are prostitutes has come to be known as "walking while trans."

While trans folks are often victimized by representatives of the criminal legal system, victimization by other civilians can be found in cases spanning the globe. This victimization ranges from rejection from family and friends, to discrimination in housing and employment (which can lead some trans people to engage in survival crimes that lead to incarceration), to the hyper-violent assaults and murders of trans people, often seen as justified because their abusers and murderers have felt deceived by their victim's gender expression. One would think that these pre-incarceration experiences of victimization would lead us to be hyper-vigilant when it comes to the treatment of trans inmates, but all too often their victimization is exacerbated behind bars.

Once an offender is convicted and sentenced, the punishment that they experience should not exceed their sentence Thus, any infliction of punishment beyond what is ordered by a judge should be considered a violation of the Eighth Amendment. Under the Eighth Amendment of the United States Constitution, inmates should not endure cruel and unusual punishment once they are confined by the State, and any indifference on the part of correctional staff in regards to the victimization of inmates is a violation of the Eighth Amendment. Further, humane punishment is rightly expected by our inmates and should be sought after as an example of the advancements of the correctional system. Thus, any unsanctioned and additional punishments that inmates face, cisgender and trans-gender alike, should not be promoted or tolerated within the criminal legal system. However, just as transgender inmates experienced victimization in their free lives, they continue to face additional and often violent victimization while they are incarcerated.

That fact that this violence often goes unrecognized speaks to the invisibility of transgender inmates, a marginalized status that begins immediately upon entering correctional facilities. Often because correctional officials simply do not know what to do with trans inmates, they face additional abuses and punishments from staff and fellow inmates. This notion of not knowing what to do with trans inmates relates specifically to outmoded classification procedures in prison. In their 2015 article discussing transgender inmates in prison, Routh et al. identified the crux of the problem with classifying transgender inmates is the strict use of binary sex categories for assigning offenders to correctional institutions. In the United States, transgender inmates are classified not by their gender identity, but by their biological sex as narrowly determined by their genitalia. This means that even if someone has been living as a woman or a man in their everyday life, if one has not undergone sex reassignment surgery they will be housed in a facility that mirrors their current genitalia – regardless of gender presentation or whether they have been on hormones or other medication, and regardless of whether the person has been presenting in a gender opposite their biological sex for one month or ten years.

The lack of knowledge about transgender men and women furthers the invisibility that these folks face regardless of whether they are inmates. For instance, relying on a diagnosis of gender dysphoria is problematic not only because it stigmatizes a trans person as having a mental disorder, but also it is often required for any subsequent related medical care, especially for those incarcerated. Although, as noted by the *American Psychological Association* identifying as transgender

> is considered a mental disorder only if it causes significant distress or disability. Many transgender people do not experience their gender as distressing or disabling, which implies that identifying as transgender does not constitute a mental disorder. For these individuals, the significant problem is finding affordable resources, such as counseling, hormone therapy, medical procedures, and the social support necessary to freely express their gender identity and minimize discrimination.

Regardless of their transition status, transgender inmates face extreme physical danger while serving time behind bars. For example, transgender inmates are more likely than their cisgender counterparts to become the victims of sexual assault while they are in prison. The National Inmate Survey, which is conducted by the *Bureau of Justice Statistics*, found that four percent of all state and federal prison inmates and just over three percent of jail inmates in the United States reported being sexually victimized one or more times. The same survey found that nearly 40 percent of transgender prison inmates and nearly 30 percent of transgender jail inmates reported sexual victimization while incarcerated. Forty percent of those attacks were committed not by other inmates, but by correctional staff.

With these disproportionate percentages in violent sexual victimization experienced by transgender inmates, questions arise regarding the impact of the Prison Rape Elimination Act (PREA) passed in 2003. The purpose of PREA is not only to provide information about rape in prison but to analyze the effect it has on inmates and to find ways in which to "protect individuals from prison rape." Oftentimes, in order to protect transgender inmates prison officials segregate them away from the general population. Although this is done under the guise of protection, PREA standards restrict this form of segregation. This speaks to the aforementioned concern that prison officials simply do not know what to do with transgender inmates in order to protect them without punishing them for their gender identity.

Through their failure to implement effective classification systems or prevent disproportionate sexual assaults from fellow inmates and staff, and enforcing isolation in segregation, correctional institutes have failed to provide proper and effective medical care for transgender inmates. Trans inmates are denied a wide range of medical necessities, including counseling, hormonal therapy and sex-reassignment surgery, which some argue should be made available to the inmate either at the inmate's cost or at the cost of the State. It is of note to mention that there have been small victories for trans inmates in the our courts such as *Fields v. Smith*, which found that a Wisconsin law that prevented inmates from having sex reassignment surgery violated the Eighth Amendment, and *Adams v. Bureau of Prisons*, which reversed what was known as the "freeze-frame" policy that prevented trans inmates from receiving any care related to their transition if the care had not begun prior to their incarceration.

In addition to these victories, there has been a modest movement within corrections to begin training for transgender competency and to implement policies regarding transgender inmates in the last few years. In fact, the *National Institute of Corrections* has released at least five research and policy publications and reports on LGBTI offenders, including one published as recently as 2015 called *Transgender, Transsexual, and Gender Nonconforming Health Care in Correctional Settings*, which is a 25 point position statement by the *National Commission on Correctional Health Care*. Among the statements made regarding transgender inmates' health, safety, and discharge planning once they are released, number six states:

> Because transgender patients may be under different stages of care prior to incarceration, there should be no blanket administrative or other policies that restrict specific medical treatments. Policies that make treatments available only to those who received them prior to incarceration or that limit transition and/or maintenance are inappropriate and out of step with medical standards and should be avoided.

Moreover, regarding sex reassignment surgery the position statement is clear: "Sex reassignment surgery should be considered on a case-by-case basis and provided when determined to be medically necessary for a patient."

This last position statement is important commentary, especially since one of the most well-known cases of transgender rights while incarcerated involved Massachusetts inmate, Michelle Kosilek, who was denied sex reassignment surgery by the Massachusetts Department of Corrections. Her case, along with other prominent cases in the media that have begun to highlight some of the issues that transgender inmates experience, will be detailed below. Many of these cases have begun to shed light on those who have lived their lives not just behind bars, but in the shadows.

Trans Inmates in the Media: Making the Invisible Visible

Though these horrific experiences behind bars were once shrouded in silence, the media has recently brought many of these issues to light, both in the United

States and abroad. This media coverage has both cast a spotlight on human rights violations against trans inmates and at times has further marginalized the trans community. The *National Center for Transgender Equality* points out that while the media attention can shed light on injustice and even cultivate positive change, transgender rights organizations have argued that the coverage of high-profile inmate cases has been done so in a way that "has relied on stereotypical images, contrived confusion over names and pronouns, and an obsession with surgery." Private Chelsea Manning, who was tried, convicted and subsequently incarcerated after a sensational Wikileaks scandal, probably best exemplifies this dichotomy. While her story raised public awareness on the issue of trans inmates, she was consistently misgendered and even referred to as a "gay man" (instead of as a trans woman) by major media outlets.

Nevertheless, there is little chance that trans inmates would receive any attention were it not for sensationalized media consideration, such as in the case of Michelle Kosilek. Kosilek, who was convicted of murdering her wife in 1990, has been at the center of a very public legal battle over her right to obtain sex reassignment surgery while incarcerated. The battle began in 2000 and ever since has seen a series of favorable rulings, all of which were promptly overruled by higher courts. She eventually appealed to the United States Supreme Court, which declined to hear her case. Though her fight has thus far not been resolved favorably, one has to wonder if her case would have made it so far were it not for the public gaze and the support that she received as a direct result of media-generated interest in her plight.

Another case that made national headlines was that of Maryland inmate Sandy Brown, who was serving a five year sentence for assault. She sued the Maryland prison system after she was sent to Patuxent Institution for a routine mental health screening and ended up spending 66 days in solitary confinement. In addition to depriving her of contact with other inmates and recreational activity, correctional officers watched her shower, called her "it," and encouraged her to commit suicide. The court ruled that Sandy's treatment was in fact a violation of the Prison Rape Elimination Act. Brown, who was the first transgender inmate to ever win a legal case under PREA, described horrid conditions. In an interview with *The Advocate*, Brown claimed that she "spent 24 hours a day in solitary and was only allowed one hour of recreation during the entire 66 days I was there. They didn't see me for the human being I am. They treated me like a circus act. They gawked, pointed, made fun of me and tried to break my spirit."

The treatment of trans inmates is gaining just as much attention in the UK as it is in the US, especially the debate over where transgender inmates should be housed. In 2011 the Ministry of Justice issued *The Care and Management of Transsexual Prisoners*, which allows any transgender inmate who has successfully obtained a gender recognition certificate through the Gender Recognition Act of 2004 to be housed in a facility that matches their gender identity. A certificate is issued once a panel approves recognition of an individual (18 or older) who has either completed transition or has been diagnosed as having gender dysphoria and has lived in their "acquired" gender for at least two years. Even though these guidelines are far more humane than any policies in the United States, transgender inmates in the UK still fear for their safety, especially if they have not yet obtained their gender recognition certificate.

Such was the case for Vicky Thompson who, at just 21 years old, was found unresponsive in a male prison in West Yorkshire, England. Prior to being sent to the prison Vicky told friends that she would commit suicide if forced to stay in a men's facility. As a result of her suicide the English government, for the first time, began collecting data on the number of trans inmates in the country. A few weeks after Vicky's death, about 160 miles away, another transgender woman by the name of Joanne Latham was found hanged in a different male prison. It is not unlikely that these two suicides were prompted by fear for their physical and emotional safety, as both occurred only weeks after another trans woman, Tara Hudson, had been moved to a female facility after over 150,000 people signed a petition to get her transferred out of a male prison. Tara, who had been on hormones for her entire adult life and had breast implants (but had not yet petitioned for her gender recognition certificate), had been experiencing severe sexual harassment from other inmates. Unlike Vicky and Joanne, Tara survived her incarceration and has continued to be a focus of British media since her release.

Of all of the trans inmates who have made headlines, the most recognizable is perhaps CeCe McDonald, a Black trans woman who was sent to a male prison after being convicted of second degree murder in 2011. After having racist and transphobic remarks hurled at her by several patrons standing outside of a bar, a woman lunged at CeCe, slashing her face with a broken bottle. When she attempted to run away, her attacker's ex-boyfriend pursued her and she ended up fatally stabbing him with a pair of scissors. Not surprisingly, trans rights groups, trans activists, and allies were outraged that she was not only sentenced for defending herself, but sent to an institution where further abuse and violence was imminent. Unfortunately, CeCe's story might never have been told or gained nearly as much attention had she not garnered support from Laverne Cox, a transgender celebrity. Indeed, one could argue that Laverne Cox has become the face of the movement for the rights of incarcerated trans people.

Laverne Cox, the Most Visible of All: Visibility, Recognition and Social Justice

Orange is the New Black (*OITNB*) premiered on Netflix in July of 2013 and quickly rose to critical and popular acclaim. In fact, while the program itself was developed based on the memoir of former federal inmate, Piper Kerman, the show almost immediately took on a life of its own; a report from *Tech Insider* found that, since its premier, *OITNB* has become the most watched original program on Netflix.

As mentioned, the storylines and character development of *OITNB* have taken on a life far beyond the scope of Kerman's memoir, encompassing continuing storylines that focus on no less than 10 characters as well as garnering several prestigious award nominations from the Emmys, the Screen Actors Guild, and the internationally recognized Golden Globes to name a few. Among the nominations, *OITNB* has won best cast from the Screen Actors Guild in 2016, and actress Uzo Aduba, who plays the character of Suzanne "Crazy Eyes" Warren, has won two Emmys and two Screen Actors Guild awards respectively.

One of the most lauded characteristics of the show itself is that the diverse cast brings more depth to the characters and, indeed, more depth in Hollywood as a whole, where most programs offer no diversity among the actors who portray the characters. *OITNB*'s cast represents women of diverse backgrounds including women of color, women representing a variety of sexual orientations, women representing a broad spectrum of socio-economic privilege, and women representing a range of gender presentations and identities. Among them is Sophia Burset, a Black transgender inmate played by transgender actress and activist Laverne Cox.

In the first two seasons of *OITNB*, Sophia's character introduces some interesting storylines and raises some important issues, but only scratches the surface of the trans inmate experience. Many scenes show her working in a prison hair salon and gossiping with other inmates, making her seem affable and thus easy to like and empathize with. One episode in the first season focuses on Sophia's backstory, including her job as a firefighter, her wife, and young son. We learn that Sophia committed fraud in order to pay for her transition and that this fraudulent activity is what lands her in prison. In addition to the minute focus that the show places on the impact her transition has on her family, the program briefly addresses Sophia's use of hormones that are eventually denied to her for not being seen as life-saving or necessary medication. When she is denied her medication Sophia points to herself and states, "I've given five years, $80,000 and my freedom for this. I'm finally who I'm supposed to be. Do you understand? I can't go back."

Later in the same episode, two correctional officers discuss whether or not they would have sex with Sophia. One correctional officer makes a crude comment about Sophia saying, "…Freaky, freaky-deaky, freaktown, cyborg pussy. I bet it's fucking perfect." The second correctional officer asks, "Don't tell me you'd hit that?" And the first correctional officer responds, "I live in the present, not in the past. Besides, she used to have a dick, and so she knows what it likes."

In Season 3 Sophia's character becomes more complex, and nearly every aspect of her story line centers around the issues outlined in the previous section – the very serious real-life issues that transgender inmates face. By this time the prison is being managed by a private corporation that would rather not be troubled with the concerns Sophia has about her health and safety. In a particularly intense scene, the other inmates confront Sophia, mocking her and refusing to leave her alone until she shows them her genitalia. After Sophia tells them that what everyone has between their legs is their own business, she is immediately attacked. Her hair is grabbed, she's called a "she-male" and while Sophia defends herself against three other inmates one yells, "See! I told you he still has his man strength!" The fight could have been stopped once a correctional officer arrives, but the new private company has cut corners on training so the officer runs to get more help despite Sophia's plea for immediate assistance. Later in the episode the executive's son tells him that Sophia plans to sue because of this lack of training. Here is their exchange:

JACK: You're saying she's threatening us? What do you want me to do, Dad? What we did in Arizona. Some time alone. Let her clear her head.
DANNY: She hasn't done anything wrong.
JACK: Well, of course not, but we can't weed out all the bullies. It's for her own protection.
DANNY: What about when she gets out? I mean, what do you think happens then? Think about the long term.
JACK: Nobody cares about the long term, Danny. Look, a year from now, Huey Strath will be CEO of CCA or fucking Best Western or some other company. All the top guys get traded around like baseball cards, you know that. The important thing is that we nail this quarter and the next one and let everyone collect their bonuses.

This scene is a chilling commentary on the lack of training and the problems associated with accommodating transgender inmates that has been recognized by the *National Institute of Corrections*, a problem that can easily be exacerbated when profit is put before people. What this scene and others also allude to, though, is that some of the "fixes" being proposed will not necessarily solve these issues – Sophia, after all, is facing these issues within the confines of a female prison. Towards the end of the 12th episode of the third season we see three correctional officers take Sophia to segregation, something that routinely happens to trans women housed in male facilities.

Season 4 exposes the mental anguish caused by prolonged segregation. Sophia completely unravels and acts out by flooding her cell, setting it on fire, and smearing the walls of her cell with blood from her wrists. Another inmate and Warden Caputo get word of Sophia's mental decompensation to her wife and she is able to pressure the facility into releasing Sophia back into the general population. The viewer ends the season with the clear understanding that Sophia is forever changed and that the damage caused by segregation may never be undone.

The evolution of Sophia Burset from Season 1 to Season 4 cannot be debated. While she was once focused primarily on her hair salon and beauty tips, as the seasons progressed so did Sophia, from her fight to receive her hormones to the fight for her own human agency as a transgender woman serving time in prison.

Her character has been truly captivating, so it comes as no surprise that Sophia Burset was ranked by *TIME* magazine as the fourth most influential fictional character of 2013, beaten out only by Katniss Everdeen, Olivia Pope, and Walter White.

While no one denies that Sophia is a groundbreaking television character, the show has been criticized for framing Sophia as a one-dimensional character. In all four seasons that have been released thus far, scenes related to Sophia's experiences both in Litchfield and prior to her incarceration have all revolved around her trans identity. Like many LGBTQ characters on television before her, she is grossly reduced to her sexual and gender identity. What sets Sophia apart from previous LGBTQ characters on television, however, is that she represents a population of which the viewing audience is very unlikely to have any real knowledge. While the viewing audience may very well have friends that identify as LGBTQ (thus, providing a reference point for characters on shows like *The L Word*), they are unlikely to have had much, if any, experience with LGBTQ persons behind bars. In this sense, a reductionist presentation of a transgender inmate may be exactly what is needed to begin a conversation that is long overdue – a conversation about the myriad challenges transgender inmates face simply because of their gender identity and a conversation that would not be where it is today were it not for Laverne Cox.

Laverne Cox has not only become a celebrated actress because of her contributions to the show, but because she has established herself as a well-known scholar and activist on a variety of issues, chief among them transgender equality. Cox herself has received nominations for her portrayal of Sophia Burset in *OITNB* as well as a nomination and a win for her documentary, *The T Word*, which highlights the experiences of seven transgender youth from New York. She is without a doubt one of the most recognized transgender women of the 21st century and has arguably become the most visible and influential transgender woman of color on television and, perhaps, in the broader movement for transgender rights. Cox's fame came to a peak at a pivotal time in the history of transgender recognition and her character Sophia invited the *OITNB* audience to consider the complex issue of incarcerating transgender offenders. Without a doubt, the intersection of reality and fiction can bring critical issues such as these to the forefront, making the invisible visible and propelling a shift towards social justice, even for those in the shadows.

References and Further Reading

American Psychological Association. (n.d.) *Answers to Your Questions About Transgender People, Gender Identity, and Gender Expression*. Retrieved from http://www.apa.org/topics/lgbt/transgender.pdf

Brown, G.R. (2009). Recommended revisions to the World Professional Association of Transgender Health's Standards of Care Section on Medical Care for Incarcerated

Persons with Gender Identity Disorder. *International Journal of Transgenderism*, 11(2), 133–139.

Buist, C.L., & Lenning, E. (2015). *Queer Criminology*. United Kingdom: Routledge

Cox, L. (2013). CeCe McDonald: Survivor and leader. April 20th. Retrieved from http://www.lavernecox.com/2013/04/20/cece-mcdonald-survivor-and-leader//

Homan, T. (2015). *Further Guidance regarding the Care of Transgender Detainees*. United States Immigration and Customs Enforcement. United States Department of Homeland Security. Memorandum. Retrieved from https://www.ice.gov/sites/default/files/documents/Document/2015/TransgenderCareMemorandum.pdf

Mathias, C. (2014). New York's largest jail to open housing unit for transgender women. *Huffington Post*. Retrieved from http://www.huffingtonpost.com/2014/11/18/rikers-transgender-women_n_6181552.html

National Institute of Corrections. (n.d.). Documents. Retrieved from http://nicic.gov/library/browse.aspx?View=CORP&CORP=National%20Commission%20on%20Correctional%20Health%20Care%20(NCCHC)%20(Chicago,%20IL)

Routh, D., Abess, G., Makin, D., Stohr, M.K., Hemmens, C., & Yoo, J. (2015). Transgender inmates in prisons: A review of applicable statutes and policies. *International Journal of Offender Therapy and Comparative Criminology*. 1–22, Advance Access.

PART 2

Racial Inequality and Prisons

Shirley A. Jackson

Social scientists have long been concerned about racial disparities in arrests and sentencing. These racial disparities exist for men and women. Stereotypes are a contributing factor to these existing disparities. However, exploring this dilemma requires moving to other often less scrutinized contributing aspects. Social class and cultural perceptions of the ideal woman versus the bad woman are two of these. The chapters in this section of the book focus on some of these elements, but also include those such as over-policing of girls of color in school, and the tendency to view girls and women who do not conform to mainstream society's cultural norms of good and virtuous.

Stereotypes of racialized minorities, specifically African American women and Latinas, have been largely negative, especially as regards the tendency to ascribe characteristics depicting them as criminals, undeserving welfare recipients, bad mothers, violent, and hypersexual. These deleterious characterizations cross age groups, and thus, have a broad impact on how the group as a whole is perceived. The mass incarceration of African American women and Latinas can be demoralizing for their families and for members of the group who are at risk for being similarly stereotyped. Heavy sentences can be a punishment aimed at women who violate social dictates regarding proper feminine behavior, further adding to their Otherness when compared to White women who are viewed as individuals while women of color are viewed as representative of the group.

Latinas and African American women find themselves disproportionately represented among those with drug convictions according to scholars such as Meda Chesney-Lind, Natalie Sokoloff, and others. *The Sentencing Project* asserts that the War on Drugs has had a significant part to play in their increasing numbers among the incarcerated. Women of color who enter the prison system as a result of the War on Drugs find themselves victims of stereotypes about "crack whores" with "crack babies" or as women who are complicit in criminal behavior as the girlfriends of men involved in the drug trade. Their over-representation among those convicted of such crimes adds to their perception as undesirable and unworthy women. As a result of their intimate connections, they end up imprisoned because they have nothing to offer the authorities to receive more lenient sentences; something their male partners are capable of providing. Instead of being perceived as unconnected, blameless, or even gullible, they are viewed as complicit gun molls who aided and abetted their drug dealing partners.

Social class and race play a significant role in how stereotypes are not only formed, but maintained. African American women and Latinas are prone to those stereotypes that can lead to lengthier sentences because of their perceived criminality and their propensity to engage in violent behavior. Stereotypes held by Latino/a adolescents of their peers are a factor in how they respond to violent situations. Perceived potential violence is met with violence (Ascencio, 1999). Within their cultural, class, and neighborhood norms, dwell their individual stereotypes about themselves and their peers. The result is a thought-provoking counter-narrative to the perceived stereotypes of their violent "nature" by outsiders. Gender-based violence and stereotypes of those who are engaged in it whether willingly or not is an important consideration when it comes to forming inflexible ideas about those who are violent and thus deserve to be incarcerated.

Relatedly, research by Vera López and Meda Chesney-Lind provides an understanding of the impact on stereotypes on how Latina girls saw themselves and perceived others to view them. Stereotypes of African American girls impact their treatment in schools as they oftentimes face suspension in schools at rates not experienced by their peers according to Michelle Morris, author of *Pushout: The criminalization of black girls in schools.* Sociologist Victor Rios has reached similar findings in his work on African American and Latino boys who are punished in and out of school based on their peer group association, race/ethnicity, and perceived association with criminal activity. Furthermore, the media can exacerbate stereotypes making it more difficult for prisoners to be viewed as worthy of compassion or even release.

In her chapter, "An Overlooked Link: Popular Media Stereotypes and the Incarceration of Black Girls and Young Women," Kristin Dukes focuses on media stereotypes by outlining the problem of the prevalence of stereotypes that are directly applied to Black girls and young women. The damaging effects of these stereotypes is important to acknowledge. Dukes pays specific attention to their treatment and not so much the criminal behavior of Black women and young girls. Once Black females are perceived to have bad attitudes and/or bad verbal comments, they suffer serious consequences. Their unwillingness to conform to acceptable notions of appropriate behavior, especially towards authorities, makes their situation even more precarious and the likelihood they will receive greater punitive treatment more certain. After all, unruly children must learn to reform their behavior and attitudes and if unwilling to do so, they lend themselves to being treated harshly or as adults. For African American girls, their unruly behavior and bad attitudes are perceived as evidence of their inappropriate socialization or unwillingness to conform to respectable behavior.

Dukes shares accounts of young African American women who were treated as though they were armed and violent criminals by authority figures who saw them as threats. She is one of several examples of African American children who are treated roughly by the police and school officials who deem them a threat to the adults' physical safety because of their verbal responses and unfortunately, their skin color. Language is an especially salient aspect of how one's actions are viewed. Many can recall the disparate characterizations during Hurricane Katrina when African Americans were perceived to be "looting" stores for food while Whites were described as "finding food" (Sommers, Apfelbaum, Dukes, Toosi, & Wang, 2006). Dukes notes that the differentiated behavior of young female juveniles is perceived in much the same way whereas White girls are simply good girls from good families who have made bad decisions. On the other hand, African American girls are from poor families, live in poor neighborhoods, and thus, are likely just mere steps away from being incarcerated.

Cheryle Snead-Greene and Michael Royster's chapter, "Popular Media Portrayal of Imprisoned Black Women" describes the impact of the War on Drugs on the incarceration of African American and Latina women. It becomes evident in their chapter that the drug war has not impacted those who are at the higher levels of the drug trade, but instead, mothers, poorly skilled women who lack job opportunities, and those who are victims of interpersonal violence outside of and within prison walls. They note that in addition to the heavy sentences handed out to these women, they are ill-equipped to remain out of prison. This is not surprising given the cycle of generational poverty and their lack of employment skills. The women are poorly positioned to avoid re-entering prison once released due to the same issues that result in their passage through prison gates.

Snead-Greene and Royster also explore how media inform the public's image of what occurs within the walls of prisons. The reality is that many people do not see what occurs firsthand; but experience it vicariously through TV shows and the big screen. When women, especially, women of color are portrayed as drug dealers, violent, and lacking in civil behavior, it serves to justify their incarceration and confirm their inability to change. The fact that they are portrayed so successfully on the screen makes it hard to see women who have been convicted of crimes similar to those in *OITNB* as anything other than deserving of their punishment. After all, even with their lengthy prison sentences, they appear to be having a good time. Because they as prisoners do not resonate with the larger population as being real women, their plights are inconsequential. Thus, calls for reform, employment training, education, and so on, may not seem necessary.

Bonnie Zare's chapter, "*Indifference is the New Black*: Season One and the Violation of Women's Solidarity" examines the way in which the majority of the population are unfamiliar with and indifferent to the realities of prison life. In large part, this indifference is situated within the complexities of race relations and stereotypes that exist regarding those who are incarcerated. Studies show that there are differences with regard to how men and women of different race/ethnic groups view those in prison and their chances of rehabilitation.

Zare focuses on an issue that some neglect to consider as an important issue for prisoners, mental health stability and the treatment of mental illness. There are several characters who either pretend to be or are mentally ill but treatment options are woefully absent. These individuals seem to be generally accepted as having "something" wrong but no attempts are made to effectively address them. There is a general tone of indifference that dismisses the severity of the matter. Using original research based on interviews with current and former female prisoners in Wyoming, Zare gives an account of how the women perceived their treatment and the ways in which they were treated as though they were insignificant. The words of the women are eerily similar to the findings of David L. Rosenhan in his landmark 1973 study on perceptions of insanity. While individuals can be labeled deviant because they are criminals and mentally ill, it appears as though the former becomes their master status (Becker, 1963). The distortion of the realities of prison life make it difficult to see the women as something other than criminals. Other identities appear to be secondary in nature.

In the three chapters that make up this section of the book the authors explore at length the intersection of race, class, gender, stereotypes, and prison. They do so using the backdrop of *Orange is the New Black*, a fictional account of a women's prison, interspersed with the realities of African American and Latina girls, and women who find themselves regarded as criminals before they are even incarcerated. During their incarceration and following their release, stereotypes continue to plague their treatment and opportunities. Without viable opportunities prior to and following their incarceration, African American and Latinas find themselves going through a revolving door where bouts with incarceration are accompanied by freedom and possibilities for re-incarceration.

References and Further Reading

Asencio, M. W. (1999). Machos and sluts: Gender, sexuality, and violence among a cohort of Puerto Rican adolescents. *Medical Anthropology Quarterly*, 13(1), 107–126.

Becker, H. (1963). *Outsiders*. New York: Macmillan.

Chesney-Lind, M. (1997). *The female offender: Girls, women, and crime*. Thousand Oaks, CA: Sage.

Lopez, V., & Chesney-Lind, M. (2014). Latina girls speak out: Stereotypes, gender and relationship dynamics. *Latino Studies*, 12(4), 527–549.

Morris, M. W. (2016). *Pushout: The criminalization of black girls in schools*. New York: The New Press.

Rosenhan, D. L. (1973). On being sane in insane places. *Science*, 179(4070), 250–258.

Sokoloff, N. J. (2005). Women prisoners at the dawn of the 21st century. *Women & Criminal Justice*, 16(1–2), 127–137.

Sommers, S. R., Apfelbaum, E. P., Dukes, K. N., Toosi, N., & Wang, E. J. (2006). Race and media coverage of Hurricane Katrina: Analysis, implications, and future research questions. *Analyses of Social Issues and Public Policy*, 6(1), 1–17.

The Sentencing Project. (2013). The changing racial dynamics of women's incarceration. Washington, D.C. Retrieved from http://sentencingproject.org/wp-content/uploads/2015/12/The-Changing-Racial-Dynamics-of-Womens-Incarceration.pdf

4

AN OVERLOOKED LINK

Popular Media, Stereotypes, and the Incarceration of Black Girls and Young Women

Kristin N. Dukes

The United States may be falling behind other nations in many important indicators of societal well-being such as infant mortality and life expectancy, but it continues to hold the "honor" of having the highest incarceration rate in the world. According to The Sentencing Project (2015a), a non-profit advocacy group, the U.S. has experienced a 500% increase in its prison and jail population in the last 40 years with the current imprisoned population estimated at more than 2.3 million. Many, such as legal scholar Michelle Alexander, have now labeled this steep increase in imprisonment over the past four decades an era of mass incarceration.

The *era of mass incarceration* has not confined all racial and ethnic groups in the U.S. equally. People of color, particularly Blacks, are disproportionately incarcerated. People of color make up more than 60% of the prison population with Blacks imprisoned at the highest rates. Hispanics are twice as likely to be incarcerated as Whites, whereas Blacks are five times more likely to be incarcerated than Whites. This racial disparity is exacerbated by gender as data from The Sentencing Project (2015a) demonstrates. While, the lifetime likelihood of imprisonment for Black men is 1 in 3 compared to a rate of 1 in 17 for White men, the lifetime likelihood of imprisonment for Black women is 1 in 18 compared to a rate of 1 in 111 for White women.

These trends in mass incarceration carry over to the juvenile justice system. Though rates of juvenile incarceration have steadily declined over the past 15 or so years from a high of 77,800 youth committed to juvenile facilities and roughly 13,000 placed in adult jails or prisons in 1999 to 35,246 youth committed to juvenile facilities and approximately 6,000 placed in adult jails or prisons in 2013, racial disparities in youth contact with the juvenile justice system and incarceration prevail. According to U.S. Census data, in 2013, Black youth made up approximately 15% of the U.S. population under the age of 18, yet 38% juvenile justice cases involved Black youth. Further, as sociologist Victor Rios (2011) estimates, Blacks represent 26% of juvenile arrests, 44% of youth who are detained, 46% of the youth who are judicially waived to criminal court, and 58% of the youth admitted to state prisons. Adult incarceration rates and racial disparities in the juvenile justice system are exacerbated by gender. Monique Morris, author of *Pushout: The criminalization of Black girls in schools* (2016), finds that Black girls experience some of the highest rates of residential detention and represent the fastest-growing segment of the juvenile justice population. As stated above, overall rates of juvenile incarceration are declining but a racial gap exists within this decline. According to data in The Sentencing Project (2015b), from 1997 to 2013, the percentage of White girls confined dropped from 49% to 41%; however, the percentage dropped at a slower rate, from 34% to 31%, for Black girls.

Pushed Out, Over-policed, and Underprotected

Over the past decade scholars and policymakers have become more invested in understanding how and why youth of color are prematurely and disproportionately incarcerated in the U.S. Some advocates have focused on the tendency for punitive disciplinary measures in schools, particularly suspension and expulsion, to increase the likelihood of a student interfacing with the juvenile and adult criminal justice systems. This phenomenon is often referred to as the school-to-prison pipeline. According to the American Civil Liberties Union (ACLU), the school-to-prison pipeline refers to the policies and practices that push our nation's schoolchildren, especially at-risk children, out of classrooms and into the juvenile and criminal justice systems. A number of factors along this pathway have been identified as contributors to incarceration. These include 1) zero-tolerance discipline policies in schools which impose severe punishments for disputably minor offenses, 2) increased reliance on police officers or school resource officers to maintain order in schools, and 3) involvement of the juvenile justice system in school disciplinary issues, that is, in-school disciplinary infractions being handled in court rather than in school. Racial disparities in school discipline, and relatedly the school-to-prison pipeline, mirror those seen in the juvenile and adult criminal justice systems. Racial differences in how school discipline is handled are well documented. For instance, a recent national survey of schools by the Department of Education Office of Civil Rights (2014) found that Black students are suspended and expelled at a rate three times greater than White students. And again, like incarceration rates in the adult and juvenile criminal justice systems, racial disparities in school discipline are amplified by gender, an observation discussed in greater detail below.

Until recently, limited attention has been placed on the *school-to-prison pipeline* as it relates to Black girls in the U.S. specifically. Recent data on critical entry points along the school-to-prison pipeline suggest that the risk of Black girls entering into the criminal justice system is increasing at an alarming rate. As legal scholar, Kimberlé Crenshaw (2016) put it, Black girls are being "pushed out, overpoliced, and underprotected." Black girls are disciplined more and receive harsher punishments than their White counterparts. For instance, U.S. Department of Education (ED, 2015) data for the 2011–2012 academic year showed that Black girls were suspended at a rate six times that of White girls. More than 12% of Black girls nationwide received at least one out-of-school suspension compared to only 2% percent of White girls. The suspension rate for Black girls exceeded that of girls of any other race or ethnicity and exceeded the rate of most boys regardless of race. The disproportionate suspension of Black students begins as early as preschool. While Black students represented 18% of preschool enrollment during the 2011–2012 school year, they represented 48% of preschool children receiving more than one out-of-school suspension. The magnitude of this differential for Black girls specifically is not reported.

This discrepancy is even more pronounced among some school districts. An examination of discipline in the Boston and New York City public school districts during the 2013–2014 school year (Crenshaw, 2016) revealed that in Boston, 61% of all girls disciplined were Black and in New York City, 56% of all girls disciplined were Black. White girls represented only 5% of girls disciplined in both districts. This translates to Black girls being eleven times more likely than White girls to be disciplined in Boston public schools and ten times more likely to be disciplined in New York City public schools. Black girls also received harsher punishments than White girls with Black girls twelve times more likely to be suspended from Boston public schools and ten times more likely to be suspended from New York City public schools. Black girls constituted 63% of all girls expelled in Boston public school and 90% of girls expelled in New York City public schools; no White girls were expelled from either school district. This translates to Black girls being ten times more likely to be expelled in Boston public schools and an overwhelming fifty-three times more likely to be expelled in New York City public schools.

This type and level of discipline in our nation's schools is astonishing given what we know about the ineffectiveness of suspension and expulsion. Evidence simply does not show that suspension or expulsion improve student behavior or school climate. The Department of Education, which acknowledges that students of color are suspended and expelled at higher rates than their peers, is raising awareness of the negative impact of suspension and expulsion, and is encouraging educators and administrators to *rethink discipline*; but are we moving fast enough to save Black girls from the school-to-prison pipeline?

As critics of the school-to-prison pipeline often highlight, school discipline is a much too easy entryway into the juvenile court system, particularly through law enforcement referrals for in-school disciplinary infractions and school-related arrest. Racial disparity in discipline and harsher punishment extends to this domain as well. While Black students represent 16% of student enrollment, as data from the DOE Office for Civil Rights (2014) shows, they represent 27% of students referred to law enforcement and 31% of students subjected to school-related arrests. Again, the magnitude of this differential for Black girls specifically is not reported.

An Overlooked Link

Data clearly indicate that, Black girls are disproportionately impacted by punitive disciplinary measures, a critical risk factor for contact with the juvenile and adult criminal justice systems; yet, the bulk of interventions developed to disrupt the school-to-prison pipeline have focused on Black boys and young men, over-looking Black girls and young women. For example, in 2014, President Obama launched the My Brother's Keeper (MBK) Initiative to address "persistent opportunity gaps faced by boys and young men of color and ensure that all young people can reach their full potential (2015)." While the language around MBK is general and seemingly inclusive of *all young people*, the prevailing connotation is that the initiative targets boys and young men of color. Few initiatives of this type exist for girls and young women of color and none of them match the magnitude of MBK. For example, in 2010 the Office of Juvenile Justice and Delinquency Prevention (OJJDP, 2012) established the National Girls Institute (NGI) as "a national clearinghouse for information and as a training and technical assistance center for gender-specific programming." The NGI received $776,000 in funding in fiscal year 2014 compared to the more than $300 million committed to MBK by private-sector and non-profit foundations, businesses, and social enterprises during the same time period. And although the White House Council on Women and Girls released a comprehensive report on challenges faced by girls and women of color in the U.S., only a few paragraphs of the over forty-page report concentrated on the disproportionate incarceration of Black girls and women.

While targeting the school-to-prison pipeline and its role in the criminalization of children and adolescents' behavior is absolutely necessary, I argue that a link critical to understanding the treatment of Black girls and young women at every point along the school-to-pipeline is being overlooked and understudied. That link is popular media and stereotypes of Black women. I contend that we have not paid enough attention to how media portrayals of Black girls and young women as aggressive and criminal may influence their introduction into and treatment within the juvenile and criminal justice systems.

Scholars are beginning to concentrate on this link. For instance, some empirical research suggests that racial disparities in harshness of school discipline may be partially driven by racial stereotypes. One study by social psychologists Jason Okonofua and Jennifer Eberhardt (2015) presented K-12 teachers with records of a Black or White student who misbehaved twice. While there were no differ-ences in perceptions of students after their first infraction, teachers felt more "troubled" after the second infraction committed by the Black student than after the second infraction committed by the White student and thought the Black student should be disciplined more severely after the second infraction than the White student. Additionally, teachers were more likely to label the Black student a "trouble maker" and state that the Black student's behavior across the two incidents was a pattern. And although the teacher perceived the infractions to be minor, they were more likely to imagine themselves suspending the Black student in the future compared to the White student. These findings suggest that racial stereotypes have the potential to not only impact how teachers interpret Black students' behavior and the type of discipline they feel is appropriate but may also lower the threshold for interpreting future behavior through a stereotypical lens. This pattern of increasingly negative evaluation of Black students over multiple interactions has been labeled the *Black-escalation effect.*

This study is valuable in that it is one of the first to examine race-related discrepancies in school discipline using an experimental paradigm and actual teachers as participants. However, this study suffers from a flaw shared by the bulk of research in this domain – it lacks an explicit emphasis on both race and gender. Accounting for the unique consequences of Black women and girls' social identities as both "Black" and "female" is required to fully grasp how they are perceived, interpreted, treated, and valued. Distinct stereotypes exist for Black women and girls apart from stereotypes of women as a gender group, Blacks as racial group, and Black men specifically, making it problematic to generalize scholarship on any of the latter groups to the former. Social psychological research on stereotyping of Black women suggests that Black women are viewed as "having an attitude", "loud", "ghetto/unrefined", and "aggressive". Yet, to my knowledge, an up-to-date social psychological analysis of the proliferation of these stereotypes in popular media and their influence on perceptions of Black girls and young women has not been conducted. Additionally, the potential link between these portrayals and attitudes surrounding the incarceration of Black girls and young women has not been fully explored.

This chapter aims to address this void by examining portrayals of Black girls and young women as aggressive that may influence perceptions of them as well as their entry into and treatment within the juvenile and criminal justice systems. Specifically, I focus on three poignant examples of Black girls and young women depicted as aggressive and criminal:

1. The violent detainment of 15-year-old Dajerria Becton, one of several Black adolescents attending a pool party in a subdivision of McKinney, Texas
2. Portrayals of Black girls on A&E's unscripted series *Beyond Scared Straight*, a television show that profiles at-risk adolescents' experiences in young offender intervention programs
3. The widely shared video clip of the vicious assault of 17-year-old Sha'Michael Manuel by 16-year-old Sharkeisha Thompson, both Black teenage girls

I argue that these examples are merely a drop in the ocean of popular media depictions that perpetuate the belief that Black girls are aggressive, unruly, and in need of taming.

"Have an Attitude" and "Loud": Stereotypes of Black Women

Stereotypic representations of Black girls and young women are commonplace in our society, particularly in popular media. According to psychologist, Carolyn West (1995), many of these representations are based on three distinct sociocultural and historical images or archetypes of Black women: the Mammy, the Jezebel, and the Sapphire. Originating in the U.S. South during slavery, the Mammy portrays Black women as domestic, subservient, and nurturing, especially towards Whites. She is often depicted as overweight, dark-skinned, unattractive by European standards, and asexual. The Jezebel also originated during slavery and was used to justify the rape of Black slave women by White male masters. The Jezebel paints Black women as sexually promiscuous and seductive with insatiable sexual appetites. The Jezebel is almost a direct contrast to the Mammy physically, depicted as slender yet curvaceous, light-skinned, exoticized, and hypersexual. Finally, the Sapphire, taking its name after Ernestine Wade's character Sapphire Stevens on the *Amos 'n' Andy* show, represents Black women as ill-tempered and emasculating. The Sapphire is often depicted as the angry or sassy Black woman.

These representations are apparent in Negin Ghavami and Letiha Peplau's (2012) psychological research on stereotypes of Black women. When asked to report stereotypes associated with Black women, participants responded that Black women are "overweight", "dark-skinned" and "not feminine" (traits consistent with the Mammy), that Black women are "promiscuous" (a trait consistent with the Jezebel), and that Black women "have an attitude", are "loud", and "aggressive" (traits consistent with the Sapphire). It is important to note that "have an attitude" and "loud" were the most frequently reported stereotypes of Black women. I assert that these general stereotypes of Black women found in empirical research extend to Black girls and young women, and that the Sapphire is a particularly dominant and recurring representation of Black girls and young women. Below I analyze three examples of the Sapphire image in popular media.

"I'm guessing he thought we were saying rude stuff to him":
The Detainment of Dajerria Becton

On June 5, 2015, police officers responded to a disturbance call at a pool party being held at Craig Ranch North, a private, predominantly White subdivision of McKinney, Texas. In an attempt to control the situation, several Black teenagers were detained by police; 15-year-old Dajerria Becton was one of these teenagers. Becton was only wearing a two-piece bathing suit when she was violently forced to the ground by Officer Eric Casebolt, a man roughly twice her size. The incident was filmed by Brandon Brooks, a White teenager attending the party, and later posted on YouTube.

Dajerria Becton recounted the events from her perspective during an interview with a local news station. She stated, "He grabbed me, twisted my arm on my back and shoved me in the grass and started pulling the back of my braids...I was telling him to get off me because my back was hurting bad." In the video, Dajerria can be heard begging for Casebolt to get off of her and crying out for someone to call her mother. When asked what prompted Officer Casebolt to tackle her to the ground, Becton responded, "He told me to keep walking and I kept walking and then I'm guessing he thought we were saying rude stuff to him." Consistent with Dajerria's assessment, just seconds before Eric Casebolt's tackles her to the ground, he angrily orders Black girls in the vicinity to "quit standing there running their mouths."

Becton's account of the encounter with Officer Casebolt suggests that her perceived bad attitude was the impetus for her detainment. A viewing of the video makes it difficult to argue that Dajerria Becton was a physical threat to the officer. She was walking away from the scene in a two-piece bathing suit with nothing in her hands. Her only *weapon* was a "bad attitude" and "loud" mouth. These traits were enough to signal aggression for Eric Casebolt. It is important to note that just prior to dragging Dajerria Becton to the ground by her hair, Officer Casebolt yelled profanities at other Black teens walking away from the party – "Get your asses out of here." He tackled at least three other Black boys to the ground and handcuffed them. Casebolt even drew his loaded weapon at several unarmed teenagers. Meanwhile, Brandon Brooks, a White teen within similar proximity to police officers arriving on the scene as the Black teens, films the entire encounter and is never once told by officers to get on the ground or move away. Brooks even noticed how differently he was treated stating, "Everyone who was getting put on the ground was Black, Mexican, Arabic. [The cop] didn't even look at me. It was kind of like I was invisible".

Supporters of Officer Eric Casebolt's actions quickly remarked that had Dajerria Becton only been quiet and obeyed the officer's commands, the situation would not have escalated. But these supporters do not question why the perceived unruly attitude and loud voice of a 14 year-old child represented an aggressive act for an officer with over a decade of experience in law enforcement. One would like to believe that Dajerria Becton's detainment was an isolated incident; however, it is merely one of many incidents of excessive use of force against unarmed Black girls that have gained visibility in recent years.

For instance, on June 9, 2015, an unidentified 12-year-old Black girl was arrested alongside her mother, 34-year-old Maya Dixon, her pregnant aunt, 33-year-old Krystal Dixon, and an unidentified 15-year-old male following an altercation with police at the Fairfield Aquatic Center near Cincinnati, Ohio. Police were called during a dispute between Krystal Dixon and staff after one of several children dropped off by Dixon was asked to leave the pool for not having appropriate swimwear. The dispute escalated and became physical. Surveillance video and cell phone footage of the incident depict the chaotic encounter between the two adults, two juveniles, and police. The footage shows the 12-year-old girl being handcuffed and pinned against a police cruiser. Shortly after the incident, a spokesperson and an attorney for the Dixon family alleged that the girl suffered injuries during the arrest. Additionally, the local news noted that several children were taken to the hospital for secondary exposure to pepper spray deployed by officers on the scene. Krystal Dixon ultimately pleaded guilty to disorderly conduct and no contest to resisting arrest. The 12-year-old girl in the incident was charged with assault and resisting arrest, and as of March 2016, her case was still pending in juvenile court.

Another example of questionable force against a Black girl was also captured by cell phone camera in late October 2015 when Senior Deputy Ben Fields, a South Carolina school resource officer, violently arrested a 16-year-old student. The incident occurred when the girl, only identified by her first name Shakara, used her cell phone in class and refused to comply with her teacher and a vice-principal's request to leave class as punishment. Deputy Fields was then asked to handle the situation. When Shakara did not comply with Fields' request to leave the classroom, he pulled Sharaka from her desk by her neck flipping her and the desk backward. Shakara suffered a fractured arm, swollen neck, back, and shoulder, and cuts to her face from the arrest. A civil rights investigation was ultimately opened by the FBI and an area U.S. Attorney's Office to determine whether federal laws were violated during the student's arrest. And while Fields was fired for using inappropriate force, Richland County Sheriff Leon Lott remarked that Shakara was partly to blame because "she started this" and was disrespectful and disruptive in class.

"I have a bad attitude and I like to fight": Black Girls on Beyond Scared Straight

Loosely based on the award-winning documentary *Scared Straight*, A&E's unscripted series *Beyond Scared Straight* is a reality television show chronicling at-risk youths' experiences in young offender intervention programs. The show profiles these youth and their families prior to, during, and after participation in young offender intervention programs. The youth are often prodded to detail their bad behavior. While there is roughly equal participation of both Black and non-Black girls in the programs featured throughout the series, there are striking cross-racial differences in the portrayals of these girls. For example, Season 1 Episode 7 profiles several teenage girls participating in the P.U.S.H. (Prisoners United Spreading Hope) program hosted by the Maryland Correctional Institution for Women (Jessup Women's prison). Although this episode features a racially diverse sample of participants, there are noticeable differences in the character-izations on these teens on the basis of race. The alleged crimes perpetrated by the

Black girls in this episode are drastically different than those done by the White girls. One black teenage girl has a juvenile criminal history that includes a second degree assault and weapon possession charges. Juxtapose this representation with that of four White teenage girls who were in the program for shoplifting. Similar offenses are even described differently across race in this episode. For instance, the caption states that 13 year-old Brandi, who is White, is in the program for "fighting" while it states that 17-year-old Cassandra, who is Black, is in the program for "assault."

Cassandra's story also *confirms* a number of Black racial group stereotypes within the first five minutes of the episode. Cassandra's pre-P.U.S.H. interview begins with her saying, "My name is Cassandra. I am 17 years-old and the crime I had committed was second-degree assault." The interview highlights that she lives in an impoverished inner-city neighborhood full of criminal activity and that many of her friends are from broken homes. Cassandra states, "My neighborhood is pretty much made up of gangs, violence, drugs, the whole nine yards. It's just ghetto around here. I can't wait to get out of here." She talks about her drug addiction, alludes to a history of prostitution, and speaks quite cavalierly about participating in an assault and robbery. Cassandra's intensive outpatient counselor Angela J. gives additional details about Cassandra's history as a runaway. Angela states, "[Cassandra] had quite of few issues going on when it comes to family…she has been from foster home to foster home. Her family has pretty much kind of turned their back on her… she was well on her way to self-destruction had she not gotten caught." Angela concludes, "If Cassandra continues on the path she's on, I believe that she can end up an inmate and for a very long time." By contrast, 13-year-old Megan and 15-year-old Alyssa are White participants in the P.U.S. H. program. The two sisters were caught shoplifting. Megan and Alyssa's mother and father are interviewed together about their behavior and characterize them as "good girls." Their mother tearfully states, "My girls have done well in this world and have never been in trouble before except for this one offense."

Even the physical location and atmosphere of the portrayals differ dramatically. Cassandra is shown walking down a barren and gray inner-city street with sirens blaring in the background. She gives her interview in a building stairwell. Alyssa and Megan are interviewed at their home, standing leisurely in a grassy yard with boats sitting in the background in one scene and sitting comfortably on their front porch in another scene. One is shown putting on makeup in her bedroom and the other is shown playing a guitar. Other episodes repeat the pattern of overtly negative and stereotypical portrayals of Black girl participants relative to their White counterparts. More times than not, Black girl participants explain that they are in the program for "being disrespectful", "having a bad attitude", and "fighting", leaving the viewer to discern if these traits are truly that common among Black girls and young women in daily life.

"Sharkeisha No!": The assault of Sha'Michael Manuel

It could be called the punch heard around the world. On November 27, 2013, video footage of a violent attack on 16-year-old Sha'Michael Manuel by another Black teenage girl only identified as Sharkeisha (Thompson) surfaced on social media. In the roughly 90 second video, Sharkeisha delivers a powerful sucker punch to Manuel and begins kicking Manuel in the head once she is on the ground. One bystander yells, "Sharkeisha no! Don't kick her in the head!" The video quickly went viral, resulting in countless shares on Facebook, a flurry of memes based on the altercation, an entry in the Urban Dictionary, and a song mentioning the fight. Sharkeisha even gained thousands of followers on Twitter after the attack. As of early 2016, the clip had garnered close to 30 million views on various social media sites.

But what does this social media fascination with Black girls' violent altercations tell us about perceptions of them? The Sharkeisha fight video is just one of thousands of clips routinely shared on the website World Star Hip-Hop, a social media platform for entertainment and popular culture videos. In fact, filming fights and uploading them to this site is so common that bystanders are often heard yelling "World Star" while capturing footage of altercations. A quick glance in the comments sections of these videos gives us a glimpse into societal attitudes about Black female aggression. Comments are often blatantly racist, and more often than not, focus on the physical toughness of Black girls. Further, when the videos feature girls and women of other races or ethnicities fighting, comparisons are commonly made with Black girls and women – "She fights like a Black girl." There is even a video of two White girls fighting named "The White Sharkeisha" suggesting that this type of violent behavior is normative for Black girls and must be labeled and explained when acted out by non-Black girls. Numerous fight videos like these circulate the internet and social media. The comments about these videos illustrate startling, but not so surprising, attitudes about Black girls and young women. It is clear that these videos reinforce the belief that Black girls and young women are aggressive, violent, and dangerous.

Conclusion

Black girls and young women represent a substantial segment of the population impacted by the juvenile and adult criminal justice systems. Harsher punitive measures for Black girls in our nation's schools increase their likelihood of coming in contact with these systems. School level interventions are no doubt critical to eliminating this trend. Still, I argue, that media portrayals of Black girls and young women as aggressive and criminal are an underexamined link to disproportionate incarceration rates for these girls and young women. Pervasive stereotypic representations like the examples I described in this chapter have the tremendous power to influence the way Black girls and young women are viewed, how their actions are interpreted, and consequently, how they are treated. These representations perpetuate the belief that Black girls and women are aggressive, unruly, and in need of taming. Unfortunately, the method of "taming" often involves unjustified use of force, prosecution, and confinement rather than social support and therapeutic interventions. Further, these representations have meaningful implications for the societal acceptance, support, and even encouragement of the incarceration of young Black women and girls.

Attention is shifting toward the treatment of Black girls in our nation's schools but more must be done. For example, The ED and DOJ spearheaded the *Rethink Discipline* campaign. In July 2015, the Departments hosted a conference with school administrators and teachers from across the country in an effort to "advance the national conversation about reducing the overuse of unnecessary out of school suspensions and expulsions and replacing these practices with positive alternatives that keep students in school and engaged in learning, but also ensure accountability" (ED, 2015) The conference built on work done by MBK, the White House Council on Women and Girls, and the Supportive School Discipline Initiative. Additionally, the DOJ launched the National Resource Center for School Justice Partnerships with the aim of advancing school discipline reform efforts and providing training and technical assistance portal for juvenile courts, schools, law enforcement agencies, and others to support school discipline reform efforts at the local level.

The ED website prominently displays statistics about suspension and expulsion rates in public schools as well as reports on the disparate use of these practices with students of color and students with disabilities. Still, *Rethink Discipline* does not focus on Black girls specifically. Rather, it provides general recommendations for improving discipline practices. Providing this type of information raises awareness, but targeted policies and actions are needed to transform the treatment of Black girls in our public schools.

As President Obama recently noted, "[Women of color] struggle every day with biases that perpetuate oppressive standards for how they're supposed to look and how they're supposed to act. Too often, they're either left under the hard light of scrutiny, or cloaked in a kind of invisibility (White House Council on Women and Girls, 2014)." Indeed, Black girls and young women are hypervisible recipients of undue punishment in school and the criminal justice system; yet, their social invisibility hinders responsiveness to unique challenges they face. Black girls' social invisibility dampens our willingness to acknowledge and engage in social movements focusing on their plight.

Focus must be placed on the profound influence that negative stereotypes like the ones described in this chapter have on societal views and treatment of Black girls and young women. To this end, some scholars have suggested interventions for teachers and administrators that encourage them to view student behavior as malleable rather than a reflection of the students' disposition or cultural competence training in conjunction with clearer standards for student behavior. However, concrete changes to school discipline and juvenile justice system policy that explicitly focus on Black girls and young women and take into account the power of stereotypes are vital for noticeable equity.

References

Alexander, M. (2010). *The new Jim Crow: Mass incarceration in the age of colorblindness.* New York, NY: New Press.

Crenshaw, K. W. (2016). *Black girls matter: Pushed out, overpoliced and underprotected.* African American Policy Forum. Retrieved from https://static1.squarespace.com/static/53f20d90e4b0b80451158d8c/t/54d2d37ce4b024b41443b0ba/1423102844010/BlackGirlsMatter_Report.pdf

Ghavami, N., & Peplau, L. A. (2012). An intersectional analysis of gender and ethnic stereotypes: Testing three hypotheses. *Psychology of Women Quarterly,* 37(1), 113–127.

Morris, M. W. (2016). *Pushout: The criminalization of Black girls in schools.* New York, NY: The New Press.

My Brother's Keeper Task Force (2015, February 27). One-year progress report to the President [Press Release]. Retrieved from https://www.whitehouse.gov/sites/default/files/docs/mbk_one_year_report_2.pdf

Okonofua, J. A., & Eberhardt, J. L. (2015). Two strikes: Race and the disciplining of young students. *Psychological Science,* 26(5), 617–624.

Office of Juvenile Justice and Delinquency Prevention (2012). National Girls Institute launches web site. Retrieved from http://www.ojjdp.gov/newsletter/238120/sf_4.html

Rios, V. (2011). *Punished: Policing the lives of Black and Latino boys.* New York, NY: NYU Press.

The Sentencing Project. (2015a). Fact sheet: Trends in U.S. corrections. Retrieved from http://www.sentencingproject.org/wp-content/uploads/2016/01/Trends-in-US-Corrections.pdf

The Sentencing Project. (2015b). Fact sheet: Incarcerated women and girls. Retrieved from http://www.sentencingproject.org/publications/incarcerated-women-and-girls/

U.S. Department of Education. (2015, July 22). Educators gather at the White House to rethink school discipline [Press Release]. Retrieved from http://www.ed.gov/news/press-releases/educators-gather-white-house-rethink-school-discipline

U.S. Department of Education Office for Civil Rights. (2014, March 21). Civil Rights Data Collection: Data snapshot: School discipline. Retrieved from http://www.ocrdata.ed.gov

West, C. M. (1995). Mammy, sapphire, and jezebel: Historical images of Black women and their implications for psychotherapy. *Psychotherapy,* 32(2), 458–466.

White House Council on Women and Girls. (2014) *Women and Girls of color: Addressing challenges and Expanding opportunity.* Retrieved from https://obamawhitehouse.archives.gov/sites/default/files/docs/cwg_women_and_girls_of_color_report_112014.pdf

5

POPULAR MEDIA PORTRAYAL OF IMPRISONED BLACK WOMEN

Cheryle D. Snead-Greene and Michael D. Royster

Introduction

The term *War on Drugs* was first used by President Richard Nixon on June 17, 1971, at which time he described illegal drugs as "public enemy number one in the United States." Nixon's drug initiative dramatically increased the size and presence of federal drug control agencies and pushed through measures such as mandatory sentencing and no-knock warrants. According to Human Rights Watch, the *War on Drugs* caused soaring arrest rates that disproportionately targeted African Americans; studies indicate that Nixon may have used the *war on drugs* to criminalize and disrupt Black and hippie communities and their leaders (NPR, 2007). In her book, *The New Jim Crow: Mass Incarceration in the Age of Colorblindness*, Michelle Alexander proclaims that the drug war has never been focused on rooting out drug kingpins or violent offenders. She contends federal funding flows to those agencies that increase dramatically the volume of drug arrests, not the agencies most successful in bringing down the bosses.

The *War on Drugs* impacts people differently based on gender and race. With more than one million women behind bars or under the control of the criminal justice system, women are the fastest growing segment of the incarcerated population increasing at nearly double the rate of men since 1985. Nationally, there are more than eight times as many women incarcerated in state and federal prisons and local jails as there were in 1980, increasing in number from 12,300 in 1980 to 182,271 by 2002. The racial disparities that exist in incarceration are just as startling but not surprising. The NAACP (2016) reports that women of color are significantly overrepresented in the criminal justice system. African Americans (men and women) now constitute nearly 1 million of the total 2.3 million incarcerated population. According to the Bureau of Justice Statistics (BJS) the total female prison population in 2011 was 1,598,780 (equating to approximately 1 in 100 African American women in prison). More specifically, the ACLU finds that Black women represent 30 percent of all incarcerated women in the U.S, although they represent 13 percent of the female population generally; and, Hispanic women represent 16% of incarcerated women, although they make up only 11 percent of all women in the U.S.

Black women within the prison system deal with various sociological issues and influences that precede their tenure within the walls of confinement. In the Netflix comedy drama series *Orange is the New Black* (*OITNB*) there are several characters who share with its audience experiences with racial disparities prior to prison. In this chapter we will look into the lives of several Black female characters in the series that were incarcerated for drug abuse. We will briefly discuss the *War on Drugs* as a war on women. We will discuss how female, Black prisoners, who were victims of the prison system and the internal dynamics of imprisonment, endured prison culture while serving their terms. Finally, we will address the physical, psychological, and internal impact that prison had on these women.

Impact of the War on Drugs Mandate

One of the effects of President Nixon's *War on Drugs* entailed a broad depletion of significant proportions of African American men from the homes and their respective communities through means of differential justice. The Moynihan Report of 1965 has left an accompanying legacy that serves as a measuring stick for elites to access African American inequality and its associated social ailments. According to Daniel Moynihan, the author of the report, family structure stood at the heart of what he notoriously labeled a "tangle of pathology".

The series *OITNB* functions as a testament to how African American women have endured the effects of the removal of targeted men, through their own loss of social capital. The absence of African American men has contributed towards families headed solely by women under economically deprived conditions. Michelle Alexander contends, "The criminalization and demonization of black men has turned the black community against itself, unraveling community and family relationships, decimating networks of mutual support, and intensifying the shame and self-hate experienced by the current pariah caste" (2010: 120–121). Furthermore, such conditions have created a shortage in viable male companions within a predominantly endogamous culture. Such combined factors have created favorable conditions for women to become accustomed to life without significant bonds to their male counterparts for the sake of meaningful emotional support. In addition, such a state has been exacerbated by the scarcity of family sustaining employment and the eroding of public assistance.

In response to the Personal Responsibility Act of 1996, welfare recipients, especially women of color, have been adversely politicized through stigmatization. Historically, African American women have disproportionately occupied low-wage employment which has been insufficient for supporting family or self. The given conditions have forced women to marry a "breadwinner" in order to avoid economic sanctions, increasingly difficult because of the reduction in the number of "eligible" partners due to mass incarceration. The aristocratically constructed "social strains" correlate with African American women resorting to criminal behavior as a response to coping with desperation while resorting to "self-medication" as a means to purge some of the pain.

In the 1980s, Ronald Reagan reignited the *War on Drugs* at a time when drug related crimes were in decline. During that time, says law professor Michelle Alexander (2010), "the media was saturated with images that seemed to confirm the worst negative racial stereotypes". The legacy of Nixon's *War on Drugs* had a direct impact on many of the drug reform policies made by the Reagan, Bush, Clinton and Obama administrations. For example, Ronald Reagan escalated the war with "tough on crime" mandatory minimum sentences. George H.W. Bush advised the country that drugs were the greatest domestic threat facing the nation while holding up a bag of seized cocaine. Bill Clinton signed laws that pushed for tougher prison sentences and stripped prison inmates of much of their legal defense rights. The Obama administration alone worked to reshape how America fights its war on drugs — to treat drugs more as a public health issue than a punitive criminal justice undertaking (Lopez, 2017).

The 1988 U.S. Presidential election indicated that Democrat candidates were likely to be defeated if they failed to make a public display of toughness against crime. Such was evident when the "Willie Horton political ad" functioned as a means to use racialized emotional manipulation towards a significant amount of the electorate to the disadvantage of the candidate Michael Dukakis. Bill Clinton in turn remembered what happened to Dukakis and was pressured to sign aggressive legislation which played a contributing role in mass incarceration, especially of African American men and women. Republican candidates have a reputation of favoring retribution rather than rehabilitation in terms of corrections. Democrat candidates face pressure to appeal to both the "Tupac Shakurs" and "Carol Bradys", metaphorically speaking. Tupac Shakur symbolizes the part of the electorate that determines which candidate will win depending on their turn out. Carol Brady symbolizes the suburban mother who wants to be reassured that someone in charge will keep their neighbor safe.

The War on Drugs is a War on Women

The so-called *War on Drugs* policy has had a critical impact on the lives of women in the criminal justice system. Not only has the policy punished women disproportionately to the harm they cause society, the policy has also branded these women as pariahs or social outcasts. In essence, as a result of the *War on Drugs* mandate, women, who are most likely to be incarcerated for a drug-related crime, are seen as society's "public enemy number one". The drug war severely punishes women, particularly mothers. Even women who do not use drugs may be punished, for example, by welfare regulations that require recipients to submit to invasive and embarrassing monitored drug testing in order to obtain public assistance. Drug use and drug selling occur at similar rates across racial and ethnic groups, yet black and Latina women are far more likely to be criminalized for drug law violations than White women. The Drug Policy Alliance (2016) finds that Black women are more than twice as likely – and Latinas are 25 percent more likely – to be incarcerated than White women.

Researchers have found that about half of women offenders confined in state prisons had been using alcohol, drugs, or both at the time of the offense for which they had been incarcerated. These women usually share a similar socio-demographic profile: Most of the women are poor, undereducated, unskilled, single mothers and disproportionately women of color, and their paths to crime are usually marked by abuse, poverty and addiction.

The emphasis on punishment rather than treatment has brought many low-income women and women of color into the criminal justice system. Women offenders who in the past decades would have been given community sanctions are now being sentenced to prison. Mandatory minimum sentencing for drug offenses has increased the numbers of women in state and federal prisons. Between 1995 and 1996, female drug arrests increased by 95%, while male drug arrests increased by 55%. In 1979, the Bureau of Justice Studies reports that approximately one in ten women in U.S. prisons were serving a sentence for a drug conviction; in 1999, this figure was approximately one in three.

Despite cultural portrayals of African American women as extraordinarily resilient to institutional constraints which results in resource deprivation, the incarceration rates of such sectors of the population indicate that there exist concrete limits to their collective navigational capital. Critical race theorist Tara Yosso has stressed that navigational capital "infers the ability to maneuver through institutions not created with Communities of Color in mind" (2005: 80). When combining the factors of African American men in prison with those who are present in the community, but disenfranchised, the ability for African American women to overcome the elements which contribute to incarceration becomes further challenged.

Incarceration in Popular Culture – *OITNB*

In the late eighteenth century, most punishment moved behind prison walls; what took place there was a mystery to most. In the modern era, people often turn to the media and popular culture to feed their curiosity about what sociologist Erving Goffman calls the total institution. In real life, prison life is ugly, grisly and unpredictable. Not wanting to get their hands truly dirty, people have opted to view the macabre of prison life on the big screen or on the small screen in the comfort of their own homes. They would rather get their "fix" by turning on the television to watch marathons of the prison documentary series *Lockup* on the cable news station MSNBC or by binge-watching *Orange is the New Black* on Netflix. No matter how they choose to ingest it, criminologist Dawn Cecil (2015) contends there are ample opportunities on television to satisfy people's curiosity about life behind bars.

The series *OITNB* depicts the story of Piper Chapman, a White woman in her thirties who is sentenced to fifteen months in prison after being convicted of a decade-old crime of drug trafficking. The show takes place in Litchfield Penitentiary, a minimum-security women's federal prison, and pays close attention to how instances of corruption, drug smuggling, funding cuts, overcrowding, and correctional officer brutality adversely impact not only the prisoners' health and well-being, but also the prison's basic ability to fulfill its fundamental responsibilities and ethical obligations as a federal corrections institution.

In this chapter we focus on several dynamic, yet unique women of color, featured in the series that were imprisoned for drug abuse. Tasha "Taystee" Jefferson, Dayanara "Daya" Diaz, and Poussey Washington are convicted drug offenders in the fictional Litchfield Prison system; they are women of color who are victims of the internal dynamics of imprisonment.

OITNB and the Imprisoned Black Woman Drug Offender

Women represent a significant proportion of all offenders under criminal justice supervision in the United States. Criminal justice researcher Barbara Bloom and her colleagues Barbara Owen and Stephanie Covington note that as the United States increased the criminal penalties through mandatory sentencing and longer sentence lengths, huge increases in the imprisonment of women have been a gendered consequence of these policies.

Drug use by any woman, whether she lives in suburban or urban areas, brings with it the psychological, social and cultural experience of stigmatization that can perpetuate the continued problem of drug use. This usage and its inherent problems violate gender expectations for women in our society. Poor women who use street-level drugs experience additional societal stigma because they do not have the protective societal buffer enjoyed by women who are insulated by their families, friends, and economic status. Those who use street-level drugs are also less protected from becoming prisoners of the *War on Drugs* because of their high visibility Although Whites use drugs at the same rate as African Americans according to public health data, African Americans make up almost half of those arrested for drug offenses and more than half of those convicted of drug offenses, causing critics such as Michelle Alexander to call the *War on Drugs* the "New Jim Crow". Between 1982 and 1996, drug law violation sentences got longer and the African American prison population doubled.

Viewers first meet Tasha Taystee Jefferson in prison in Season 1; she works in the hair salon. Almost immediately, viewers see past Jefferson's orange jumpsuit and recognize that the Taystee character is witty, intelligent and creative.

Jefferson is also, unfortunately, the young Black woman who is incarcerated due to her reluctant participation in a drug ring culminating in a drug trafficking conviction. In Season 1, Episode 9, Jefferson is released from Litchfield but finds that her support network is missing. By Episode 12 in the same season, unable to adjust to life outside, Jefferson commits a crime and returns to Litchfield. Jefferson's story serves to illustrate that even in real life, it is a never-ending "merry-go-round" from the time prisoners are sentenced to the time they are released and then resentenced again. Sadly, the rate of recidivism among women prisoners is on the rise. In July 2002, the Bureau of Justice Statistics (BJS) released a Special Report, *Recidivism of Prisoners Released in 1994*, describing the recidivism patterns of 272,111 female and male former prisoners (Langan & Levin, 2002). Within three years, almost 68% of all released prisoners were rearrested; 47% were reconvicted; and 25% were resentenced to prison. There are many external factors that contribute to recidivism for women offenders with the most common factors being substance abuse and mental illness, especially Post-Traumatic Stress Disorder.

Dayanara "Daya" Diaz is also in prison for drug related offenses. She was unwittingly involved in a drug operation literally taking place on her kitchen table. Daya was sentenced to 36 months in prison. Mandatory minimum sentencing strips judicial discretion and imposes unduly long prison sentences on minor offenders, violating common sense and fundamental notions of justice and morality. It is important to note that according to Drug Policy Alliance, the most egregious example of mandatory minimum sentencing is the sentencing disparity between crack cocaine and powder cocaine drug law violations.

In Season 4, we learn that Daya's mother, Aleida, who is also incarcerated in Litchfield, was a silent partner in the drug ring operation taking place in Daya's home. While inside Litchfield, Daya and her mother continue to clash. Although rare, there are a few relatives sharing prison dorms and even prison cells. Of the estimated 600,000 parents of minor children in the nation's state prisons in 2004, half had a relative who was currently or used to be incarcerated, according to a Bureau of Justice Statistics report.

Poussey Washington is in prison after being busted over a small amount of marijuana. Studies have shown that African Americans and Hispanics are significantly more likely than Whites to be arrested for possession and sale of marijuana, targeted for arrest by the police, and to receive a conviction and criminal record, despite the fact that the majority of regular marijuana users are non-Hispanic Whites. Cannabis is the most widely used illicit substance, with 29 million Americans using it at least once a year. Though 74% of regular marijuana users are non-Hispanic Whites and 14% are Black, Drug Policy Alliance reports that African Americans make up 30% of all marijuana arrests.

While in prison, Poussey becomes depressed and turns to alcohol, even making her own "hooch" to satisfy this addiction. In Season 2, another inmate approaches Poussey about selling her homemade "toilet hooch", but Poussey rejects the offer and, as a result, is psychologically and emotionally punished by the inmate. The toll that this abuse takes on Poussey is revealed in many of the uncharacteristic behaviors that she exhibits in later seasons. Like Poussey, many prisoners are forced to undergo increasingly harsh policies and conditions of confinement in order to survive in the prison. These prolonged adaptations to the deprivations and frustrations of life inside prison lead to certain psychological changes. The person who suffers the acute pains of psychological or emotional abuse from other inmates may develop post-traumatic stress disorder or other forms of disability which may be in the form of what criminology scholar Gresham Sykes has referred to as diminished sense of self-worth and personal values.

Whether their crimes were petty or significant, all three of these women will forever be labeled as drug offenders; they will forever be seen by society as "public enemy number one". This is the one offense that keeps hurting women over and over again, because thanks to the *War on Drugs* mandate, the punishments drug offenders face often extend far beyond the prison walls or the parole officer's office. According to Michelle Alexander, author of *The New Jim Crow: Mass Incarceration in the Age of Colorblindness* this scenario is not unique. Alexander implies that this war has been waged almost exclusively in poor communities of color and that today we see millions of poor people and folks of color who are trapped, yet again, in a criminal justice system which is treating them like commodities, like people who are easily disposable.

The social reverberations of mass incarceration do not stop with the prisoners themselves. The consequences can be even greater for children, family members, and associates attached to those who are imprisoned. The family of a woman incarcerated in prison is socially impacted, for the worse. Families are made of two or more people who share responsibilities. Traditionally women took on roles in families such as cooking, cleaning and childbearing. In each of those roles socializing occurs that shares these roles with other members of the family. If women are not present to complete those roles due to incarceration, those roles might not be completed. Today women have more of a financial impact than ever before. Women are working full time jobs, and earning more wages than they were in previous decades. The United States Department of Labor reported that women are projected to account for 51 percent of the increase in total labor force growth between 2008 and 2018 and 66 million women were employed in the United States; additionally, 73 percent of employed women worked on full-time jobs, while 27 percent worked on a part-time basis (United States Department of Labor, 2010, p. 1.). Women socially impact families. If a woman with minimal education can barely meet her basic needs in life, imagine the consequences for a woman with symptoms of mental illness and less education. Education may be one way to reduce the incarceration rates of Black women. The following educational statistics of women in the criminal justice system from *The Sentencing Project* speak volumes:

- 44% of women in state prisons have neither graduated from high school nor received a GED.
- 14% of women in state prisons have had some college-level education.
- Half of women in prison participate in educational or vocational programming – only one of every five women takes high school or GED classes.
- Only half of women's correctional facilities offer post-secondary education.

Some prisons offer limited educational programs to model inmates. Vocational training or career technical education programs in prison are designed to teach inmates about general employment skills or skills needed for specific jobs and industries. The overall goal of vocational training is to reduce risk of inmates' recidivating by teaching them marketable skills they can use to find and retain employment following release from prison. In their research on educational programs, researchers David Wilson, Catherine Gallagher, and Doris MacKenzie found vocational and technical training programs can also reduce institutional problem behaviors by replacing inmates' idle time with constructive work. On *OITNB*, the warden attempts to offer educational courses to the Litchfield inmates in order to give them something useful to do during their incarceration; as a result of budget cuts, the formal education program is replaced with a more cost-effective vocational training program. Sadly, most of the women in Litchfield choose not to take advantage of the training program; however, in a Season 4 flashback, we see Taystee and other inmates using the vocational training program to prepare for Litchfield's Mock Job Fair, an annual event sponsored by a nonprofit called Dress for Success. The mock job fair gives Taystee a chance to show off her business smarts with a Philip Morris representative in a mock interview (interestingly, she manages to spin her drug-running experience as a net positive). She is named the Job Fair's winner to a thunderous ovation only to learn that the coveted job is a fake...simply a prison myth.

In prison census studies conducted by economists Lance Lochner and Enrico Moretti (2003) it is estimated that schooling significantly reduces the probability of incarceration. The authors further suggest that the impacts are greater for Blacks than for Whites. For example, one extra year of schooling results in a.10 percentage point reduction in the probability of incarceration for Whites, and a.37 percentage point reduction for Blacks. To help in interpreting the size of these impacts, they calculate how much of the Black–White gap in incarceration rates in 1980 is due to differences in educational attainment. Differences in average education between Blacks and Whites can explain as much as 23% of the Black–White gap in incarceration rates.

People who go to prison are removed from educational opportunities, families, neighborhoods, the workplace, and friendship networks, leaving their children, partners, friends, and neighbors to bear greater economic burdens and social challenges in their absence. The devastation for families and communities has been enormous – especially for black Americans, whose daily lives and economic fortunes bear the brunt of the prison boom.

Conclusion

The United States is the world's leader in incarceration with 2.2 million people currently in the nation's prisons and jails – a 500% increase over the last forty years according to *The Sentencing Project*. The first feature of mass incarceration is simply the sheer number of African Americans behind bars. From 1995 to 2002 the average annual rate of growth of the female inmate population was 5.2%, higher than the average 3.5% increase in the male inmate population. Since 1995 the total number of male prisoners has grown 27%; the number of female prisoners 42%. By year end in 2002, women accounted for 6.8% of all prisoners, up from 6.1% in 1995. More than 60% of the people in prison today are people of color. Black men are nearly six times as likely to be incarcerated as white men and Hispanic men are 2.3 times as likely. For Black men in their thirties, 1 in every 10 is in prison or jail on any given day. The rate of imprisonment for Black women far outpaces that of both White and Latina women; for example, in 2014, *The Sentencing Project* reports the imprisonment rate for African American women (109 per 100,000) was more than twice the rate of imprisonment for White women (53 per 100,000), as compared to Hispanic women who were incarcerated at 1.2 times the rate of White women (64 vs. 53 per 100,000). The explosion of both the prison population and its racial disparity are largely attributable to aggressive street-level enforcement of the drug laws and harsh sentencing of drug offenders.

Punishment changed in the United States in the last third of the twentieth century. The indicators of this change are well-documented and widely agreed upon. Prison populations soared, correctional and rehabilitative goals were largely supplanted in official and popular discourse by concerns with public safety and victims' rights, penal policy became highly politicized, and public sentiment toward criminals hardened. As a consequence, criminal punishment touched the lives of more Americans than ever before in the 1990s, a decade characterized by "mass imprisonment".

Imprisonment is a widespread punishment all over the world, but prison is for most of us an unknown experience and anything we know is mostly through media and cinema representations. Therefore, it is very likely these representations play an important role in the formation of our social representation of this matter. Prisons have typically responded to female criminal behavior with little thought to the unintended consequences for women, their children, and the community. Since prisons for women have been modeled after their "louder and bigger brothers," they damage women incommensurately with the level of threat most convicted women present to society says John Irwin, author of *The Warehouse Prison: Disposal of the new dangerous class*. For women, life in prison is a harsh reality. U.S. studies on women in prison reveal that female inmates incarcerated in U.S. prisons and jails share a "superfecta" of characteristics: undereducated; low-income; unskilled with sporadic employment histories; and histories of alcohol and substance dependency.

Though *Orange is the New Black* may exist within the heightened reality of prison, it still manages to downplay "real prison life". *OITNB* also works to understand the nuances and the specificity of female friendship in ways that make the women and their relationships meaningful, no matter their circumstances. The relationships in *Orange is the New Black* are forged for a variety of reasons, which include convenience, safety and protection, and genuine affection. The reasons for their friendships are important in understanding them, but they are also only one aspect of what bonds them.

Prison life experienced by, and seen through the eyes of inmates like Taystee, Daya and Poussey is both colorful and revealing. Many of the women incarcerated in Litchfield are intelligent, expressive, have strong personalities, and have formed close bonds with some of the other inmates; still others are cunning, manipulative, diabolical, and self-proclaimed predators on the weak. But this is not to say that these women are naïve and oblivious to the machinations of prison life in Litchfield. In *OITNB* we see that Taystee, and the others, have either witnessed or been a victim of the violence, intimidation, fighting, back-biting, and racial divide that occurs at Litchfield. None of these women are strangers to the pitfalls of being locked up; but all is not bad in Litchfield. Because of their backstories, it could be surmised that these inmates view Litchfield as "home". Litchfield provides their basics needs (food, shelter and security) and it also provides them with a makeshift "family", no matter how dysfunctional and unconventional that may be.

Current research has established that women offenders differ from their male counterparts in personal histories and pathways to crime. African American women have many challenges to overcome if they find themselves confined by prison walls. This brief overview of the Netflix comedy drama series *Orange is the New Black* depicts the lives of several African American women incarcerated in prison. *OITNB* attempts to give these women a voice; it attempts to share with its audience, in a lighthearted manner, the social injustice, the gender inequalities, as well as the racial disparities that exist in prison. All of the imprisoned women of Litchfield are different, yet they share similar stores. For example, many of them have experienced the foster care system early in their childhoods. Many of them have been either physically, emotionally or sexually abused; and many of them have experimented with drugs. All of them have struggled to adjust to life inside Litchfield prison.

Finally, it must be noted that *OITNB* takes place in a fictional prison setting, thus, serving as entertainment for the viewers. It is a fictional representation of women behind bars. Let's face it, *OITNB* glamorizes life in prison and people have always been enamored with crime and punishment. Actual prison life can be worse than what one sees in the show; and people do not want to be a part of that particular reality, especially since many of them support long-term jail offense for people of color regardless of whether or not the crime was petty or serious. Viewers can laugh and cry with TV prisoners or shun and support them because at the end of the hour they shut off the television set and forget about these characters until the next episode. Historically in America, people have always been curious about what goes on behind the locked gates of prisons; they have always had a fascination with tales of prisoners, punishment and escapes, and have flocked to the big screens to gorge themselves (i.e., *Escape from Alcatraz, Cool Hand Luke, Shawshank Redemption*, etc.). Viewers may use *OITNB* to gingerly escape prison reality without guilt.

References and Further Reading

Alexander, M. (2010). *The New Jim Crow: Mass incarceration in the age of colorblindness.* New York: New Press.

Bloom, B., Owen, B., & Covington, S. (2004). Women offenders and the gendered effects of public policy. *Review of Policy Research*, 21(1), 31–48.

Cecil, D.K. (2015). Prison life in popular culture: From the big house to *Orange is the New Black.* Boulder, CO: Lynne Rienner Publishers.

Drug Policy Alliance (2016). Fact sheet: Women, prison and the drug war. Retrieved at: http://www.drugpolicy.org/sites/default/files/DPA_Fact%20Sheet_Women%20Prison%20and%20Drug%20War%20%28Feb.%202016%29.pdf

Goffman, E. (1961). *Asylums: Essays on the social situation of mental patients and other inmates.* New York: Anchor Books.

Harrison, P.M., & Beck, A.J. (2003). *Prisoners in 2002.* Bureau of Justice Statistics Special Report, NCJ-193427, U.S. Department of Justice, Washington, DC.

Irwin, J. (2005). *The warehouse prison: Disposal of the new dangerous class.* Los Angeles, CA: Roxbury Publishing Company.

Kerman, P. (2013). *Orange is the new black: My year in a women's prison.* New York: Spiegel & Grau Trade Paperbacks.

Langan, P.A., & Levin, D.J. (2002). *Recidivism of prisoners released in 1994.* Bureau of Justice Statistics Bulletin, NCJ-200248, U.S. Department of Justice, Washington, DC.

Lochner, L., & Moretti, E. (2003). The effect of education on crime: Evidence from prison inmates, arrests, and self-reports. Retrieved at: https://eml.berkeley.edu//~moretti/lm46.pdf

Lopez, G. (2017). How Obama quietly reshaped America's war on drugs. Retrieved at: https://www.vox.com/identities/2016/12/19/13903532/obama-war-on-drugs-legacy

NAACP (2016). Criminal justice fact sheet. Retrieved at: http://www.naacp.org/criminal-justice-fact-sheet/

NPR (2007). Timeline: America's war on drugs. Retrieved at: http://www.npr.org/templates/story/story.php?storyId=9252490

Wilson, D.B., Gallagher, C.A., & MacKenzie, D.L. (2000). A meta-analysis of corrections-based education, vocation, and work programs for adult offenders. *Journal of Research in Crime and Delinquency*, 37(4), 347–368.

Yosso, T.J. (2005). Whose culture has capital? A critical race theory discussion of community cultural wealth. *Race Ethnicity and Education*, 8(1), 69–91.

6

INDIFFERENCE IS THE NEW BLACK

Season One and the Violation of Women's Solidarity

Bonnie Zare

Prison has four ostensible purposes: punishment, deterrence of future actions, segregation and rehabilitation. Of these, American prisons generally neglect the last one; few remember the origin of the word penitentiary, a place to be penitent. Yet every prisoner who is released will live in someone's neighborhood. Since no one wants their neighbors to be unskilled, under-confident, and conflicted then we cannot help but desire incarcerated American citizens to possess positive interpersonal skills and have access to education. However, our prisons are not run this way, partly because women in the general population have not identified the incarcerated stranger as ourselves.

While many people are aware the US cages more people per capita than any other nation, far fewer likely realize that the vast majority of females behind bars have not engaged in violent crime and thus do not pose a safety risk to the general public. As the ACLU (2015) reports, approximately 74% are confined because of drug crimes (using or selling), burglary or fraud. Owing mainly to the adoption in the 1980s of federal sentencing guidelines that increased sentences for drug related crimes and restricted judicial flexibility in sentencing, we know from Ruby Tapia (2010) that from 1977 to 2010 the number of women prisoners increased by over 700%. At least half of incarcerated women are people of color, and this is part of why the average White middle class and liberal US citizen knows little to nothing about the inner lives of this group of people. Prisoners are not solely geographically and institutionally isolated but are Othered by their physical appearance and economically deprived circumstances. It is *not* simply a matter of ignorant White women forgetting about their privilege; it would seem that as fear of the economic future deepens, so does a desire on the part of the general public to "stay in a bubble." For a women's movement with the greatest possible inclusivity, it is imperative to extend a hand to our sisters behind bars; our society as a whole can only transcend divisions based on racial identity, economic class and carceral status if we do so.

To illustrate the limitations of the general discourse surrounding this population it is instructive to analyze the beginning episodes of the first highly successful television drama about female prisoners, *Orange is the New Black* (*OITNB*). This contemporary popular culture artifact perpetuates mainstream misunderstandings about women of color and influences American ideology about incarcerated women generally, omitting crucial information about repeated patterns of economic and social injustice that lead to the disproportionate imprisonment of non-white women. After exploring the first six episodes' limits as a piece of artivism, a term for art that promotes social justice, this chapter will outline elements that need to receive increased attention to advance dialogue about our sisters behind bars. Suggestions about needed changes will be informed by several sources, including seventy interviews conducted by my colleagues and myself, the basis of a forthcoming book, *Outlaw Women: Prison, Rural Violence and Poverty on the New American Frontier*. Interlocking oppressions often combine to prevent women from re-establishing productive lives, and there is an urgent need to listen to what women themselves say they need to become skilled and constructive community members.

Orange is the New Black

OITNB first aired on Netflix in July 2013 and has been a staple of popular culture references including parodies and memes since that time. The series was nominated for a GLAAD award for its portrayal of a trans inmate, and its main actress, Taylor Schilling, has been nominated for a Golden Globe award and Satellite Award, and the show has won a People's Choice Award and several awards from the Writers Guild of America. TV critics have praised it for its "authenticity" and "bracing originality." *Washington Post* TV critic Hank Steuver called it "thoroughly engrossing" and said while prison life is miserable it "is also filled with the entire range of human emotions and stories, all of which are brought vividly to life in a world where a stick of gum could ignite either a romance or a death threat". While Netflix does not release audience numbers, all of this suggests a high general approval among white liberal viewers. The show is also being aired in two majority White countries, Australia and New Zealand.

As is well known, the show is based on a prison memoir by Piper Kerman, a White woman who went to prison for one year. We follow this yuppie affluent New Yorker who now is named Piper Chapman as she has recently been sentenced to 15 months in a women's federal prison because ten years earlier she had transported a suitcase with money for her former girlfriend, who was an international drug smuggler. This crime under the influence of misguided love is the only crime Piper ever committed, and she had moved on to a typical elite lifestyle in Manhattan when one day her past catches up with her, and she must turn herself into the police. The script creates comical moments by demonstrating Piper's naiveté about prison conditions and contrasting elements of Piper's former life, such as a passion for expensive and exotic gourmet food items, with that of her current life where jail food is barely recognizable as food.

OITNB has weight and heft: it does not shy away from exposing the racist thoughts of inmates and the racist acts of correctional officers or from showing that sexually exploitive and sadistic people often become correctional officers and seek to control and punish the inmates, thereby committing their own crimes, such as infringement of privacy, molestation, and rape. In addition, it has rightfully been admired for its sympathetic portrayal of Sophia Burset, a transgender woman who feels "right in her body" for the first time only after surgery.

Unfortunately, however, the show often gives a nod to progressive thought but then ultimately is okay with audience indifference as it structurally returns to predictable power dynamics. For example, in one episode the main character, Piper, sees a chicken inside the prison yard, and the resulting interest in finding and possessing it plays upon national and racial stereotypes – the Russian must want to make chicken Kiev, the Blacks must want to eat fried chicken, etc. At one point, the Russian cook chides Piper, saying it is racist to think the Black inmates want the chicken for food. The cook turns around and says that since "all black people are addicted to heroin," really they must think that the bird has heroin hidden it. Before Piper can reply, the Russian continues her parade of bigotry: "The Spanish ones won't even eat it [the chicken]. They'll just cut it open and drink its blood for some kind of superstitious thing." If the show permitted a reply from Piper there could be an interesting confrontation, but instead, in service of comedy, the camera glibly pans to Piper's surprised face and then shows a group of Black women childishly running after the chicken. As the episode unfolds we become complicit in a structure in which we repeatedly see people of color living for the moment as infants do and the White character, Piper, acting more of the adult and worried about getting unfairly punished for creating tension amidst the inmates. The scriptwriters assume our main concern is whether the pitiful middle class White girl will get framed and not on how the other prisoners are being verbally confined through such insistent stereotyping.

Another offensive aspect of the early episodes is the depiction of people struggling with mental instability. Consider, for example, the incomplete character of "Crazy Eyes" Warren. Crazy Eyes is a lesbian woman who is very energetic and insistent. Correction officers make comments about her incomprehensible speech and unpredictability. At first she appears generous because she does favors for our main character, Piper. Quickly we learn that Crazy Eyes desires Piper to be her new "wife" or long-term girlfriend, and that she will only take yes for an answer. Piper finally asks her to stop stalking her but tries to do it as gently as possible, and she remains a mysterious figure who may show up at any moment either to haunt or help Piper. Crazy Eyes knows what she likes and is well liked by viewers because of her character's intensity. However, it should be noted that, early on, the show establishes that the only person who is marked as pathologically crazy has the darkest face in the prison. Other characters may appear delusional or unstable or unsettled but are not called outright crazy. Admittedly, later in the show, Crazy Eyes has moments of utter gravity and areas in which she demonstrates talent and creativity. Still, audiences who only see a few early episodes take away an image of a disturbed woman with exaggeratedly childish movements and predatory sexual behavior.

OITNB gets a bit more thoughtful in later episodes, when audiences learn why inmates are there, and we see some of the abusive family members and difficult situations they experienced before they were incarcerated. However, the offensive choices it makes for the sake of comedy and sensationalism when approaching such a vulnerable and misunderstood population violates women's potential solidarity and thereby exposes how easy it is to stereotype this particular group of people.

Realities of Imprisonment for Female Inmates

As postcolonial critic Gayatri Spivak (1988) famously asked, how can the subaltern person make her voice heard? Many people who have experienced prison firsthand are so disenfranchised that they are structurally silenced; moreover, as advocates for prisoners justly note, it is impossible for any set of stories to represent with accuracy the extremely varied individuals inside. Having been a part of an intensive project at one of the country's most remote prisons, the Wyoming Women's Center (hereafter WWC) in Lusk, it is instructive to examine how a representation of prison life such as OITNB contrasts with the ideas shared by the women we spoke with. Between December 2014 and August 2015 three University of Wyoming faculty members and one graduate student interviewed forty women who are incarcerated at the WWC and thirty women who were formerly incarcerated there. The resulting report for the Department of Corrections listed twelve pressing issues from the data. Owing to space constraints, this chapter will confine itself to demonstrating the inmates' inadequate mental health and post-traumatic experience rehabilitation and their frustration with the therapy unit, an intensive behavioral modification program aimed at former drug and alcohol users.

Addressing Mental Health Conditions

Before discussing the mental health situation in detail, it is important to consider the similarities amongst women in prison. In fact, as Margaret Malloch and Gill McIvor have found, crossing all national boundaries a striking uniformity exists among imprisoned women who share the following: a) A prevalence of mental health issues, b) Substance misuse, c) Experiences of abuse from family members or intimate partners, d) Substitute care while growing up and e) High levels of self-harm. Given that a severely disadvantaged population enters prison and cannot immediately erase traumatic memories, prison conditions would need to be highly specialized to avoid any aggravation of the above or repetition of the crime. Society does not recognize that a lack of community resources helped create the conditions for the crime to be committed, and they do not redouble their efforts for the confined women. Once typed as a criminal, the state lowers its obligations towards that person.

Many of the women spoke about their perceptions regarding the WWC's failure to assist women with mental illnesses, partly due to the reality that this unmet need permeates so many other parts of daily life. The women spoke of how rarely they see a caseworker or counselor. On paper, they should be able to see their counselor at least once every 2–3 weeks. In reality, these sessions which are a meager 30 minutes might happen monthly or even less often, despite the prominent conditions the majority of women struggled with, which often included post-traumatic stress disorder, depression and bipolar disorder. It was reported that if anything more urgent came up with another mental health patient, that person's appointment would be cancelled. Another person reported that they hardly ever knew when their appointment would be, and thus they might have just awakened and could not prepare for it sufficiently. Another challenge was not being able to work with the same counselor. As one person said, "They make us change counselors so much. I don't know why. I guess its turnover."

Repeatedly we heard that the inability to have regular counseling sessions impacted women struggling to move past addictions and an addict's way of thinking. One person spoke of how even all of the 12-step programs that met inside the Center were not that well-known, with the weekly Debtor's Anonymous meetings being poorly advertised and thus not well attended. Several women spoke of the need to have counselors who had themselves experienced addiction because "going by the book counseling" was less effective. Another person asked, "Why don't we have sponsors while we are inside the prison?" It's a fair question: the small town (population 1,617) of Lusk lobbied to have the prison located there to provide employment. It appears no thought was given to how few experienced 12-step sponsors or leaders would be available for the inmates, despite the large number of women who are imprisoned for drug-related charges.

Insufficient Programming for Survivors of Abuse

A typical woman we spoke with who had experienced abuse or violence had had a disrupted childhood, a home situation that was unstable. This instability typically included references to economic need (with parents working multiple jobs to feed large families), neglect (with one or more parents in a state of addiction), and to abuse (often as a byproduct of being high or drunk or as a byproduct of the strain the addiction was putting on the family). As she describes her childhood, the circumstances often do not permit the speaker a healthy path towards building autonomy, self-efficacy and a sense of oneself as a singular individual. Instead, fear is often the backdrop as a girl or teen struggles to avoid a parent or stay on the good side of an unreliable, impulsive and often angry parent. Some had many younger siblings and had to take on the role of adult caretaker while still a child, not only for their sisters and brothers but for a drunken parent who forgets to eat or bathe. These women suffered from tremendous pressure at having to grow up rapidly. Other women lived in constant fear of physical violence from drunk or high parents, and a few were exposed to sexual events or used in sexual situations. The interactions with the women in speaking of their family life were filled with references to how powerful the influence of their natal family was: as one woman said, [I wish] "I had had a stable foster home where I was safe...I wouldn't have run away...I definitely wouldn't be sitting here now if I had had a different childhood".

Several of the women talked about families that were cult-like with many kids, living in isolated areas, and home-schooled (or some version thereof) at times. In many, parental support and supervision was rare. Sometimes a crisis, such as the death of a supportive relative or a rape would start a youth spiraling downwards, descending into drug use. Whether such a crisis occurred or not, abusive home situations, with or without drug using family members, would lead them to periodically try to escape; in some cases the escapes themselves might lead to drug or alcohol experiences at very young ages.

As adults, the women were highly influenced by the compulsory heterosexual script that includes a wedding and children: this was a very prominent expectation in people's mainly rural communities, and divorce was a mark of failure. About a third of female survivors had married in their teens; some had married someone at least nine years older than they were, beginning with a pronounced power imbalance. Whether the age difference was striking or not, many talked about being dependent on men as they grew, first, through the act of marriage itself and difficult economic circumstances and eventually from the desire to avoid being a single parent, both because of potential stigma and the sheer hard work of being alone and raising children. One person spoke of how she was shunned after her divorce, simply when walking into a high school basketball game: "He was Mr. Wonderful outside but they don't know what he was like inside when I was married to him."

This type of lifelong secondary status contrasted with how many women felt now, whether through changing circumstances outside or through prison life itself. For instance, one woman reflected on how she felt like a princess when holding her cell's TV remote control in her hand with no one else determining what she watched. Another woman described turning herself over to the police and feeling that "the day I lost my freedom is the day I gained my freedom...I'm 55 years old...Even though I lived [with] that 25 years, I've been in this facility for five years [and] done more in five years with myself than I did in that 25 years a marriage."

The perceived newness of women's greater independence was highlighted as the residents talked about women nowadays being "thrown into a role of the dominant and I don't believe…women know how to step into that role well." A general theme was the idea of "I'm used to having a man run me around" and not make any decisions on my own. One woman explained her marriage seemed great to her as measured by the idea she "could work 40, 50, 60 hours a week and still take care of my home and cook him a hot meal every day, you know, and pack his lunch in the morning."

While prison has programs on various kinds of wellness, including boundary setting, grief and loss, anger management and pre-release (which one inmate compared to L. Ron Hubbard's "Pursuit of Happiness" videos); there was a paucity of counseling for domestic violence survivors.

> We need women's issue counselors! Domestic violence, sexual assault, abandonment – do you know how many people've been abandoned [here]?
>
> We're in a women's prison. There's not one domestic violence program here. When I got out of here and went out on probation or parole, they didn't offer one domestic violence class. One person to deal with domestic violence. Domestic violence doesn't just come from a spouse. It comes from a boyfriend, it comes when you're 13 and you're dating someone who's 16 so you can get their drugs. Domestic violence is huge. We are in a women's prison – not one program. Not one. How does that happen?
>
> The parole board knows nothing about domestic violence…We're in a women's prison. There's not one domestic violence program here…It needs to be here, and it needs to be on the outside. It needs to be a continuous program…How are we supposed to get better? How are we supposed to continue in a law-abiding life, when our patterns recreate themselves every time?
>
> This place doesn't have any type of transition program for women who've been through domestic violence. I was here for five months and I didn't even see a domestic violence class…One of the biggest problems of women incarcerated is because they're usin' drugs because they're gettin' the shit beat outta them.

An Nuytiens and Jenneke Christaens (2016) interviewed late-onset female offenders whose sole vulnerability was to an abusive partner (rather than having also experienced childhood abuse or economic deprivation). They note this group is difficult to identify and reach in a prevention mode because they do not have high-risk profiles and are often isolated. In our interviews we noted how the isolation is not just geographic but psychological: it results from the actions of partners combined with women's belief in the value of a/the partner and simultaneously their own low value. In summary, an overinvestment in traditional femininity, promoted in their small rural towns, prevent women from identifying as strong agents who are competent to make decisions. They then enter a confined environment without much formal discussion of their violent relationship and ways to avoid a similar future partner.

Strengths and Weaknesses of the Treatment Unit

Another high area of concern centered on the Intensive Training Unit (ITU), an area set apart from the other halls to form a self-contained community of 54 women focusing on behavior modification. On the one hand, the program has a lot of benefits and introduced or reintroduced the 12-step program to its participants, as this speaker notes:

> It's helped me with forgiveness, and it's helped me with a lot of them [the steps]. Another thing I like is...the women. You might think it would suck living with 54 women, and sometimes it does, but like I have 53 other people and they support me so much, like spiritually, with my family, they push me in the right direction, because they want to see me do better.

Women's general views on ITU's benefits were decidedly mixed, however. Significantly, the program is essentially non-voluntary and the prison administration tries to place as many prisoners as possible within ITU. The resulting environment, as one woman points out, contains women with sharply contrasting levels of motivation:

> They have to be in a place in their life where they're willing to say enough is enough, I need help. And, I'd say six out of every ten in there is not at that point.

Another agreed, saying:

> I think the biggest downfall for ITU is that people are made to go in there that aren't ready and so they become fake or they do what they need to do because they think it's going to get them home, you know, and I think it's unfortunate because, um, it really is I think a great program if you apply yourself.

One woman elaborated further:

> I believe that it bein' made a voluntary thing would do a lot more good, because I honestly believe that you could force somebody to go into a program like that but it doesn't mean they're gonna change. So I feel like if they're not gonna bother changing, then you're wasting a lotta time.

For this speaker every forced and disgruntled participant is taking up valuable bed-space from a person who desires treatment. Aside from increased tension, these arrangements pose practical concerns for the unit at large: inviting discord through clique-ish behavior and groupings, and more seriously, the potential for uncertain release dates. Most women are court ordered to complete the program successfully before they can exit the prison, yet the available bed space in this wing may delay their release time, preventing women from reuniting with children or family members and casting the program as a disruptor before the women even participate.

Other negative perceptions of ITU were based on the contradiction between the obligation of program secrecy while mandating participant divulging of intimate or painful life experiences, obligatory games women regarded as infantilizing, and being given the punishment of "ghost" status or silent treatment. Regarding this status one person said:

> What really scares me the most is ghost status. To me that seems like the most humiliating and shaming thing…I think what really bothers me is that one of the girls that had that status a few weeks ago, she had a very abusive childhood, you know, so it triggered a lot of stuff for her cause you have to sit under the stairs in a chair all day and just look down.

Another woman spoke of a common punishment: a way of humiliating a group member by making them read a children's book to the entire group or sing a children's song many times over. These acts that framed women as children were problematic particularly for women who had lived in abusive circumstances while growing up.

Furthermore, several women saw ITU as too rigid. The program did not acknowledge a context for criminal behavior.

> First of all…you have to get somebody to talk to them that knows and understands it, that gets that they've created this survival thinking. And they're still in their survival thinking. ITU doesn't address survival thinking. They only address the addiction.

Many of the crimes that landed women in prison readily comport with the above idea of "survival thinking". For instance, driving factors behind women's eventual use or sale of drugs were poverty, medical expenses, untreated mental health issues, violence and other exigencies. For some participants, the inability of the ITU to contextualize criminal behavior was a glaring weakness.

Another aspect of the program the women questioned repeatedly was the lack of professionally trained addiction counselors and caseworkers associated with ITU, and the control that incarcerated women in the program could exert over each other.

> We are inmates because we have not been the most upstanding character, and to give somebody so much power over another person, they don't need that. They take it and run with it. There's staff in that program for a

reason...you should probably use those staff. I also don't think there should be any of that degrading, pulling people down.

The Assistant to the Warden explained that they used to have staff run the entire ITU program but with staff turnover and understaffing being such a persistent problem, they chose to make willing women who had passed the program the instructors for the next group, since other programs in the US have used this method. While it may have positive sides, the many comments about favoritism suggested that using inmates as instructors was risky and did not enhance feelings of unity or cohesion between women in the group. This kind of feeling can persist long past the program. For instance, a group with splintered loyalties does not mirror the 12-step groups likely to be available to join on the outside, which means some women may not pursue similar opportunities which aid them in staying healthy when they are out in the world.

How to actively prevent victimized women from engaging in actions that lead towards incarceration including partner choice, alcohol and substance abuse and complicity with a partner's crimes is an unanswered and important question. Early intervention for people experiencing intimate partner abuse is vital. Furthermore, we can and should certainly do more to help the legal system respond to the effects of trauma and polyvictimization. Lastly, greater funding should be channeled towards community based recovery services; they truly help women keep the gains they made in prison while away from their former life of abuse.

Conclusion

Prisons by definition hide the people inside them. Perhaps that is why entertainment producers seek to write stories about them: they are mysterious. As prison rights advocate and scholar Jodie M. Lawston and Ashley Lucas (2011) have pointed out, by and large, prison officials control what gets told about the prison to the outside world. People can voyeuristically peep into female prisoners' lives without harm; out of all of female citizens, these women have the least voice in our nation. While *OITNB* contains hints of what our study exposed, it hardly prepares audiences to learn that the majority of women inside are receiving little to no counseling, that a prison may provide little information on avoiding future abusive relationships and that behavioral modification programs are run by inmates to save money on staff and thereby may become places of inconsistency and sometimes even exploitation.

The prison is a microcosm of US society: it devalues the difficulties of impoverishment and skin-color based discrimination and thereby lays bare our false claims to democracy, freedom and the availability of the American dream. Rather than mining prisoners' lives for humor or playing to preconceptions about groups based on racial background, class or mental health status, *Orange is the New Black* could have been as thoughtful as the memoir it was based on. It is time we bring the edge to the center and create new dialogue so that people both inside and outside of prison may join in solidarity.

References and Further Reading

ACLU. (2015). Facts about the over-incarceration of women in the United States. Retrieved from https://www.aclu.org/facts-about-over-incarceration-women-united-states

Lawston, J.M., & Lucas, A.E. (2011). *Razor Wire Women*. Albany, NY: SUNY Press.

Malloch, M., & McIvor, G. (Eds.). (2013). *Women, Punishment and Social Justice: Human Rights and Penal Practices*. London: Routledge.

Nuytiens, A., & Christaens, J. (2016). Female pathways to crime and prison: Challenging the (U.S.) gendered pathways perspective. *European Journal of Criminology* 13(2): 195–213.

Solinger, R., P.C. Johnson, M.L. Raimon, T. Reynolds, & R. Tapia, (Eds.), *Interrupted Life: Experiences of Incarcerated Women in the United States*. Berkeley, CA: University of California Press.

Spivak, G. (1988). Can the subaltern speak? In C. Nelson, & L. Grossberg (Eds.), *Marxism and the Interpretation of Culture* (pp. 271–313). Champaign, IL: University of Illinois.

Tapia, R. (2010). Introduction. In R. Solinger, P.C. Johnson, M.L. Raimon, T. Reynolds, & R. Tapia (Eds.), *Interrupted Life: Experiences of Incarcerated Women in the United States* (pp. 1–10). Berkeley, CA: University of California Press.

PART 3

Pregnancy and Parenting for Female Inmates

JaDee Carathers

Parenting is hard. Parenting from prison, however, is a difficult reality that the majority of incarcerated women endure. Imprisonment often interrupts parenting, imposing barriers to communication and physical visitation – removing mothers from everyday care and responsibilities, and the closeness that such proximity may impart. The very idea of family may be reshaped by the extenuating circumstances of residential instability, as children move from caregiver to caregiver, and potentially in and out of the foster care system. Mothers risk losing their children to the state altogether in too many instances, and often cannot depend on fathers to provide primary support.

Societal norms shape ideas about 'good' mothering that are both class-based and racialized. Popular culture and media play an integral role in disseminating the discourse of 'good' mothering, providing visual representations for mothers to measure themselves against. The 'good' mother fulfills the timeless duties relegated to the domain of mothering – the mundane minutia that makes daily living possible, like clean laundry and hot meals – and the sentimental markers of mothering, like emotional intimacy and nurturance. Gendered cultural messages steeped in biological essentialism tell us good mothers belong in the home according to sociologist Evelyn Nakano Glenn.

Women of color have historically been excluded from the ranks of good mothers by economic necessity – working outside the home, perhaps even providing the sole income for the family. Laboring in the public sphere serves to masculinize, and therefore problematize, the femininity of women of color, further distancing them from the cultural markers of delicate (white) womanhood. The issue of domestic labor presents a quandary, for example, when women of color are employed to care for White (middle-class) children and are subsequently stigmatized for being away from their own children. In this way, race and class are key to examinations of mothering discourse and the racialized stigmatization of 'bad' mothers according to historian Rickie Solinger.

But what happens when mothering is denied, interrupted by a criminal justice system that disproportionately punishes racial minorities and those living in poverty? The experience of pregnancy and childbirth while serving a prison sentence has rarely been explored in popular culture and media. The following chapters trace the experiences of Dayanara and Maria, two *OITNB* characters who deal with pregnancy while imprisoned, highlighting the issues of quality healthcare, nutrition, and postpartum support.

In "Baby Bumps in Litchfield: Pregnancy in *Orange is the New Black* Series", Rebecca Rodriguez Carey demonstrates how *OITNB* misses an opportunity to explore critical issues connected to pregnancy in prison, including the lack of prenatal healthcare. As Daya's pregnancy progresses, for instance, we see how she is able to circumvent the rules in order to access nutrient-rich spinach to supplement an abysmal prison-food diet. Carey also points out the important role of "pseudo-families" in this context, who may be a primary – if potentially inaccurate – source of information on pregnancy and childbirth. Daya's pseudo-family concocts a home remedy for constipation, a common ailment during pregnancy, again breaking the rules in an attempt to assist her. Carey emphasizes the lack of autonomy present among women giving birth while incarcerated, noting how their role may be minimized to that of a mere "spectator" at the event.

In "Pregnancy Postpartum Life Behind Bars: What's Present and What's Missing in *Orange is the New Black*", Janet Garcia-Hallett focuses on two issues that *OITNB* might have better addressed: shackling during pregnancy and prison nurseries. Although a number of states do prohibit women from being shackled during childbirth, enforcement varies. *OITNB* omits imagery of laboring women being shackled, but we do see a corrections officer in the hospital room with Daya postpartum – a scenario likely to be uncomfortable for her. Garcia-Hallett notes that shackling during pregnancy, delivery, or postpartum is an unnecessary and inhumane procedure, while also reminding us that women in prison may lack access to information about their rights. *OITNB* also omits depiction of prison nurseries, which are both not a new concept and also not the standard of care. As Garcia-Hallett notes, some nurseries allow women and infants to co-reside – a protective measure that precludes the potential negative effects of mother–child separation that may include anxiety and depression in children. Importantly, prison nurseries demonstrate how it is possible to keep infants with their mothers, in an effort to prevent situations where parental rights are threatened by the state.

Focusing on intersectional inequalities in mothering in "Pregnancy, Parenting and Prison: Mothering while Incarcerated", Jeanne Holcomb asks if all women are allowed to be 'good' mothers. Imprisonment, it seems, holds the potential to mar the traditional femininity of women as mothers, hardening them and their children to the inevitable pains of separation. Mothers often play a primary role in maintaining responsibility and safety for their children, and when absent, they may experience increased stress because they cannot function in this primary role from afar. Holcomb notes that though most women in prison are the primary caregivers for their children, most children do not see their mothers while imprisoned. Lack of communication and engagement with their children may increase parental stress and negatively impact mental health.

Holcomb also explores the portrayal of Daya's experience as institutionalized sexual abuse; reminding us that though women should legally have access to abortion while imprisoned, there are myriad reasons why they might choose to hide a pregnancy to avoid punitive repercussions. When medical care is provided, bias and discrimination may sometimes manifest against the mother and child. Particularly troubling are instances of imprisoned women giving birth alone, separated from personal support and medical care – to the detriment, and even potential death, of the child. Perhaps unsurprisingly, Holcomb notes the increased risk of postpartum depression and psychosis that may accompany giving birth in prison.

Taken together, these chapters present a number of problematic issues to address related to pregnancy and parenting in prison including the need for pre-natal care and a nutritious diet, reexamination of the practices surrounding birth and postpartum that deny mother–infant dignity and bonding, and alternative forms of rehabilitation that keep families together. Pregnancy is often celebrated culturally as a time of beautiful growth and feminine reflection, but this exalted form of fertile femininity is not equally accessible (nor necessarily desirable) among all women. In many ways, cultural representations of 'good' mothering in the contemporary US are part of a racialized discourse centered on middle-class, heterosexual, White families that marginalizes alternative experiences outside of the 'nuclear' tradition. While OITNB tackled the contentious issue of pregnancy and parenting in prison through the characters Dayanara and Maria, problematic aspects of their portrayal remain as an indictment of the harsh realities many prisoners face every day.

References and Further Reading

Chodorow, N. J. (1978). *The Reproduction of Mothering*. Berkeley: University of California Press.

Glenn, E. N. (1994). Social Construction of Mothering: A Thematic Overview. In E. N. Glenn, G. Change, & L. Forcey (Eds.), *Mothering: Ideology, Experience, and Agency* (pp. 1–29). New York: Routledge.

Rich, A. (1986). *Of Woman Born: Motherhood as Experience and Institution*. New York: W. W. Norton.

Ruddick, S. (1995). *Maternal Thinking: Toward a Politics of Peace*. Boston: Beacon Press.

Solinger, R. (2005). *Pregnancy and Power: A Short History of Reproductive Politics in America*. New York: New York University Press.

7

BABY BUMPS IN LITCHFIELD

Pregnancy in the *Orange is the New Black* Series

Rebecca Rodriguez Carey

The popular Netflix television series *Orange is the New Black* (*OITNB*), based on Piper Kerman's best-selling memoir that detailed her time spent in federal prison, is known for bringing to light the incarceration of women, an area that has long been understudied in the field of criminology. While this show focuses on a wide variety of issues facing the incarcerated and their families, it also highlights an area that is rarely discussed in both research and popular culture: the incarceration of pregnant women. This chapter considers critical ideas that remain underexplored throughout the series in regard to pregnancy, particularly the quality of healthcare that pregnant women receive behind bars.

The series follows lead character Piper Chapman who is sentenced to fifteen months in Litchfield, a fictional federal correctional institution, for her involvement in an international drug ring five years earlier. Throughout the series, the audience is introduced to a variety of characters, including two pregnant inmates: Maria Ruiz and Dayanara "Daya" Diaz. Maria is introduced in Season 1, as a young Latina inmate, who is visibly pregnant in her third trimester. With assistance from her peers, who serve as her pseudo-family in prison, Maria labors in Litchfield; later in the series, Maria struggles with the separation from her new daughter. Fan favorite Daya is also a young Latina who later becomes pregnant in prison from a correctional officer. When the soft piano music plays, fans are immersed in the romantic relationship that has quickly blossomed between Daya and John Bennett, a young White correctional officer who served in the military; as the two lovers secretly exchange heartfelt notes and drawings, they envision a fairytale life together outside the prison gates. Their relationship changes gears when Daya becomes pregnant with Bennett's child. These two storylines provide a glimpse into the pregnancy experiences behind bars.

OITNB's portrayal of pregnancy is important and warrants further examination because of the staggering growth of women under correctional control. Evidence from Heather C. West, William J. Sabol, and Sarah J. Greenman with the Bureau of Justice Statistics indicates that approximately 114,000 women in the U.S. are currently incarcerated, due to expansive criminal justice efforts, including a crackdown on female criminality and tougher sentencing (West et al., 2010). Consequently, a number of women are also pregnant while incarcerated. Bureau of Justice Statistics statistician Laura M. Maruschak estimates that, in 2004, four percent of state prisoners were pregnant, while three percent of federal prisoners were pregnant upon admittance. National statistics regarding the number of women who become pregnant from correctional officers, as in Daya's case, are largely unknown, as national statistics regarding this information are not well-maintained. While the show has unarguably brought attention to the incarceration of women, it is argued that the show's portrayal of pregnancy in prison ignores critical issues that incarcerated pregnant women face. Although Maria and Daya are fictional characters, it is important to consider the lives of those who are actually pregnant and incarcerated.

Since Maria is a minor character in OITNB, this chapter will primarily focus on Daya and her pregnancy; however, it is worth noting that Maria is the first pregnant inmate viewers meet; additionally, Maria's storyline also brings to light important considerations that are outside the scope of this chapter regarding how OITNB depicts pregnancy with regard to race and the role of fathers as caregivers.

Daya's storyline initially centers on seemingly harmless flirtatious encounters that lead to a romantic and sexual relationship with Bennett, which ultimately results in her becoming pregnant. However, keeping their relationship a secret becomes increasingly difficult once she becomes pregnant, especially given that relations are not allowed between correctional officers and inmates. Once pregnant, Daya's storyline shifts its focus to center on devising a plan to explain how she became pregnant in prison. In OITNB, Daya faces a quandary; if she reports the pregnancy to prison officials, then Bennett could be imprisoned as well, due to the Prison Rape Elimination Act, which criminalizes sexual relations between correctional staff and inmates. In this case, if Bennett becomes incarcerated, then Daya's unborn child would grow up without a father. Daya views the potential absence of Bennett as concerning because she desires a two-parent household for her unborn infant, especially since her own father was absent. Yet, by keeping the pregnancy hidden from the correctional staff, Daya is unable to receive pre-natal care and the necessary nutrients to optimize the likelihood of a healthy pregnancy.

With each episode, devising a plan becomes more pressing, as Daya gradually becomes unable to conceal the pregnancy because of her growing "baby bump." Daya's peers arrange a plan that involves seducing George "Pornstache" Mendez, a crooked correctional officer, into having sexual relations with her, so the pregnancy can be pinned on him. With assistance from her peers, it is arranged for the correctional staff to walk in on Mendez and Daya having sex in a prison utility closet. With the pregnancy now pinned on Mendez and Mendez incarcerated on rape charges, this allows Bennett to be scot-free, at least until Daya feels guilty for framing Mendez. Mendez' mother also enters the picture in later episodes, which further complicates matters.

Since the incarceration of pregnant women is largely closed off from society, Daya and Maria's storylines deserve further consideration. *OITNB*'s depictions of pregnancy are significant because they illuminate the ways in which individuals shape their views of the criminal justice system and the incarceration of women, especially those who are pregnant and incarcerated. For those without close ties to the criminal justice system, individuals may receive misinformation about the criminal justice system from television, and therefore, an examination of the *OITNB* series regarding pregnancy is important.

Accessing Prenatal Care

In order to better understand pregnancy behind bars, a focus on pregnant inmates' healthcare is necessary. Since the audience is introduced to Daya prior to her becoming pregnant, viewers are able to see the entirety of her pregnancy unfold in prison. Throughout her pregnancy, Daya's health is marked with increased stress, as a result of having to grapple with several major decisions related to her pregnancy, such as whether to report her pregnancy to correctional administration, whether to reveal the true identity of her unborn infant's father, and decisions related to selecting the best caregiver for her unborn infant. However, throughout these nine months, Daya is not seen accessing prenatal care, which is troubling. As anthropologist Sallie Han noted in her research that centered on the experiences of pregnant women, accessing healthcare is viewed as a requisite to both reducing potential complications and optimizing health outcomes. As such, an examination of Daya's healthcare in *OITNB* is important because it speaks to the larger issue of healthcare among the incarcerated, particularly those who are pregnant and incarcerated.

Evaluating pregnant inmates' healthcare is difficult given that there are mixed research findings regarding the quality of healthcare pregnant inmates receive. As childbirth educator Barbara A. Hotelling argued in her research on pregnant inmates, incarceration may provide protective health benefits for women and their unborn children. This is because prison offers shelter, meals, and healthcare, necessities which may not be guaranteed for women on the outside. As such, incarceration may minimize the stresses associated with securing these necessities, since inmates are provided these essentials. Likewise, for women who use drugs during pregnancy, incarceration may further provide protective health benefits because it (theoretically) eliminates access to illicit drugs. However, for others, the experience of being incarcerated may reduce the likelihood of having healthy outcomes, due to various stressors related to imprisonment, including poor healthcare. These stressors may negatively impact both maternal and fetal health, as Hotelling noted in her research. For women with high-quality healthcare on the outside, they may experience markedly inferior healthcare in prison.

Furthermore, research by health scholars Anita G. Hufft, Lena Sue Fawkes, and W. Travis Lawson, Jr. on pregnant offenders illustrated how pregnant prisoners receive knowledge regarding bodily changes concomitant with pregnancy from their pseudo-families in prison or from inmates who serve as mentors, since little pregnancy educational material is provided in prison. Pseudo-families or mentors may provide information regarding the "interpretation of symptoms, self-diagnosis, the need for clinical appointments, use of self-remedies, evaluation of treatment, and belief in professional explanation" (Hufft et al., 1993, p. 57). It is important to note that this information may be inaccurate thereby potentially complicating health outcomes.

The reliance on peers for information concerning pregnancy is evidenced in *OITNB*, as Daya's mother, Aleida, who is also incarcerated in Litchfield, is the one who informs Daya that she is pregnant; Daya's "positive pregnancy test" is based on her mother's interpretation of her symptoms rather than the reliance on a traditional pregnancy test to inform her that she is pregnant. Gloria Mendoza, the pseudo-mother to the Latinas in Litchfield, also provides information to Daya regarding the use of home remedies to relieve her pain. Incarcerated pregnant women may be forced to rely on home remedies from other inmates, such as Gloria, to relieve pain during pregnancy because traditional healthcare may be poor or absent.

Moreover, inmates may be forced to circumvent prison rules, in order to both provide and receive this care. This circumvention is evident in *OITNB*, as Aleida sneaks into an administrative office to access ingredients to assist Gloria with making a home remedy for Daya to relieve her constipation. Although Litchfield's correctional officers frequently circumvent rules and procedures themselves, the inmates could have received a formal reprimand for circumventing prison rules to create these home remedies.

Furthermore, pregnancy is marked as a period that places a particular emphasis on the consumption of food that is rich in nutrients for the betterment of one's health, as Sallie Han (2013) further noted in her research. Han's findings are evident in Season 2, Episode 3, as Daya reads an article in the prison library about the importance of consuming folic acid during pregnancy, due to its benefits on a developing fetus. This particular scene is significant because prior to Daya reading this article, her only means of receiving knowledge regarding her pregnancy was through her peers. Since Daya has consumed little to no folic acid, she becomes increasingly worried about the health of her developing fetus.

Bennett tells Daya not to worry about her lack of prenatal care, such as folic acid, because his mother did not take prenatal vitamins when she was pregnant with him; he also tells Daya that it is safe to assume that Aleida did not take prenatal vitamins either when she was pregnant with Daya. Bennett rationalizes that the health of the fetus will be fine, even in the absence of prenatal vitamins, because he and Daya "turned out okay" without prenatal care. However, Daya views Bennett's logic as unacceptable because she wants their unborn child to have the very best of everything, including prenatal care. Understanding Daya's concerns, Bennett utilizes his prosthetic leg to serve as a vessel to secretly deliver raw spinach, which is high in folic acid, to Daya. Given the absence of food rich in nutrients, Daya and Bennett are forced to circumvent the prison rules, so Daya can optimize her health outcomes.

As such, one of the reasons Daya feels compelled to report her pregnancy to officials involves the receiving of healthcare for her fetus; in Daya's mind, once she reports her pregnancy, a magic door that provides healthcare will open. However, once prison officials became aware of the pregnancy, viewers do not see Daya receiving healthcare. This is ironic given that prenatal care is especially important for Daya, so she can give her unborn child the best life possible, including during in utero. Thus, viewers are left with questions regarding Daya's healthcare: is this an oversight by *OITNB* or did Daya truly lack healthcare? The absence of care becomes more problematic given that the audience follows Daya throughout the entirety of her pregnancy, including during the final weeks, when it is recommended that pregnant women have weekly prenatal appointments. It is difficult to speculate the extent of Maria's healthcare, while she was pregnant, as viewers only saw her pregnant in the initial episodes of the series.

For incarcerated pregnant women without their own Bennett to deliver healthy food, they must rely on other methods to receive food that is rich in nutrients. In *OITNB*, the kitchen is a frequently sought after job because working in the kitchen helps to ensure that one has access to food rather than being at the mercy of other inmates who work in the kitchen. This is because other inmates have the power to refuse to serve those they dislike. The importance of having access to the kitchen or a good working relationship with the kitchen workers is evident when Piper, the lead character, becomes "starved out" by the kitchen workers. However, since Daya is employed in the kitchen during her pregnancy, she has frequent access to food, including the ability to gather additional food as needed.

Still, despite working in the kitchen, accessing food that is rich in nutrients may be dependent upon the availability of prison funds. As an example, when Litchfield becomes a private prison, the quality of food suffers substantially, and it is obvious that the women's health suffers as a result. Although the women can buy additional food from the prison commissary in *OITNB*, the food available for purchase appears insufficient with regard to nutritional value, and furthermore, the women do not necessarily have the financial means to purchase this food.

In Litchfield, healthcare for all women is limited. Thus, it is somewhat surprising that the women do not ask their Women's Advisory Council representative to seek improved healthcare. In one scene, Maria, a member on the Women's Advisory Council, requests a second pillow, presumably to ease the pain associated with her pregnancy; however, other inmates on the Women's Advisory

Council inquire about more trivial issues, such as wanting doughnuts and additional television programming rather than issuing requests concerning more serious matters, such as the need for improved medical care for all inmates and pregnant women in particular.

While *OITNB* does not show Maria and Daya during delivery, it does show them laboring with the support of their pseudo-family members in prison. Both women are transferred to a hospital to give birth. In legal scholar Kelly Parker's research that focused on how prison practices negatively affect pregnant inmates, Parker noted that transferring women to a hospital to give birth is a relatively common practice among pregnant inmates, since many prisons are ill-equipped to deliver infants. The quality of women's healthcare during pregnancy, including during labor and delivery, is largely dependent upon resources available at each particular prison. It is also dependent upon pregnant women's interactions with medical personnel, such as nurses and doctors, and the correctional personnel, particularly those who accompany the women to the hospital.

As historian Rickie Solinger argued in her book, *Pregnancy and Power: A Short History of Reproductive Politics in America*, incarcerated pregnant women have limited decision-making concerning their healthcare. This includes decisions pertaining to the location of birth, e.g., hospital, birthing center, or home, in addition to few choices regarding the methods of relieving pain and decisions pertaining to the presence or absence of select individuals in the room during labor and delivery, as examples. The lack of autonomy in decision-making influences the healthcare received during pregnancy, as incarcerated women may be viewed as spectators of their own pregnancies rather than active participants.

As health scholar Jennifer G. Clarke and her colleagues indicated in their research that focused on reproductive healthcare among incarcerated women, many of the pregnancies of incarcerated women are considered high-risk, due to a variety of risk factors, such as a possible combination of prior drug and alcohol use, prior sexual abuse, limited healthcare, poor nutrition, and the presence of sexually transmitted diseases. Therefore, examining the ways in which pregnant women's healthcare is portrayed in *OITNB* is important because it calls into question larger issues concerning the quality of healthcare incarcerated women receive, particularly special needs populations, such as pregnant women. For fictional characters Daya and Maria, their lack of healthcare is certainly a cause for concern; however, it is important to remember that for many incarcerated individuals, this is their reality.

Conclusion

While *OITNB* is considered a fictional television show, albeit based on the true story of Piper Kerman, the show has undoubtedly contributed to the public discourse regarding the incarceration of women. Since the event of experiencing a pregnancy in prison has not received adequate attention from scholars, it is important to consider how *OITNB* serves as a powerful medium that provides knowledge regarding how pregnancies unfold behind bars. These experiences are also important because they may be significantly different from the pregnancy experiences among women who are not incarcerated. Throughout this chapter, it becomes clear that experiencing a pregnancy behind bars is often more complex than depicted in a television show. This chapter contributes to an understanding of how the criminal justice system affects women, especially since female criminality is often overlooked in comparison to male criminality. This chapter also considers important issues regarding incarcerated pregnant women, primarily their health-care. With every television show, it is important to consider the ways in which television shows influence public policy considerations, especially with regard to incarceration.

References and Further Reading

Chesney-Lind, M., & Pasko, L. (Eds.). (2013). *The female offender: Girls, women, and crime.* (3ʳᵈ ed.). Thousand Oaks, CA: SAGE Publications.

Clarke, J. G., Hebert, M. R., Rosengard, C., Rose, J. S., DaSilva, K. M., & Stein, M. D. (2006). Reproductive health care and family planning needs among incarcerated women. *American Journal of Public Health*, 96(5), 834–839.

Han, S. (2013). *Pregnancy in practice: Expectation and experience in the contemporary US.* New York, NY: Berghahn Books.

Hotelling, B. A. (2008). Perinatal needs of pregnant, incarcerated women. *The Journal of Perinatal Education*, 17(2), 37–44.

Hufft, A. G., Fawkes, L. S., & Lawson, W. T., Jr. (1993). Care of the pregnant offender. In J. A. Gondles, Jr. (Ed.), *Female offenders: Meeting needs of a neglected population* (pp. 54–59). Laurel, MD: American Correctional Association.

Maruschak, L. M. (2008). Medical problems of prisoners. *Bureau of Justice Statistics.* Retrieved from http://www.bjs.gov/index.cfm?ty=pbdetail&iid=1097

Parker, K. (2004). Pregnant women inmates: Evaluating their rights and identifying opportunities for improvements in their treatment. *Journal of Law & Health*, 19(2), 259–295.

Solinger, R. (2005). *Pregnancy and power: A short history of reproductive politics in America.* New York, NY: New York University Press.

West, H. C., Sabol, W. J., & Greenman, S. J. (2010). Prisoners in 2009. *Bureau of Justice Statistics.* Retrieved from http://www.bjs.gov/content/pub/pdf/p09.pdf

8

PREGNANCY AND POSTPARTUM LIFE BEHIND BARS

What's Present and What's Missing in *Orange is the New Black*

Janet Garcia-Hallett

Introduction: Female Inmates as Mothers

Public perceptions of incarcerated women can be shaped by media representations, whether these images claim to be real-life showcases or mere entertainment. Such influence can be used to enlighten individuals about critical issues in the criminal justice system while further testing the waters of emphasizing humor and amusement. The Netflix series *Orange is the New Black* (*OITNB*) has managed to accomplish a little bit of both. Though it caters to public fascination with drama and female sexuality, it has also sparked interesting discussions in classroom settings, in the workplace, and among members of the public at large. Such discussions may include the show's race-based commentary on criminality, examples of mothering practices behind bars, and prevalent issues with the privatization of prisons – to name a few.

Two interconnected matters that have been depicted in *OITNB* consist of: (1) pregnancy during incarceration and (2) motherhood after delivery. This chapter examines the media's portrayal of pregnant incarcerated women and mothering in *OITNB* and the realities of women who are pregnant and mothers behind bars. I begin by briefly reviewing the stories of two women who experienced pregnancy during the first three seasons of this Netflix series – Maria Ruiz and Dayanara Diaz. In doing so, I explore aspects of the women's experiences that are consistent with existing literature in the field of criminology about motherhood while incarcerated. Then, I highlight key criminal justice issues that were understated in the Netflix series despite their importance in legal and social justice matters.

Managing Motherhood

Through the stories of two pregnant women, *OITNB* makes an attempt to capture prevalent issues women encounter when becoming mothers during their incarceration and while they navigate adapting to motherhood. In 2013, a group of Registered Nurses published a research article on "Contemporary women's adaptation to motherhood." In this article, Cynthia Aber and her colleagues explained: "Adaptation to motherhood initially deals with the transition from being a nonparenting woman to becoming a parenting woman; that is, a mother. When the woman becomes a mother for the second time, her transition is from parent of one child to parent of more than one child, and so on for subsequent children" (2013, p. 344). This adaptation to motherhood is not limited to the time during pregnancy and the point of delivery, but may also entail the months after delivery and last over a wide timespan. While this transition is acknowledged within nursing research, Aber and her colleagues argue that there is "an assumption that the process of adaptation is universal and context-free rather than evolving within the life and societal context of women across generations" (ibid.). Instead, they suggest that this transition is not normative in nature and should be understood according to social, physical, emotional, and practical factors that may shape women's experiences in adapting to motherhood. *OITNB* has tapped into these four components by displaying Dayanara's maternal concerns in anticipation of her daughter's arrival and by demonstrating Maria's postpartum attempts to navigate maternal care from a distance.

When women are incarcerated while pregnant, the living arrangements of their newborn children are common concerns, as they often must decide the most suitable caregiver while they finish their sentences. Impregnated during her incarceration by a correctional officer, Dayanara's case is unique as it portrays an ongoing intimate relationship with a correctional officer and, arguably, dramatizes the nature of such sexual relations for the sake of media. Nonetheless, for the purpose of this piece, I will focus on Dayanara's experience in the Netflix series after the point of conception. For instance, while Dayanara was pregnant during her incarceration, she was unable to rely on the father to be the primary caretaker once their daughter was born. This is a common experience among incarcerated mothers who often see little caregiving accountability from their children's fathers and face the practical reality that they cannot depend on the fathers for such responsibilities during their incarceration. In fact, reports by the Bureau of Justice Statistics demonstrate that children of incarcerated women are more likely to reside with their grandparents than their fathers. In the absence of the fathers or grandparents who may care for children, incarcerated mothers may find themselves in a bind. *OITNB* presented a scenario in which Dayanara temporarily considered putting her daughter up for adoption once she was born, believing: "It ain't right for me to keep the baby if I'm not gonna be around." Eventually, however, she changed her mind and decided to leave her newborn child under the care of a man with whom Dayanara's mother maintained a domestic partnership. This living arrangement did not last for long as the third season concludes with a drug raid in which the temporary caregiver was arrested and Child Services was called for Dayanara's daughter (who was present at the time of the arrest).

This not only hints at the residential instability and complications that children encounter during maternal incarceration, but it also draws attention to mothers' experiences with navigating postpartum care from a distance during their imprisonment.

The Shackling of Pregnant Women

While *OITNB* depicts common issues faced by incarcerated mothers during and after their pregnancy, it has glossed over the shackling of pregnant women that is still prevalent in correctional facilities across the country. When Maria was in labor, she was shown breathing heavily with her face shining from sweat as she held her stomach in discomfort. After a few moments, a nurse approached Maria and informed her that there was a hospital van waiting at the facility. She was seated in a wheelchair and, as she was transported off the screen, Maria was told: "Let's get you to the van. Everything is going to be okay." There was no further illustration of her transportation to the hospital or her experience as a pregnant incarcerated woman in a hospital setting. Did she enter the hospital van without shackles while she was in labor? Were shackles in place as she entered and maneuvered inside the nearby hospital? Was she shackled to the bed during or immediately after her delivery? Did she return to the correctional facility in shackles? These questions remain unanswered as this was not illustrated regarding Maria's experience.

The only direct reference to the shackling of pregnant women occurred in reference to Dayanara's unborn child; specifically, the father was asked if he wanted Dayanara to be taken away to another facility before delivering their baby in shackles. Though mentioned briefly here in reference to Dayanara's potential experience, this was not part of the visual storyline. Instead, Dayanara—unlike Maria—experienced some complications during labor and was later placed in an ambulance rather than "the van." Fast-forwarding postpartum, the Netflix series illustrated Dayanara holding onto her newborn daughter without visible shackles and telling her daughter that she loves her. In this depiction, there was a correctional officer inside Dayanara's hospital room who was posted by the entrance door. According to an investigation conducted by the non-profit organization, the Correctional Association of New York, mothers view the presence of correctional officers in delivery rooms as a source of discomfort given the already restricted nature of the hospital room in addition to the emotional, psychologically difficult, and physically demanding circumstances of delivery.

While the Netflix series did not depict Maria's experience after leaving the correctional facility and was unclear regarding the matter of shackling, it did follow Dayanara as she was leaving the facility and after her delivery. Yet, the prevalence of shackling was minimized in the representations of pregnancy and postpartum experiences even though shackling remains a considerable legal issue. In fact, the full shackling of women around the wrists, waist, and feet increases the potential of falling while pregnant and potentially harming the unborn child, while simultaneously decreasing mothers' chances of protecting themselves (and the baby) in such situations. For these reasons, the shackling of pregnant women is cruel and inhumane. Such shackling is also excessive given the womens' physical condition and the fact that women offenders are typically incarcerated for non-violent offenses and pose little threat. As many as 28 states do not prohibit the shackling of pregnant incarcerated women. While the remaining states have anti-shackling laws banning shackling during labor, they are often weak concerning other stages of pregnancy and recovery, and are overcome by issues with adherence to such laws – as is the case with New York State.

The Case of Shackling in New York

New York State passed a law in 2009 prohibiting the shackling of pregnant women during childbirth. Yet, research conducted by the Correctional Association of New York (2015c) demonstrated that the law was not being implemented and women were still shackled despite the law banning this very act. In fact, they found that women were shackled throughout their pregnancy. Of the 27 women they studied, 23 were still shackled while in transport to the hospital during labor, immediately after giving birth during their postpartum recovery, and while in transportation back to the facility. The lack of implementation is potentially triggered by a lack of education on behalf of the correctional officers and a lack of enforcement to ensure facilities adhered to this law. This is also further complicated by the lack of information given to incarcerated women about their rights. After a series of local outreach efforts associated with an anti-shackling movement, Governor Cuomo signed the 2015 Anti-Shackling Bill to strengthen the preexisting 2009 Anti-Shackling Law. According to a news report by the Correctional Association of New York:

> The new law fortifies an existing 2009 ban against shackling during labor and delivery, and, most significantly, extends the law to include all stages of pregnancy....The new law, in addition to widening the pool of protected women, also: bars correctional staff from the delivery room unless the woman or medical personnel request their presence, institutes yearly reporting of all incidents in which guards have deemed shackling necessary, [and] requires rigorous training of all staff about the policy.

While progress is being made in New York, other states are at a standstill without laws that prohibit such shackling throughout the pregnancy and recovery period postpartum. Although viewers may likely interpret media representations differently given varying political affiliations and preconceptions about incarcerated individuals, the shackling of pregnant incarcerated women could have sparked interesting discussions and potentially inspired inquiring minds to seek further information.

In other words, *OITNB* missed an opportunity to bring the shackling of pregnant women to the forefront of public attention.

Mothering Behind Bars: Prison Nurseries

"Is the baby gonna be staying with us?" Before Dayanara learned of her own pregnancy while incarcerated, she was shown asking about the anticipated plans for Maria's unborn daughter and inquiring whether the newborn would be staying with them in the correctional facility. Presented as an impractical circumstance, her question was answered with a rhetorical question: "You see any babies around here?" The answer was no; it was not a possibility for the mothers to remain with their babies after their delivery because there was no prison nursery program. Later in the Netflix series, the incarcerated women were in a common recreational room in which they were shown socializing loudly, reading magazines, playing cards, and engaging in a game of foosball – a depiction that is not representative of incarceration. Maria was then shown seated in a wheelchair and wheeled into the large room by a correctional officer. The room that was previously filled with sounds of laughter and chatter had transitioned into a room of silence as the women turned to look at Maria after she had delivered her baby and returned to the correctional facility without her newborn daughter.

OITNB presents viewers with knowledge that many pregnant incarcerated women are unable to keep their newborns with them in a correctional facility. In fact, mothers who do not have someone to take care of their newborns may find their babies placed in foster care. Yet, the Netflix series does not communicate the reality that some correctional facilities in the United States (and abroad) have nurseries in which incarcerated mothers may co-reside with their newborn children for a period of time after delivery. While the show's intent may have been to demonstrate the downfalls of delivery while incarcerated, an accurate portrayal of prison nurseries could have provided viewers with knowledge about alternative programs that are achievable but often unknown or unclear to the public. In essence, an opportunity was missed to convey increasing efforts to support mothering in the criminal justice system.

The literature on incarcerated women has extensively examined women's experiences, both positive and negative, at various stages pre- and post-delivery. This literature is often catered to practitioners in an effort to assist women during their pregnancies and during the early stages postpartum. Despite the numerous efforts to help pregnant and postpartum mothers, this interest is seldom associated with incarcerated women and is frequently obscured within media representations of prison life. Recently, however, scholars have drawn attention to the implementation and impact of prison nurseries, examining their effects over time for both the infants and the incarcerated mothers. While research and media attention is given to the effects of maternal incarceration on children, less attention is devoted to the mother–child separation at birth due to the mother's imprisonment. This, too, limits discussions about the presence and prospect of prison nurseries as pregnant incarcerated women are often overlooked.

Nurseries have been implemented within correctional facilities to provide a space in which newborn children can avoid the detrimental effects of being separated from their mothers and, instead, develop attachments to their mothers. There is a consensus across various fields that the first year after birth is crucial for infants to develop attachment behaviors. During this time, infants have a need for nourishment and cleansing but, unable to tend to themselves, they must rely on others to fulfill this need for them. According to an array of psychoanalytical literature and social learning theorists, infants become attached to mother-figures through these early social interactions. John Bowlby, a pioneer in attachment theory, presents infants' attachments to their mothers as a biologically driven need to maintain close proximity in order to remain safe and increase their chances of survival. Whether a social learning or biological perspective, scholars are in agreement that attachments to mothers are instrumental in infants' subsequent social development but mother–child separation may influence an array of nega-tive behavioral responses from the children. For instance, in her article *The Bond Between Mother and Child,* psychologist Beth Azar (1995) notes that a lack of maternal attachment during infancy interferes with infants' social stimulations and subsequently impairs their ability to manage otherwise normal social interactions. Thus, prison nurseries have been implemented as a means to help children establish attachments to their mothers during this crucial developmental stage – despite the mothers' physical restrictions to correctional facilities in which they must complete their penal punishments.

While prison nurseries have been implemented to act in the best interest of the infants, advocates of prison nurseries have also argued that incarcerated women should be able to serve their punishment without being further reprimanded by forced separation from their newborns. Yet, involvement in a prison nursery program is still regarded as a privilege. When children are (or are expected to be) born while the women are under custody, the women must undergo a range of evaluations before potential involvement in a prison nursery. For instance, the mothers likely do not have histories of mental health issues. As a precaution against potential harms to the newborns, women with a record of violent crimes or crimes against children are typically prohibited from the benefits of having their newborns in prison nurseries. Once a part of a prison nursery program, incarcerated mothers are likely held in areas that are separated from the general population of other incarcerated women. Living quarters, vary however, as some facilities provide space for mothers to co-reside solely with their children and others require multiple mothers to share and co-reside with their children. The following sections present selected benefits and issues with prison nurseries, incorporating quotes from formerly incarcerated mothers in New York with previous involvement in such programs.

Benefits of Prison Nurseries

As briefly captured in *OITNB*, in the absence of a prison nursery program, incarcerated women may dread the expected separation from their newborns and later find the separation to be an abrupt and traumatic experience. Angelina Chambers, a Certified Nurse-Midwife and Professor, conducted interviews with incarcerated postpartum mothers and explored the impact of forced separation policies on the women. Chambers found that despite existing knowledge of the expected process, women described a painful realization of the separation as their children were taken from their arms at the hospital. Through interviews with formerly incarcerated women who gave birth during imprisonment, Stephanie Fritz and Kevin Whiteacre found that the mothers were denied immediate information from correctional officers about the whereabouts of the intended caregivers, which contributed to the traumatic separation from their children. What is not captured in *OITNB* is how this mother–child separation may be averted when a prison nursery program is available for incarcerated women. Instead of being separated from their children at birth, women may return to a designed area of the correctional facility along with their newborns and experience some benefits to their involvement in a prison nursery program.

> I did 18 months in the nursery. They spoiled us. We had everything we needed.
>
> Then, you know, they love the babies; so, they love the babies, they love the parents.
>
> *– Lucinda*

Created in the best interest of infants, prison nurseries typically incorporate a range of resources for the mothers, such as access to childbirth education, day care, breastfeeding support, and parenting classes. Often fraught with negative relationships and a lack of social support pre-incarceration, mothers find the supportive nature of prison nurseries to be an encouraging environment as they are often not accustomed to this level of attention and help. In fact, in their study, Fritz and Whiteacre discovered that mothers in prison nursery programs described staff as caring individuals who took a genuine interest in listening to them and helping them with concerns. It is also not assumed or expected that motherhood is a natural transition for all mothers. Thus, educational parenting classes are typically a requirement of prison nurseries in which mothers can learn about child development and receive practical maternal support with childrearing and breastfeeding. Katy Huang, a Registered Nurse and Lactation Consultant previously with the New York City Department of Health and Mental Hygiene, conducted an exploratory study on the significance of breastfeeding to incar-cerated pregnant women. Huang and her colleagues discovered that desires and plans to engage in maternal behaviors like breastfeeding allow incarcerated women to create "a new start in motherhood and give women the opportunity to redefine their maternal identity and roles" (2012, p. 145). In another study of parent education programs for incarcerated mothers, Patricia González and her colleagues found: "mothers who took part in the parenting education curriculum demonstrated a marked increase in their sense of parenting proficiency, done by improving parenting skills and increasing their overall parenting knowledge" (2007, p. 357).

> [My daughter] was the only thing that kept my spirits up, kept me looking forward to something. She was the only thing that made me realize that I do have a future.
>
> When at that moment I felt that everything around me was tumbling, she's what kept everything up….She's what kept me going.
>
> – *Ana*

In addition to the parenting resources typically provided to incarcerated women while in prison nursery programs, the act of co-residing with their children comes with its own benefits. Incarcerated mothers may find meaning in life while co-residing and establishing a bond with their babies through the prison nursery. Advocates of prison nurseries note that co-residing with their infants provide incarcerated mothers with incentive to engage in constructive behaviors. In fact, there is some research to support this claim. In his review of a prison nursery program in Nebraska, Criminologist Joseph Carlson found a decrease in reports of misconduct once women were allowed to reside in the prison nursery, as opposed to the general population of incarcerated women. Carlson notes that the lower number of misconduct reports may be associated with mothers' behavioral changes to maintain co-residing arrangements with their children and avoid removal from the prison nursery. In addition, scholars have also found lower rates of recidivism among mothers involved in prison nursery programs compared to the general population of incarcerated women and pregnant incarcerated women who were unable to reside with their infants in prison nurseries. It is possible that the lower recidivism rates may be attributable to the supportive nature of prison nursery programs that encourage maternal activities, which may persist post-incarceration as constructive behaviors evading recidivism.

> I went to jail in 1995. I had my youngest daughter in prison with me for a year….
>
> That was the best year of my life 'cause I wasn't there for the first years of my two oldest.
>
> – *Onika*

In addition to the personal gain mothers obtain from their involvement in a prison nursery program, there is also some research demonstrating the benefits of prison nurseries on the children. Some mothers encounter an array of socio-economic obstacles in the community that may hinder or interfere with their ability to adequately care for their children. Having their newborns with them may function as a slight do-over as they may be able to provide better care of their child under the guidance of the prison nursery program. According to an investigation of California's mother–infant prison programs that was conducted by the support organization, Legal Services for Prisoners with Children (LSPC), mothers perceive their children to be better situated with them in these prison programs. These mothers' perceptions have also been supported by existing research on the outcomes of 100 infants who spent time in prison nurseries. Specifically, nursing professor Mary Byrne and her colleagues suggest that due to the numerous risk factors incarcerated mothers encounter in their communities, the prison nursery serves as somewhat of a buffer in which their infants may be shielded from such socio-economic disadvantages like poverty and residential instability. Through the parenting classes offered in prison nursery programs, infants are able to receive resources that are not readily accessible or financially attainable to this population after their incarceration. In fact, Byrne and her colleagues found that "mothers in a prison nursery setting can raise infants who are securely attached to them at rates comparable to healthy community children" (2010, p. 357). Moreover, they also found that children who spent time in prison nurseries were less withdrawn and had less anxiety and depression compared to those who were separated from their mothers. Thus, infants in prison nurseries may be protected from risk factors in the mothers' communities, may develop the attachments to their mothers that are crucial for later social development, and may also face no adverse effects as a result of their involvement.

Issues Regarding Prison Nurseries

The transition to motherhood may be difficult at times and, as a result, there are extensive efforts by practitioners to support women in this transition. The transition to motherhood, however, is not experienced similarly by all women and is shaped by access to a social support network that may provide mothers with valuable information, practical assistance, and emotional support during times of need. Yet, less attention is directed to the experiences of women in the criminal justice system and the unique circumstances they face as they transition to motherhood.

> I breastfed my daughter, so I was always in the spotlight 'cause no one breastfed their kids.
>
> – *Ana*

The establishment, continuation, and display of breastfeeding are common issues faced by mothers, but the setting of a correctional environment may further complicate this. It is likely that mothers may receive breastfeeding advice and support from other incarcerated mothers with breastfeeding experience, but this social support network may not offset the lack of readily available healthy food options in a correctional facility. In his report, *Children Imprisoned by Circumstance*, Oliver Robertson notes that the selection of food availability is limited during incarceration and "because of the often limited quality of prison diets, prisoners may be unable to breastfeed or to produce enough milk for their babies." Although policies are imposed upon some facilities demanding that they provide incarcerated mothers with healthy food items, this is not always implemented in practice. In addition, when mothers are not breastfeeding their newborns, it is imperative that the babies receive proper nutrition through other sources.

> I felt like [my daughter] was treated unfairly because her mom was in prison kind of thing.
> Like, she didn't get the treatment a regular person—a regular civilian—would have received, and I didn't appreciate that.
>
> – *Madison*

Inadequate access to proper health care alongside potential judgments from practitioners may both pose additional obstacles to incarcerated mothers who are co-residing with their children in prison nurseries. The receipt of adequate medical care for their children is a common issue mothers discuss. In fact, some mothers within prison nurseries may purposefully request their children to be transferred out of the nursery and into the care of other family members when their children are not receiving the best medical care. Due to limited health services within correctional facilities, children co-residing with their mothers in prison nurseries may also receive such limited services. In a 2010 report written by Karen Shain and her colleagues of the Legal Services for Prisoners with Children (LSPC), it is noted that incarcerated mothers may be denied or delayed transportation to a nearby doctor when they believe their children are ill. Once taken to nearby practitioners outside the confines of correctional facilities, mothers may also find that their children are treated differently and carelessly with knowledge that their mothers are under custody. While some critics may argue that prison nurseries are not the proper setting for infants due to this inadequate medical attention, it can also be argued that this should be motivation to improve the medical conditions within correctional facilities given that proper health care is a human right. As stated by Oliver Robertson of the Quaker United Nations Office (QUNO) Women in Prison and Children of Imprisoned Mothers research project: "Whether they live in prison or remain outside, the children of prisoners have committed no crime and should suffer for none. It is the responsibility of all involved in the criminal justice process to ensure that this is so" (2008, p. vi). This has implications for practitioners as proper care should be provided without prejudice towards incarcerated women, and their children should be given proper medical attention without biased assumptions of wrongdoing on behalf of the mother.

> [The separation] kinda worked out anyways 'cause I had to send her home 'cause I had to go to [another state].
>
> – *Madison*

Prison nursery programs are time-limited and subject to termination, potentially presenting mothers with emotional difficulties when the mother–child pair is removed from the nursery program. Newborns are only allowed to remain with their mothers for a restricted amount of time – typically up to 18 months. While facilities like Bedford Hills try to minimize this transition by having expected guardians visit and spend time with the baby to build acquaintance, this mother–child separation may still be difficult for the mothers. Specifically, this delayed separation may be difficult for mothers as they remain in the correctional facility and are then relocated to the general population of incarcerated women outside the prison nursery program. Transitional planning may prepare both mothers and their children for the separation that awaits them – particularly for the children who must then transition to a different environment with a different caregiver. While transitional planning is present in some prison nursery programs, it should be the norm for all cases of mother–child separation.

Childcare Beyond Prison Bars

Maria is another mother in *OITNB* who has her baby while incarcerated, but unlike Dayanara—and many incarcerated mothers—she is able to leave her daughter in the care of her daughter's father. While the Bureau of Justice Statistics reports that most incarcerated women have some contact with their children by phone, mail or visitation, updates about newborns are at the discretion of the caretakers who must speak on their behalves (Glaze & Maruschak, 2008). Initially, Maria was able to see her daughter somewhat frequently when her partner brought her for visitation at the correctional facility. In the first visitation depicted, Maria was portrayed asking her partner if their daughter was a good baby, if she slept okay, and if she was eating. These questions attempt to capture the reality that incarcerated mothers may miss the development of their children over time, unless caretakers share this information with them in their absence. Maria was also shocked at how different her newborn daughter looked since she had last visited. Her commentary and stunned facial expression portrays the time lapse in which incarcerated mothers can see their children in person.

During visitation, Maria was shown with the baby in her hands, kissing her several times and telling her daughter that she was her mother, she loved her very much, and they would be "spending lots of time together" in the near future. However, realizing that she had six more years to serve of her sentence, Maria believed there was a chance that her daughter could be calling someone else "mommy" by the time of her release. This conflict between expectation and experience arises for many women as the mother–child relationship they expect upon their release may have been established with another mother figure during their absence.

Eventually, Maria was shocked and angered to learn that her partner decided to keep their daughter from visiting her. He thought it would be best to cut such visitation to prevent their daughter from believing a prison setting was normal. He also noted that he came to this decision upon doing some reading, but did not clarify what kind of sources he referred to for this information. In addition to other scenes within *OITNB*, this scenario captures the reality that, for a variety of reasons, many incarcerated mothers do not receive visits from their children. For instance, Professors Karen Casey-Acevedo and Tim Bakken report in their article *Visiting Women in Prison: Who Visits and Who Cares?* that as many as 61% of incarcerated mothers do not receive visits from their children. This can be attributed to the long distances between family members and correctional facilities, the considerable expenses associated with travelling, and the limited availability or desire of the children's caretakers to arrange and complete such visitations. Although Maria does not see her daughter anymore and would "give anything" to see her for merely five minutes, Maria states that at least she knows her daughter is with her family rather than with strangers. Her commentary is consistent with existing research demonstrating that incarcerated women find solace in having their children reside with family members, viewing this living arrangement as superior.

After some time leaving her partner multiple angry messages about his decision, Maria came to better recognize her own emotional standing in regards to the distance between her and her daughter: "She's gonna be okay. I'm not freaking out because she needs me, I'm freaking out because I need her." In fact, Certified Nurse-Midwife Angelina Chambers found that feelings of emptiness, loneliness, and depression among incarcerated mothers can occur early postpartum when the newborns are expected to be taken away. The impact of this forced separation may be particularly difficult after delivering their babies and returning to the correctional facility without their newborns in order to finish serving their sentences. Though most newborns and older children remain with family members when the mother is incarcerated, a foster home or agency is also a reality for minor children with incarcerated mothers. When a child is in the foster care system for 15 of the previous 22 months, mothers may have their parental rights terminated according to the Adoption and Safe Families Act (ASFA). This is particularly problematic for incarcerated mothers who, on average, spend longer periods of time incarcerated than the allotted time before their parental rights are terminated. Restrictions of imprisonment may also hinder mothers' ability to meet socially constructed measures of parental "fitness," shaping the process of maintaining and regaining parental rights into a battle that is waged against them.

OITNB attempts to capture the complexities of the foster care system for incarcerated mothers as Dayanara was shown saying, "Kids that go into the system is like flushin' a goldfish down the toilet. They don't swim back up." With her own child in foster care, Dayanara appeared to be emotionally distraught and at a loss of hope. In these ways, the Netflix series demonstrates how the forced separation between incarcerated mothers and their children may not only create emotional turmoil but may also shape legal changes in parent–child relationships.

Conclusion

Some scholars may suggest that media efforts to educate its viewers may be unsuccessful in outweighing the numerous other sources of flawed and inaccurate portrayals of prison life. Despite the prevalence of flawed and inaccurate portrayals, this should not legitimize further contributing to such misrepresentations by failing to address the realities of incarceration. *Orange is the New Black* has flourished in its ability to entertain its viewership by depicting the often-unfamiliar setting of correctional facilities for the sake of amusement. Though embedded in a hyper-sexualized and comical backdrop, this Netflix series still reveals some of the issues with pregnancy during incarceration and with having a newborn on the outside whilst the mother is still incarcerated. As described in this chapter, mothering behind bars is crucial for children's social development and long-term emotional health, and may also function as an educational, motivational, and constructive force in the mothers' lives. Void of the social and structural support needed to ease this process, however, mothering behind bars may become devastatingly overwhelming. Thus, pregnancy and postpartum life behind bars have serious implications for policymakers and practitioners working with incarcerated mothers and their children.

While media representations of incarceration typically cater to public fascination with drama, efforts can be made to redirect this focus and serve as mediums for penal reform. For instance, in view of legal dialogues and local efforts that often go unnoticed by the general public, *OITNB* could have also demonstrated the reality of shackling for pregnant women or communicated the possibility of prison nurseries. Given its large and diverse viewership, this Netflix series has a unique advantage to trigger public discussions about the criminal justice system. It is a shame when this platform is not used to its advantage to further the potential for penal reform across a variety of affairs.

References

Aber, C., Weiss, M., & Fawcett, J. (2013). Contemporary women's adaptation to motherhood: The first 3 to 6 weeks postpartum. *Nursing Science Quarterly*, 26(4), 344–351.
Azar, B. (1995). The bond between mother and child. *American Psychological Society*. Retrieved from http://www.thelizlibrary.org/liz/APA-Monitor-attachment.html

Byrne, M. W., Goshin, L. S., & Blanchard-Lewis, B. (2012). Maternal separations during the reentry years for 100 infants raised in a prison nursery. *Family Court Review*, 50(1), 77–90.

Byrne, M. W., Goshin, L. S., & Joestl, S. S. (2010). Intergenerational transmission of attachment for infants raised in a prison nursery. *Attachment & Human Development*, 12(4), 375–393.

Carlson, J. R., Jr. (2001). Prison nursery 2000: A five-year review of the prison nursery at the Nebraska correctional center for women. *Journal of Offender Rehabilitation*, 33(3), 75–97.

Casey-Acevedo, K., & Bakken, T. (2003). Visiting women in prison: who visits and who cares? *Journal of Offender Rehabilitation*, 34(3), 67–83.

Chambers, A. N. (2009). Impact of forced separation policy on incarcerated postpartum mothers. *Policy, Politics & Nursing Practice*, 10(3), 204–211.

Correctional Association of New York. (2015a). Correctional Association of NY hails new law ending shackling of incarcerated women throughout all stages of pregnancy. Retrieved from http://www.correctionalassociation.org/news/correctional-associatio n-of-ny-hails-new-law-ending-shackling-of-incarcerated-women-througout-all-stages- of-pregnancy.

Correctional Association of New York. (2015b). It's time for New York to end shackling: Women share their stories [Video file]. Retrieved from https://www.youtube.com/wa tch?v=63bTTnkSy6M.

Correctional Association of New York. (2015c). Reproductive injustice: The state of reproductive health care for women in New York state prisons. Retrieved from http:// www.correctionalassociation.org/wp-content/uploads/2015/03/Reproductive-Injustice- FULL-REPORT-FINAL-2-11-15.pdf.

Fritz, S., & Whiteacre, K. (2016). Prison nurseries: Experiences of incarcerated women during pregnancy. *Journal of Offender Rehabilitation*, 55(1), 1–20.

Gonzalez, P., Romero, T., & Cerbana, C. B. (2007). Parent education program for incarcerated mothers in Colorado. *The Journal of Correctional Education*, 58(4), 357–373.

Huang, K., Atlas, R., & Parvez, F. (2012). The significance of breastfeeding to incarcerated pregnant women: An exploratory study. *Birth*, 39(2), 145–155.

Robertson, O. (2008). *Children imprisoned by circumstance*. New York, NY: Quaker United Nations Office.

Shain, K., Strickman, C., & Rederford, R. (2010). *California's mother-infant prison programs: An investigation*. Legal Services for Prisoners with Children. Retrieved from http:// www.prisonerswithchildren.org/wp-content/uploads/2013/01/CA-Mother-Infant-Pri son-Programs_report.pdf

9

PREGNANCY, PARENTING, AND PRISON

Mothering While Incarcerated

Jeanne Holcomb

Introduction

Our culture seems to place a great deal of value on motherhood, and, more specifically, mothering behaviors as carried out by biological mothers or otherwise "good" mothers. However, what about women who are denied the opportunity to mother their children? How does the cultural emphasis on mothering fit with the increases in rates of women who are incarcerated? This chapter will briefly review background information regarding women in prison, then focus on mothers in prison, and then shift specifically to women who are pregnant and give birth while serving their sentence. It concludes with an exploration of how pregnancy and childbirth are portrayed in mass media, as seen in *Orange is the New Black* (*OITNB*).

Background Statistics

There has been a dramatic increase in women who are incarcerated, in jail, or under some form of supervision by the criminal justice system. According to *The Sentencing Project* (2012), the number of women in prison increased by 646% between 1980 and 2010, with over 200,000 now women being held in prison or in jail. While there have been increases in the numbers of both men and women being incarcerated, the number of women in prison is growing at a faster rate than that of men.

Research shows that women offenders commonly have life experiences that include poverty, abuse, and drug or alcohol dependency, and limited job skills, and there are significant variations in incarceration rates by factors such as race and geographical location. According to *The Sentencing Project*, a research and advocacy organization, the lifetime likelihood of a woman being incarcerated is about 1 in 56, but for Black women this likelihood increases to 1 in 19 and for White women it decreases to 1 in 118. Incarceration rates also vary by geographical location, with Maine having the lowest rate of women in prison, and Oklahoma the highest.

Drug or property related offenses are the leading reasons for women's incarceration. According to the American Civil Liberties Union, in 2000, 40% of criminal convictions of women were for drug-related offenses, 34% were for non-violent offenses (such as burglary or fraud), 18% were for violent offenses, and 7% were for public order offenses (such as driving under the influence and liquor law violations).

Imprisoned Mothers

Within the larger context of the significant increase in the number of women experiencing incarceration is a subpopulation of particular interest – mothers who are incarcerated. According to the US Department of Justice, about 65% of women who are incarcerated have at least one child, and 71% of mothers in prison were the sole primary caregivers for their children prior to their incarceration (Mumola, 2009). In some ways, they are fairly similar to the broader population of women in prison; for example, minority status and incarceration as the result of drug offenses are typical. However, there are significant nuances, especially when related to parenting stress. When fathers are incarcerated, it is common for the children to remain with their mothers; however, when mothers are incarcerated, children most often live with grandparents, other relatives, or foster homes.

Research has indicated a connection between having an incarcerated parent and numerous adverse outcomes for children. For instance, truancy, withdrawal, aggressive behaviors, drug and alcohol use, declines in academic performance, and disruptions in regular eating and sleeping patterns are not uncommon experiences among those who have a parent who is incarcerated. Children may also experience internalized consequences, such as anxiety, grief, shame, guilt, embarrassment, sadness, and low self-esteem. Furthermore, children whose mothers are imprisoned are likely to encounter numerous home and school displacements as their caregivers change, and this can negatively impact abilities to develop secure attachments, as well as academic performance and relationships with peers. Two factors are worth noting here, though. First, these children's families often face multiple difficulties, including high rates of poverty and issues related to addiction and criminality that may impact multiple persons within the extended family unit. Second, although many children with an incarcerated parent experience negative outcomes, it is important also to recognize the resiliency that many children exhibit.

In addition to the impact on child outcomes, criminologists conclude that separation can also result in numerous negative outcomes for the mother, including experiencing maternal distress, depression, guilt, and helplessness. For example, mothers may feel as though their authority and ability to make legal and educational decisions for their children are undermined by their time behind bars, and mothers often worry about their children's current living conditions, safety, and emotional development. Researchers have found that enforced separation leads to increased parental stress and poor emotional regulation; stress related to one's competency as a parent was associated with higher rates of mental health symptoms as well as higher rates of rule-breaking while imprisoned (see Tuerk & Loper, 2006).

Several researchers have also noted the need for the criminal justice system to create more programming to assist mothers in developing and maintaining positive relationships with their children, especially regarding positive communication patterns. For example, research indicates that contact with children during incarceration is the best predictor of successful reunification, yet as criminologists note, 54% of mothers in state prisons and 42% of mothers in Federal prison never receive visits from their children, largely due to transportation costs and the resistance of caretakers to allow children to visit. Even if children can physically visit, there can be other difficulties, including lack of play spaces and continued physical separation, such as with a glass barrier. Given the difficulties of physical visits, research has focused on how to increase the effectiveness of letters and phone calls, with some research indicating that parental stress can be reduced through letter writing. For example, research shows that mothers often report difficulty communicating with their children and maintaining positive co-parenting alliances with the caregivers of their children, with common barriers to effective communication including geographical distance, restrictions relating to visitation days and times, and policies related to phone calls, including cost as well as limits on length and number of calls.

Pregnancy and Birth in Prison

As we have seen, there have been significant increases in the number of imprisoned women, leading to questions regarding the impact of incarceration on mother/child relationships. Among this group of women, though, is another group of particular interest – those women who experience pregnancy and childbirth during their sentence. Despite policies and standards that are supposed to assure women of appropriate care during pregnancy, birth, and postpartum experiences, many women report a lack of systematic quality care. Guiding standards and policies are complicated, and occur at various levels, including national standards, federal laws, state laws, and institutional policies. Pregnancy-related health care standards have been established by the National Commission on Correctional Health Care, the American Congress of Obstetricians and Gynecologists, as well as the American Public Health Association. These standards uphold that women who are pregnant while incarcerated should be provided with counseling and assistance, whether she chooses to keep the child, use adoptive services, or to have an abortion. Furthermore, adequate prenatal care, including medical exams and nutritional guidance, should be available, and all of these standards recommend against the use of restraints during labor. Furthermore, there are several relevant federal laws, but one of particular interest is the Prison Rape Elimination Act (PREA). PREA stipulates that victims of sexual abuse should receive timely medical care, including pregnancy-related health care and abortion services. While organizational standards and federal laws offer some framework, there is significant variation by state, and further variation in actual implementation, as discussed in the following sections. Taken together, the national standards, federal laws, and state laws indicate that some attention has been given to the needs of pregnant women who are incarcerated.

Precise statistics regarding the number of incarcerated women who are pregnant are currently unavailable due to inconsistencies in reporting requirements, but, according to research by medical professionals Dr. Jennifer Clarke and colleagues, between 6 and 10 percent of incarcerated women are pregnant and scholar Diana Kasdan (2009) suggests that about 10,000 pregnant women are in jail or prison. Pregnancies among this group of women are frequently unplanned and high risk due to a variety of factors, including a lack of prenatal care, drug or alcohol use, poor nutrition, high rates of STDs, and mental health illness and fetal exposure to teratogenic medications. There are numerous understudied areas related to the topic of pregnancy and childbirth while in prison, but two are worth briefly noting here. First, pregnancy as the result of sexual assault while already in prison is virtually unacknowledged, but legal scholars note that women in prison experience "institutionalized sexual abuse" and the law offers them little protection or mechanism for redress. To follow this point, little is known about the availability of emergency contraception or abortion services for women in prison. Although there may be a legal agreement that women "must have adequate access to abortion care", researchers have found that women's efforts may be thwarted due to a lack of assistance in setting up necessary appointments, payment, or transportation. With those limitations in mind, the following sections explore the experiences of pregnant women who are imprisoned, including various aspects of prenatal care, childbirth, and postpartum care.

There are numerous issues associated with being pregnant and giving birth in prison, one of which is appropriate and timely medical care. Social science researchers, Stephanie Fritz and Kevin Whiteacre found that mothers reported largely negative experiences with prenatal care. Women felt like they were on an assembly line, with the nurses and doctors not taking the time to develop relationships with them as patients or adequately addressing health concerns. Furthermore, many of the women in this study complained of delays in medical attention because all requests had to be approved by the infirmary. Bureaucratic delays and unsympathetic authority figures left the women feeling as though they were not provided with adequate prenatal care.

It is well known that pregnant women are encouraged to pay particular attention to their nutrition during pregnancy. Pregnant women are encouraged to increase caloric intake by about three hundred calories, being careful that the increased intake comes from healthful foods; medical professionals encourage mothers to eat more fruits, vegetables, and foods high in protein but are cautioned about foods high in sugars and fats. Women are also cautioned about eating some types of seafood and lunch meats, and nutritional deficiencies in pregnancy can lead to numerous adverse health outcomes, including increased risk for gestational diabetes and anemia. In social scientist Kristina Sadler's (2012) study of nutrition among pregnant inmates in a Texas prison, she found that they were not given fresh fruit or vegetables of any kind. Instead, servings of fruit were coming from fruit juices, which are often high in added sugars. Further concerns were the frequent use of lunch meat, such as baloney, and the high prevalence of empty calorie foods, such as white bread, Ramen noodles, sugary drinks, and hot dogs. Although this is only one example, there is scant research on the dietary intake of pregnant inmates, and it likely highlights pervasive concerns regarding the quality of food available to pregnant inmates (and all inmates for that matter).

It is evident thus far that incarcerated women who are pregnant experience difficulties obtaining reproductive services and prenatal care, but there are indications that the birth process is also fraught with inconsistencies and a lack of recognition of women's needs. Women often report giving birth alone; even when birth coaches such as a spouse, female relative, female friend, or appointed doula are allowed, they often cannot make it to the birth due to distance and a lack of timely communication. Some women have filed lawsuits because of their mistreatment during birth; in one media reported case, a woman in Texas filed a lawsuit because she gave birth in a jail cell after her numerous attempts to seek assistance were ignored, and in another media reported case, a woman filed suit because she gave birth in solitary confinement (see Townes, 2015). Her child was born with the umbilical cord wrapped around its neck and was later pronounced dead.

One particular area that has received increased attention is the practice of shackling women during labor. Twenty-one states have passed legislation banning the practice of shackling during labor and delivery, and numerous organizations, including the American College of Obstetricians and Gynecologists (ACOG), the American College of Nurse Midwives, the American Public Health Association, and the American Medical Association, have make statements against the practice. However, despite fairly widespread condemnation of the practice as both a violation of human rights as well as an interference in medical care, women report a wide range of actual practice (see Dignam & Adashi, 2014). For instance, one woman in Stephanie Fritz and Kevin Whiteacre's study reported being handcuffed for an extended period of time, despite the written policy indicating that handcuffs should be removed upon admittance to the hospital, while another reported that she was rarely restrained by the mandated ankle chain.

Most mothers who give birth while serving a prison sentence are separated from their child after birth. In most cases, mothers may have twenty-four hours with their infant in the hospital, but then the child is placed with relatives or in foster care, and the mother returns to prison. Medical professionals suggest that this early separation has negative consequences for both mothers and children, as the early bonding period is disrupted. For children, this can result in lifelong difficulty with life stressors, and for mothers, has been shown to increase rates of recidivism. Research has shown that the traumatic nature of the separation was exacerbated due to a lack of clear communication; some women said that the guards could not tell them when a family member arrived to pick up the baby, due to security concerns. Mothers reported being handcuffed while watching their infants being taken away, and not having much information about where the infant was going.

Breastfeeding is another topic that is highly significant in discussions surrounding mothering, but has many more nuances when focused on incarcerated mothers. The American Academy of Pediatrics recommends breastfeeding exclusively for six months, and including breast milk in an infant's diet for at least the first year of life. These recommendations are based on research that indicates that breastfeeding has health benefits for infants, including decreased rates of respiratory tract infections, urinary tract infections, and infant mortality, among many others. Some studies also suggest that breastfeeding enhances infant cognitive and psychological development, and other research focuses on health benefits for the mother, including reductions in postpartum blood loss and protective effects against some types of cancer.

However, because of the quick separation most incarcerated mothers experience, it is very difficult to maintain breastfeeding behaviors. Social scientists Stephanie Fritz and Kevin Whiteacre have studied differences in breastfeeding behaviors between mothers who were allowed to stay with their infants in a prison nursery program and mothers who met eligibility requirements for the nursery program but were incarcerated before the program's implementation. Breastfeeding rates among those in the nursery program were double the rate among those who could not participate in the nursery program. Mothers in the nursery program reported support from lactation consultants and ready availability of electronic breast pumps. Among mothers in the group who could not participate in the nursery program, barriers included the cost of supplying their own breast pump, concerns about appropriate storage, and the costs associated with either mailing breastmilk or transportation for someone to come pick it up.

Furthermore, mothers who give birth while in prison may be at a higher risk for experiencing postpartum depression and psychosis. According to medical professionals, such as Lorry Schoenly, postpartum depression tends to be higher among women who have past histories of mental health concerns like anxiety or depression, have poor social support systems, and have experienced recent life stressors, and all of these are fairly common among female inmates. The National

Commission on Correctional Health Care likewise states that incarcerated women are at a higher risk for postpartum depression and psychosis due to the trauma of being separated from their newborn and the prevalence of underlying mental health illnesses. They recognize, though, that despite this awareness, postpartum screenings are not routinely performed.

One area of further concern is the maternal rights of the mother. As discussed earlier, children of women who are incarcerated are often cared for by other family members, such as grandparents, or are placed in the foster care system. Under the Adoption and Safe Families Act (ASFA) of 1997, states can terminate parental rights after a child has been in foster care for fifteen of the last twenty-two months. Incarcerated women serve, on average, a sentence of eighteen months, meaning that their parental rights can be terminated while they are serving their sentence. Schlager and Moore (2014) further point out that, in addition to length of sentence, prison policies related to visitation, mail, and phone contact make it extremely difficult for parents to maintain consistent and ongoing contact with children. While the intention of ASFA was to prevent children from lingering in the foster care system and to promote more permanent arrangements for children, scholars suggest that some child welfare policies end up undermining the parental rights of incarcerated parents.

It is clear that pregnant women who are incarcerated often experience great difficulties in obtaining adequate care, and that the entire process raises concerns about how to balance what some may see as a need for punishment for violating the law with the basic human rights of mothers and infants. When we listen to women's experiences, it is clear that there is considerable room for improvement in the treatment and care of pregnant women who are incarcerated. There are numerous areas for improvement, including, but of course not limited to, prenatal medical care and nutrition, dignified treatment during birth, reexamination of separation so quickly after birth, and postpartum screenings and care.

Nurturing the Mother/Infant Relationship

One mechanism through which the significance of mother and child relationships is recognized in the criminal justice system is through prison nurseries. Prison nurseries actually have a long history in the United States, with the first program being opened in 1901 at the Bedford Hills Correctional Facility in New York. As of 2015, ten states had some type of prison nursery program: New York, California, Illinois, Indiana, Ohio, Nebraska, South Dakota, Washington, West Virginia, and Wyoming. The main premise is that these programs allow mothers to stay with their babies; the length of time that mothers and children can stay in the programs varies from thirty days to three years, and most programs have strict criteria that make violent offenders and mothers with a history of child abuse or neglect ineligible to participate.

Research indicates positive outcomes for those who participate in prison nursery programs. Benefits can include increased attachment between the mother and child, improved parenting skills, and reduced recidivism rates. Mothers are allowed to serve their time, while also participating in programming that helps them meet the health needs of their children, develop realistic expectations, provide intervention as needed, and generally learn skills to help them be responsible parents. Research suggests that prison nursery programs, while certainly important in developing parenting skills, can also help mothers develop skills that will be needed in successful reentry, as well as to engage in other self-development activities. Another point of consideration is cost; while these programs can be expensive, the costs associated with having children placed in foster care are also considerable, not to mention the costs associated with familial separation.

Despite the research that shows positive outcomes, there are some concerns with prison nursery programs. Some legal scholars and social scientists are concerned that children's rights advocates have been largely absent from the conversation about these programs and suggest that prison nurseries do not have the child's best interest as a top priority. Furthermore, prison is seen as an unhealthy and hostile environment that is an inappropriate setting for young children. A 2010 investigation by Shain and colleagues of prison nursery programs in California highlighted concerns related to a lack of effective, child-centered programming; the physical conditions of the buildings (such as mold problems); inadequate food; and the quality of medical care, among others. While prison nursery programs may be an alternative to separation during incarceration, concerns related to the conditions of these programs are pervasive.

Others suggest that beyond creating space for mothers to be with their children within the prison system, as in prison nurseries, there should be more emphasis placed on alternative, community-based rehabilitation programs. Indeed, Karen Shain and her colleagues who, authored the report on California's mother–infant programs, urge the creation of alternatives outside of the jurisdiction of the state corrections system. Likewise, legal scholars Una Stone and colleagues (although focusing more specifically on Australia), note that mothers often encounter enormous difficulty in meeting all of the demands placed upon them suddenly at the time of release, such as organizing appropriate housing, finding employment, reuniting with family and meeting child protection demands, and fulfilling all the other requirements of parole. They, too, argue that there needs to be an increase in the availability and usage of community based alternative programs to prison, particularly for mothers of young children. On a global scale, the UN Rules for the Treatment of Women Prisoners and Non-Custodial Measures for Women Offenders, known as the Bangkok Rules, recommend that "non-custodial measures should be preferred where possible and appropriate" (2010, p. 4). However, pregnancy and parenting are rarely taken into consideration in the U.S. legal system, and, as we have seen, even where it might seem as though there are some standards or legal protections in place, women's experiences often illustrate experiences of trauma, insufficient care, and enormous negative impacts on the family unit.

Orange is the New Black

Orange is the New Black (*OITNB*) offers several interesting examples of experiences of pregnancy, childbirth, and postpartum experiences of incarcerated mothers. In the first season, we briefly see the experience of a minor character, Maria, giving birth. She mostly endures the early stages of her labor by herself and with her fellow inmates; she is taken to the hospital by ambulance and then we see her returned to her prison unit by wheelchair. Later, in Season 2 of the show, we see Maria holding her child during a visit in the main visiting area. Although these scenes are relatively minor in the grander scheme of the show, they illustrate several points. First, women are often isolated and alone during labor, with medical care coming relatively late into the process. Second, women are often separated after the birth, with women returning to prison, and infants being cared for by family members, entering the foster care system, or being adopted. In this case, it seems as though the father of the child is taking care of the infant. There is no mention of postpartum physical or mental health checks. Lastly, visitation between mothers and infants is often highly restricted and not child-friendly; in this case, although the mother can hold the child, there do not appear to be any child-friendly play spaces. Rather, the family must sit at the table for the visiting period, something that could be challenging with infants and toddlers. Her example illustrates the lack of attention given to the overall well-being of pregnant women and family development.

Dayanara's ("Daya") character offers a deeper exploration of pregnancy and childbirth. Although her experience illustrates many of the same points, it also highlights other factors worth considering. First, she was not pregnant at the time she entered prison, but rather became pregnant as the result of consensual sexual activities with a correctional officer. Because of the risk that it may pose to the father's job, Daya resists telling prison staff early on about her pregnancy, but she realizes that this may not be the best course of action. We see in Season 2 that she is concerned about her prenatal care and questions whether something could be wrong; she really does not know because she has not had any prenatal care. Daya learns about pregnancy through material in the prison library, and understands the significance of prenatal nutrition and vitamins, but feels that appropriate medical care is beyond her grasp.

Daya's birth and postpartum experiences are as what would be expected – she labored in her prison unit for some time before she was transported by ambulance to the hospital. In the hospital scenes, viewers do not see shackles, but we do see the lack of family or support persons; birthing is largely a lonesome endeavor. She is allowed some time with her newborn, but they are separated quickly, as the newborn is passed on to family and Daya returns to her unit. No mention of breastfeeding is made, although one would expect that she was in a great deal of discomfort when her milk came in, and likewise, there is no mention of postpartum care.

At the end of Season 3, we see an example of the precarious nature of family placements. While Daya is under the assumption that her child is well cared for by family members, many of her family members are involved in selling drugs, and the family residence is raided. During the raid, the officials pick up her infant, along with other children present. While the scene (and the season) ends there, it remains unclear who will obtain caretaking responsibilities and if Daya will be informed.

A certain paradox then presents itself: on the one hand, we seem to exist in a society that places a high emphasis on mothering and family values. Medical recommendations about appropriate care during pregnancy and related to infant care abound, yet some mothers seem to be excluded from being able to follow that advice if they wanted to do so. Can incarcerated mothers follow advice regarding prenatal nutrition? Can they breastfeed? Are their children afforded the "best start"? Are they able to develop positive maternal identities? The larger question then becomes: Is it possible that inconsistencies in the implementation of policies, and in some cases, the lack of attention given to some areas of concern, are systematically disadvantaging some mothers and children (who, as we have seen, are more likely to be poor and from minority racial backgrounds)?

References

Clarke, J.D., Hebert, M.R., Rosengard, C., Rose, J.S., DaSilva, K.M., & Stein, M.D. (2006). Reproductive health care and family planning needs among incarcerated women. *American Journal of Public Health*, 96(5), 834–839.

Dignam, B., & Adashi, E. Y. (2014). Health rights in the balance: The case against perinatal shackling on women behind bars. *Health and Human Rights Journal*, 2(16), 13–23.

Fritz, S., & Whiteacre, K. (2016). Prison nurseries: Experiences of incarcerated women during pregnancy. *Journal of Offender Rehabilitation*, 55(1), 1–20.

Mumola, C.J. (2000). *Incarcerated Parents and their Children*. Washington, DC: US Department of Justice, Bureau of Justice Statistics.

Sadler, K. (2012). *Texas Jail Project*. http://www.texasjailproject.org/2012/09/harris-coun ty-jail-nutrition-provided-to-pregnant-inmates/

Schlager, M.D., & Moore, B. (2014). Risk and resiliency of incarcerated mothers. *Families in Society: The Journal of Contemporary Social Services*, 95(2), 100–106.

Shain, K., Strickman, C., & Rederford, R. (2010). California's mother-infant prison programs: An investigation. *Legal Services for Prisoners with Children*.

Stone, U., Liddell, M., & Martinovic, M. (2015). Jumping hurdles: The myriad of issues and barriers for incarcerated mothers to regain custody of children. *Justice Policy Journal*, 12(1), 1–23.

The Bangkok Rules. (2010). United Nations Office on Drugs and Crime. https:// www.unodc.org/documents/justice-and-prison-reform/Bangkok_Rules_ENG_ 22032015.pdf

The Sentencing Project. (2012). Incarcerated women. http://www.sentencingproject.org/doc/publications/cc_Incarcerated_Women_Factsheet_Sep24sp.pdf

Townes, C. (2015). Woman allegedly forced to give birth on jail cell toilet, alone. http://thinkprogress.org/justice/2015/04/10/3645529/woman-births-son-on-jail-cell-toilet/

Tuerk, E.H., & Loper, A.B. (2006). Contact between incarcerated mothers and their children: Assessing parenting stress. *Journal of Offender Rehabilitation*, 43(1), 23–43.

PART 4

Prisons, Hegemony, and Patriarchy

Madhavi Venkatesan

Women represent the fastest growing segment of the U.S. prison population. In the last forty years, the growth rate in U.S. female incarceration has exceeded 640 percent. Since the 1980s, the number of women incarcerated in the United States has multiplied at a dramatic rate. The data shows that two-thirds of women in prison have been incarcerated for nonviolent crimes. Compared with men, women are sentenced more often to prison for nonviolent crimes. According to the Bureau of Justice data (Glaze & Marschak, 2010), approximately 55 percent of women in prison have committed property or drug crimes relative to about 35 percent of male prisoners, making the increase in female incarceration rates appear inconsistent with the significance of the crime. Prevailing gender roles in combination with the direct assessment of the role of patriarchy and the subsequent dominance of hegemonic masculinity provides a contextual basis for understanding current trends and seemingly also provides a foundation for enabling gender equity.

According to the Women's Prison Association, in addition and correlated with race, poverty is also an important demographic of incarcerated women, as many women (48 percent) were unemployed at the time of their arrest. Furthermore, many were documented as having been residing in economically disadvantageous areas. This attribution appears related to their crime, as many incarcerated women were arrested for economically driven crimes such as property, prostitution, and drug-related offenses.

Consistent with male-centricity enabled through a patriarchal system, scholars note that the same characteristic is not true of male prisons, which in general terms have been better equipped and funded over historical time compared to female prisons (see Freedman, 1974). The characteristics of female inmates are both environmental and institutional, as both influence sentencing decisions to the extent that they are supported by White male perceptions of female value and appropriate behavior. There is a correlation between race, educational attainment, and poverty. Further, racial stereotypes, whether manufactured or environmentally established, promote a noticeable variation in the punitive component of female incarceration, with White women less likely to be incarcerated and/or serve a length of sentence comparable to their non-white counterpart.

The circumstance leading to female incarceration and the living conditions faced by female inmates, scholars argue, has been little understood, and has minimally engendered mainstream social interest (see Bonnett et al., 2001). To the focused observer the assessment and evaluation of individuals comprising this segment of society has paralleled hegemonic masculinity as it relates to socio-economic status, race, and gender stereotypes related to women. Further, feminist scholars argue that the embedded patriarchal framework that supports the social perception of a male-centric view of society has by definition limited a contrary view or even questioning of the attributions of female incarceration. In contrast, the authors included in this section evaluate female incarceration as projected by the media, and in *Orange is the New Black* in particular. Each author offers that the media through either news or entertainment channels can be a significant conduit for prompting both societal awareness of prevailing perceptions as well as subsequent modification of the same. In essence, in the same manner in which the media has promoted prevailing societal norms, the channel may also be able to foster and even catalyze modification.

Orange is the New Black (*OITNB*) depicts the life of a 30-something, White female convict who is sentenced to imprisonment for a drug related crime. The main character, Piper, is depicted as attractive and her development is crafted to be both identifiable and sympathetic to the broad viewing audience. She has a fiancé, but has had a lesbian relationship; at the same time she is educated and can be characterized as middle class. The series incorporates elements characteristic of female prisons, highlighting stereotypes, relationships, brutality, impact of overcrowding, and funding cuts, against a background of the rationale for prison as means to promote rehabilitation and societal re-entry. In this regard, *OITNB* provides a communication vehicle to address the oppression faced by women that contextualizes incarceration and prompts the address of hegemony and patriarchy as it relates to both acceptance of and increase in female penal representation.

In her chapter, "I'm in here because of bad choices: Patriarchy and Female Incarceration in *Orange is the New Black*", Sabrina Boyer focuses on the societally pervasive patriarchy that both establishes gender-roles and acceptability based on a male perspective of female objectification. Boyer frames her discussion on a definition of patriarchy inclusive of three components: male dominance, male identification and male centricity. She promotes the credibility of *OITNB* with respect to the show's representation of the dominance of societal patriarchy through an analysis of the character development of the show's female inmates. Describing both the pre-incarceration character development as well as the conditions of selected characters while in prison, she surfaces the prevalence of the patriarchal framework and engages in a discussion of the parallels within *real world* present society. Boyer notes a vicious cycle. Specifically, she addresses a male-centric society that sends women to prison, as being the same society that defines what crimes are and are not while also controlling the institutionalization of rehabilitation.

Tracy L. Hawkins prompts an evaluation of societal patriarchy in her contribution "Prison Privatization through the Lens of *Orange is the New Black*: Piper Sells Dirty Panties." Hawkins focuses on this storyline embedded in *OITNB* and details how the show raises relevant issues related to profit-taking and cost-minimization, as well as the outcomes of a financial focus: overcrowding and prisoner abuse. Detailing specific episodes, she advocates for the show's realistic depiction of prison life, inclusive of the societal acceptance of the marginalization of the incarcerated, and notes the call to action or at minimum contemplation resulting from the show's storylines. Embedded in her analysis is the prevailing societal framework that determines human value based on financial return alone. Her assessment ultimately prompts the recognition of the vulnerability of the incarcerated along with the institutionalized marginal status of inmates, which compounds the punishment being served for their crime.

In "Executing Women: Media Explanations of Female Criminality" Sarah Lazzeroni evaluates the role of the media in establishing and promoting a perception of women on death row. The chapter highlights the significance of both media attention and subsequent characterization of females in shaping perspectives, promoting the direct linkage between patriarchy and societal perception of women convicted of crimes consistent with a death row judgment. Lazzeroni defines the acceptable standard of femininity as conveyed through the media and extrapolates the relationship between conformity and nonconformity to this standard as embodied in the social acceptance of both punishment and retribution for defined criminal acts or allegations. Using case studies in conjunction with media (discourse) analysis, she highlights the relevance of often omitted context in facilitating understanding in lieu of the more common simplified villainization of criminal acts perpetrated by women.

All three authors address prevailing social perceptions, incorporating both explicit and implicit attribution of patriarchal perspective on the status conveyed to incarcerated women. The discussions surfaced clearly increase awareness of the embedded socialized and institutional framework that reflexively pervades and influences perception of the acceptability and judgment of the defined criminal actions of women. Each essay promotes increased cognizance and recognition of the need for scrutiny with respect to how society evaluates women within the context of crime and punishment.

References and Further Reading

Bonnett, D.K.W., Bounds, D., Paese, K.R., & Houser, S.H. (2001). Women in prison tell it like it is. *Off Our Backs*, 31(2), 9–12.

Buck, M. (2004). Women in prison and work. *Feminist Studies*, 30(2), 451–455.

Dirks, D. (2004). Sexual revictimization and retraumatization of women in prison. *Women's Studies Quarterly*, 32(3/4), 102–115.

Freedman, E.B. (1974). Their sisters' keepers: An historical perspective on female correctional institutions in the United States: 1870–1900. *Feminist Studies*, 2(1), 77–95.

Glaze, L.E., & Maruschak, L.M. (2010). Parents in prison and their minor children. Retrieved from http://www.bjs.gov/content/pub/pdf/pptmc.pdf

Women's Prison Association. (2004). *Focus on Women & Justice: Trends in Arrests and Sentencing.* Retrieved from http://www.wpaonline.org/pdf/Focus_Trends_May2004.pdf

10

"I'M IN HERE BECAUSE OF BAD CHOICES"

Patriarchy and Female Incarceration in *Orange is the New Black*

Sabrina Boyer

According to sociologist Allan Johnson, patriarchy is based on male dominance and identification and is centered on males. As a system, patriarchy encourages men to continue the oppression of women, as well as accept male privilege, that it is mostly men who dominate in positions of power in society. Within the context of the television show *Orange is the New Black* (*OITNB*) that takes place in a women's prison, the women are at the mercy of masculine control, dominance, identification, and centeredness. Even the female correctional officers Susan Fischer and Wanda Bell as well as the once assistant to the warden Natalie Figueroa are under male dominance and control.

As the viewer is exposed to the stories of the female inmates and characters, all the characters are in prison as a direct result of male privilege and dominance. It is trying to exist within the patriarchal system that directly results in these women being incarcerated. It is easier to let a few women hold positions of power than to give up male privilege and benefits from a patriarchal society. This type of system encourages women to adapt and accept their oppression at the hands of patriarchy, and does so by creating the illusion that women who are oppressed within a patriarchal system are so because of their own personal choices rather than because of a system that does not provide room for upward mobility or change.

Within the context of the show, each character is viewed in relation to men and their stories; as we learn more about the background of each character, we learn that the choices they made that landed them in Litchfield are a direct result of choices made in relation to a man or male dominance and control. For example, though Piper carried a bag *one time* assisting Alex to smuggle drugs, we learn that Alex met and became involved in the drug smuggling business because she went to meet her "real" father, who ended up being a drug addict and over the hill musician. There, she meets the man who will be the link to encouraging and recruiting her to join the drug selling and smuggling business, and thus eventually lands her in jail. Despite her wealth and privilege, Piper experiences the effects of her love affair with Alex both before and within her time spent in jail, particularly from the point of view of corrections officer Sam Healey, who clearly exhibits misogynist viewpoints in terms of lesbian sex, as he tells Piper, almost as a warning, that "you do not have to have lesbian sex." Many of the other characters, viewers learn, are incarcerated as a direct result of male control and dominance within their lives and the show speaks to a larger issue that most women, as recent data suggest, experience sexual and/or physical abuse prior to incarceration.

This chapter will aim to demonstrate that women are often incarcerated as a direct result of systemic patriarchal oppression, and draws on Allan Johnson's definition and framework of patriarchy from his text *The Gender Knot: Unraveling our patriarchal legacy* and examines this fact through the characters of *OITNB*. In section one, I examine the aspects and definition of patriarchy. In section two, I summarize the history of women's incarceration and imprisonment. In the last three sections, I separate the three tenets of patriarchy and examine how specific character story arcs align with the specific aspects of a patriarchal system and society. As this chapter will show, these character's stories and incarceration are a direct result of existing within a patriarchal system designed to benefit heterosexual, white, cis-males.

Patriarchy: A Lasting Legacy

Patriarchy, as we know it, is a type of society that includes both men and women, but also caters to and enforces male privilege; it is a system that is a set of cultural beliefs and behaviors that associates masculinity with being human and positions femininity as marginal. As sociologist Allan Johnson describes it, it is a system that encompasses three main tenets: male dominated, male identified and male centered. Male domination refers to positions of authority and institutions that are male-led, positions and institutions like the military, politics, the justice system, education, religion, and economics. Within these realms, males may claim dominance which leads to higher income, control, and power. Additionally, it is a system of White male superiority; race factors into the discussion of patriarchy as marginalized men do not have the same access as White, cis-male, straight, men. In other words, those who are non-white and non-male are excluded from these positions of power and privilege.

The second focus of patriarchy is a society that is male-identified. Ideas about what is good or desirable in a culture are aligned with cultural ideas about men and masculinity. The way our society uses language, creates standards of living, considers what is good and bad, and what behavior is or is not accepted is directly defined in relation to male identity. Our core cultural values are directly tied to what it means to experience manhood and male experience. It is the standard measurement against identity description and expression. Anyone who is not male is marginalized and described as "other." Other to what or whom? Maleness. Additionally, within such a system women's value is also defined in relation to maleness: how much sexual desire a woman incites; her power lies in her sexuality and appearance, as that is what is most valuable to heterosexual men. Women are seen as valuable in other ways, but the more power women wield the less sexually desirable they are. Furthermore, women who do wield power (arguably, those who are allowed to) must embrace patriarchal values. In other words, for women to achieve the same level of authority and identification, she must uphold the patriarchal structure that keeps her from ascending fully in the first place.

The last tenet of patriarchy that Johnson describes is that of male centeredness: the focus within our culture is male experience and existence: who they are and what they do. They are at the center of attention, and cultural myths, stories, and representations often circle around straight, White, male experience. We see this in both macro and micro levels, from small microaggressions in conversations between males and females (interrupting, mansplaining) to media: news coverage of male politicians, films centered around male experience. Further, what underlies this centeredness is the issue of control and for some men, control is key to their self identity. As a result, women, in a patriarchal society, are oppressed and their experience is a form of slavery and social control.

As we examine the issues of a patriarchal culture and how they affect women's experiences, it is important to acknowledge that "male" and "female" are categorical labels assigned to us at birth based upon the biology of our bodies. Further, it is acknowledged that patriarchy creates a system of binaries, either/or, especially in relation to sexuality and gender performance. This has much to do with creating the reality and social behavior in which we engage, often created through male domination and control. When someone defines themselves not in relation to a man (queer, trans, genderqueer), they are effectively denying male privilege and centeredness, and thus denying the patriarchy. It is this that creates such backlash like homophobia and sexism, because in these ways of being, male privilege and experience are denied. It is also important to note that not every woman in a patriarchy suffers from the consequences. Men suffer under such a system as well, but they do not suffer because of their gender. However, women do. As we analyze the experiences of the female-identified inmates of Litchfield, we will begin to see this patriarchal knot unravel.

The Prison System

As we have examined, patriarchy is a system that categorizes and controls a group of people; this system is not unlike the United States Prison System, as it is a reflection of this society. This is evident in the growing number of incarcerated women in the United States. Between 1980 and 2014, according to *The Sentencing Project*, a nonprofit advocacy group, the number of incarcerated women increased by more than 700%, and over one million women are under the control of the criminal justice system, accounting for 7% of the population in state and federal prisons. In terms of race, women of color were three times more likely to be imprisoned than their white counterparts, representing 30% of all females incarcerated. In relation to male inmates, women were less likely to be employed before incarceration, with lower wages, and are more likely to have experienced abuse. According to sociologists Rebecca Reviere and Vernetta D. Young, over 70% of women were incarcerated due to drug use, property theft, or public order offenses, but typically non-violent.

To give some context, as women's liberation and struggle for equal rights began, it resulted in unintended consequences for women and the criminal justice system. The criminalization of domestic violence, the arrest of both offender and victim, and harsher drug penalties contributed to the increase in female incarceration. As women worked toward more equality, it seems the criminal justice system, as an institution that is male-controlled and identified, swept women up in its wake, punishing women for their gender and the difficulties that resulted from lower wages and bearing the responsibility of family care. As scholars note (see Kurshan, n.d.), prisons serve as agents of social control and reflect upon the broader patriarchal society in which they exist. Furthermore, women's crimes are rooted in patriarchy because they are at the mercy of patriarchal control. So, imprisonment serves as a warning to women to stay within their designated and assigned social sphere. It seems that women are often punished for the experiences of being a woman in a patriarchal culture.

Historically, as long as there have been patriarchal and gender-based assumptions, women have experienced different punishments. In late Middle Ages, historians noted that women were burned at the stake if they committed adultery, but if they were pregnant, they could "plead leniency." The ideological assumptions of the subordination of women affected the ways women experienced punishment. Furthermore, perhaps one of the most famous punishments against women because of patriarchal society were the witch hunts of the 16th and 17th centuries. Historians estimate that over 80% of people killed were women. In other words, fear of women's equality and sexuality often spurred the punishments received. Puritan society was hierarchical and women were considered man's "helpmate." Women were seen as disposable when they were not serving their rightful role as a "helpmate" or as a mother or reproducer of heirs. When women do not serve the patriarchy, they become disposable.

As the 19th century took hold, women were often thrown into wings or areas of existing men's prisons, and suffered from filthy conditions and overcrowding. As women shared space with men in predominantly male prisons, sexual abuse, and vulnerability at the hands of male correctional officers became rampant. As the 19th century progressed, women's imprisonment and criminalization continued to rise because of the Civil War, industrialization, and burgeoning sexual freedom of Victorianism. As a result, women were often held to double standards of

Victorian morality. Additionally, people of color were disproportionately targeted in the North, and in the South, after slavery, Jim Crow laws were used to keep people of color in line and punished for even the most minor of offenses. As women's population in prisons grew, the need for separate prisons for women began to emerge. Custodial camps were introduced to house prisoners with no emphasis on rehabilitation. The majority of women in these camps were women of color, and eventually, separate women's prisons and reformatories were developed. Many women were incarcerated due to felony charges like property crimes and petty theft. Women in reformatories, conversely, were mostly convicted of public order offenses, like sex out of wedlock, adultery, and intoxication. It seems most of these institutions were in place to control and monitor women's sexuality and public and private behavior as a form of social control.

At the turn of the century with the Progressive movement, reformatories began to grow in response to the harsher conditions of the prison campus and as a result of prison reformers wanting to improve the penal system for women. Most women in these reformatories were working class, predominantly White women. Women of color were not expected to act lady-like and thus were not arrested for public offenses at the same rate as White women. Women were often incarcerated for violating moral codes. These offenses are related to exploitation and control/abuse by men and based on patriarchal assumptions of women's behavior. These reformatories worked, then, to train and foster more appropriate social and lady-like behavior and teach "wifely" skills. Further, parole was used as a domestic, patriarchal weapon, as paroled women were regulated to domestic jobs as another form of social control.

Even when prisons were headed by women, they still worked for a patriarchal male prison system. According to social scientists Stephanie Covington and Barbara Bloom, the prison system and its sentencing laws are based on male characteristics and male crime and ignore women's experiences. Women are largely invisible within this system, and that also acts as a form of oppression. As we examine the narratives of the women in *Orange is the New Black*, it is evident that these systems of social control and patriarchal influence are still intact, and women are still suffering at the hands of a patriarchal system.

Sociologist Alan Johnson describes patriarchy as having three focal points. As we examine the characters within the show, it is clear that most characters (arguably all) are incarcerated as a result of trying to and existing as a woman in a patriarchal system. Predominantly, women are incarcerated because of living within a patriarchal system that does not value or provide support for her lived experience. These experiences are unpacked through the character stories we have been introduced to within the show.

Piper Chapman (played by Taylor Schilling)

As *OITNB* begins, we are introduced to Piper as currently living with her fiancé Larry and learn that in her past, during her relationship with a woman named

Alex Vause (a drug smuggler), she participated in drug smuggling with Alex. After Alex was caught, Alex implicated Piper in order to negotiate a lighter sentence. As lesbians, Alex and Piper's relationship was already an affront to patriarchy; both, at the time of the relationship, were in love and did not need a man to sexually satisfy them. However, Piper admits that she was "22 and in love." As a character, Piper exemplifies, and the show arguably plays up, her whiteness and privilege. As an inmate, Piper is positioned as a woman who made a mistake, while the other women, especially the women of color, are positioned as the other, and those who "deserve" to be there, at least, until we begin to learn their backstories.

In the first episode, Yoga Jones tells Piper that surviving in prison is "all about perspective." Red tells Piper, before Piper insults her cooking, that she's "one of us." It isn't until Piper insults Red that she is ostracized. This inclusion seems only to be true for women who, like Piper, made a mistake or a bad choice, but not for the women who, through trying to survive in the system, end up in prison. In the beginning, Piper is correction officer Healey's favorite, that is, until she exhibits lesbian behavior. As someone in charge of the female inmates, and especially in the episode "WAC Pack," he encourages Piper to run as a candidate to be in charge of the women who get to work with Healey to advocate for minor needs. Piper, through Healey, is seen as a woman who is different than the other inmates, as he states, "I understand where you come from." That is, until she participates in "lesbian activity" that Healey describes as "attempted rape" of a fellow inmate, Alex Vause. This attempted rape is nothing more than explicit dancing to which they both clearly consent, and Piper ends up in solitary confinement. As the viewer learns, Healey has a deep hatred of lesbian behavior, and as the show progresses, it is read as deeply misogynistic and sexist. In a confrontation with Healey, Piper realizes that he is jealous of her relationship with Vause, whom he describes as "sick."

The male domination of prisons creates a micro-society reminiscent of the larger patriarchal order. As with Healey, he himself has difficulty with women, as his own wife is a mail-order Russian bride who only married Healey to come to America. In retaliation, Healey calls Piper's finance, Larry, and tells him she is engaging in lesbian activity. After she is released from solitary, Piper sleeps with Alex, arguably in part, to respond to Healey's homophobic response.

Of course, when these women can step out of the chains that bind them, they are only given illusory control and nice treatment to placate them in order to give them the semblance of power and control. The system will allow for some changes in order to give the perception of fairness and equity. In other words, women are given the illusion that they have a say or some "give" within this system; however, this "give" is only to maintain male domination. Thus we learn that Piper is a casualty of male-domination, despite her white privilege.

Alex Vause (played by Laura Prepon)

In Season 1, Episode 9 of *OITNB* the viewer finally learns how Alex Vause became a drug smuggler in an international drug cartel. She meets her father, who is a sub-par has-been musician who is addicted to drugs. She goes backstage at one of his shows and he says to her "I can't believe you're my kid. You got a nice rack though. I could have accidentally f#!@ed you." While crying in the bathroom, Alex meets his drug dealer. She opens up to him about how awful meeting her father is, and he tells her "Most people are better in the abstract. Alex, right? Fari." At first the viewer is left to think that Alex will begin to use as well, just like her biological father, but instead she moves through the ranks of drug smuggling.

The War on Drugs had a significant impact on the imprisonment of women. According to *The Sentencing Project*, the population in state prisons for drug offenses increased by 828 percent for African-American women, 328 percent for Latinas, and 241 percent for white women. In *OITNB*, Alex is juxtaposed to Nicky Nichols, another lesbian in prison who stole a taxi in search of heroin and is incarcerated instead of sent to rehabilitation. Similarly, *OITNB* inmate Tricia Miller overdoses on heroin as part of a drug-smuggling ring inside the prison, instigated by Officer Mendez, or "Pornstache," a male correctional officer who frequently forces inmates to perform sexual favors in exchange for pills, drugs, commissary goods, or whatever the inmates may need. He exploits them for his own advantage as part of the system. This demonstrates the correctional officers having total authority and reign over these women.

In Alex's case, though she was not a drug user, she participated in the patriarchal system of drug smuggling, typically run by men. As a woman, she was an interloper, and took the fall for the operation. It is alluded in the *OITNB* series that Alex becomes involved as a reaction to her father and the sheer let down of who he is and what she imagined him to be when she finally met him backstage. He was a low-life drug user ex-rock star who was barely lucid enough to realize the magnitude of the moment. Her father was not a part of her life, and it can be read throughout the series that his absence was felt and sought after through her superficial relationship with Fari, her drug smuggling contact. He operated as a faux father-figure, and it is suggested that Alex was involved in drug smuggling as a way to cope with an absent father figure. Additionally, *The Sentencing Project* states that women are more likely than men to serve time for drug offenses even though women are less likely than men to play a central role in drug trafficking. This is mirrored in Alex Vause's story.

Another character, Poussey Washington, faced homophobia as she got involved with the daughter of her father's base commander while her family was stationed in Germany. Once her relationship with said daughter was discovered, her father and thus her family were reassigned to the United States. She was ultimately caught with a small amount of weed, and became a casualty of the system that lays harsher punishments upon women for the same crimes as men.

Sophia Burset (played by Laverne Cox)

Sophia's story perhaps encompasses direct experience with male identification and centeredness. As a trans character, Sophia was formerly a male firefighter married to her wife, Crystal, with a son; she transitions from male to female and commits credit card fraud to finance her operation and hormone therapy. Ultimately, she is turned in by her son. Throughout *OITNB*, Sophia struggles to maintain access to her hormone treatment medication; she gets her medication taken away from her as it is deemed not necessary, nor does it have to be distributed to her while in prison. As Sophia navigates prison, she runs the in-house "beauty salon" yet struggles with sustaining her gender identity as later in Season 3 she is ostracized by the other women in the prison and begins to be the subject of transphobic treatment and slurs, with other inmates boycotting her salon. She is placed in solitary, supposedly "for her own protection."

Allan Johnson explains that how we think about the body is shaped by patriarchal ideas. For example, Sophia is, for the most part, at least in the beginning of the series, accepted and treated as a woman. It is when she is not allowed her medication and subsequently threatens a fellow inmate that she begins to experience transphobia from the other women in the prison. Sophia's experience in solitary for her own protection is really for the protection of the correctional officers and the prison itself so that they do not have to deal with her. Feminists note that controlling female sexuality is central to a patriarchal society. Sophia's identity and personhood affronts male control and male centeredness. LGBTQ+ individuals almost always experience harassment and abuse because they challenge the patriarchal view of manhood in sexual terms. Sophia subverts and rejects this manhood and maleness, thus rejecting patriarchy itself.

Suzanne "Crazy Eyes" Warren (played by Uzo Adoba)

When we first meet Suzanne, she almost immediately falls for Piper. As we come to know Suzanne, nicknamed "Crazy Eyes," we learn she becomes emotionally attached to people rather quickly. This keeps other inmates at bay, and as we get to know Suzanne, we learn she responds to kindness and acceptance, and has a great talent for writing poetry and fiction and performing. She can be dangerous when she perceives others being mean to her, and through her later relationship with Vee in Season 3, demonstrates she just wants to be accepted and loved. It is hinted within the show that she suffers from mental illness, with intense mood swings, aggressive outbursts, possible hallucinations, and inability to regulate emotions. It is mentioned in the show that Suzanne has the emotional maturity of a six-year-old, but is clearly extremely intelligent. She represents a large portion of the incarcerated population that suffers from mental illness.

Many scholars estimate that up to 70% of women in state prisons suffer from mental illness. Suzanne was adopted by two rich, White parents who lived in the suburbs. One day she brought home a friend to play with but would not let him leave and he accidentally fell off their fire escape. As someone suffering from mental illness within prison, and as a woman of color, though she can visit the psychiatric ward as often as she wants to. According to *The Sentencing Project*, it is still important to note that fewer than 25% of women who suffer from mental illness actually receive mental health services. Instead of incarceration, inmates like Suzanne would benefit from treatment. However, prisons have become a catch all for housing women who, even in the 21st century, behave outside of their moral expectations.

Galina "Red" Reznikov (played by Kate Mulgrew)

Known as head chef at the beginning of the *OITNB* series and as leader of a group of women named "Red's Girls," we learn she is a former owner of Dmitri's Russian Market in Queens, New York. Her husband is a low-level worker for the Russian mob and she struggles to fit in with the mob wives. She ends up punching the breast implant of one of the Russian mobster's wives after she overhears them laughing at her, and it is alluded to that she began to climb the ranks of the organization after providing advice to the higher-ups. It is implied that she is in prison for murder after police find a freezer full of corpses, supposedly because of her affiliation with the mob. It's interesting that Red gets caught working for an historically male-centered and identified organization, taking the fall for men, much the same way that Alex Vause takes the fall for the drug smuggling organization she works for. Red is another example of a woman taking the fall and receiving harsher punishment than her male counterparts.

Janae Watson (played by Vicky Jeudy)

Perhaps one of the most heartbreaking stories is that of Janae Watson, a former track star in high school who was rejected by boys and began to hang around with mischievous boys from her school; with a track scholarship waiting for her, she participated in robbing a store and purposefully chose to slow down while running from police officers in order to allow her male accomplice to get away. Perhaps a clear-cut story of wanting the approval and desire of males, Janae's story is one of covering for a man and taking the blame.

Claudette Pelage and Tiffany "Pennsatucky" Doggett (played by Michelle Hurst and Taryn Manning)

These two characters are paired together because both experienced sexual assault within the series. In terms of Claudette, though we only see her through Season 1, her backstory is one with specific patriarchal influence. As we learn, she was an illegal child laborer who was sent to the United States to pay off her family debt;

later, we see her as an older woman who runs a maid cleaning service and discovers one of her workers, also illegal servants paying off debts, suffered a severe beating (and possible sexual assault) from one of their clients. She takes it upon herself to beat him to death, and that is why she is incarcerated. Claudette is shown as expendable as she is essentially given up as a child in return for her labor, like domestic workers in the 19th century who were assigned domestic labor as part of their parole.

Conversely, Tiffany "Pennsatucky" Doggett is at first shown as a young girl who grew up poor and experienced bullying due to her poor upbringing. Her mother used her to exploit money out of welfare, forcing her to chug a Mountain Dew before her meeting so she could get compensation for her child with ADHD. Further, her mother's sex advice consisted of it feeling "like a bee sting" and that men would come to expect it of her. Throughout her teenage years we see Pennsatucky having sex with men as a response to this male expectation, void of sexual pleasure for her, until the one man who gave her sexual pleasure but who moves away. Her previous boyfriend ends up raping her in a bathroom, and even later, as a young woman, we see her post-coital and using crystal meth and scheduled to get her fifth abortion. A casualty of a system that continuously undervalues women's work and contributions, and economically marginalizes women, inmates like Doggett often have little to no knowledge or access to birth control or education due to their economic situation. She ends up murdering the woman at the abortion clinic who joked that she should get her fifth abortion free since she's there so often, and gets swept up in a Christian defense as pro-lifers take up her cause and her court costs, and becomes a born-again Christian. We later see her raped again by an inmate who thinks the rape was a consensual sexual encounter and continues to pursue her.

As social scientists, Stephanie Covington and Barbara Bloom note, if you are sexually abused in prison, it is impossible to escape your abuser and rarely are assault investigations taken seriously. Furthermore, it is said that when women do engage in violent crime, they often do so due to domestic violence or sexual/physical abuse. Women are much more likely to kill in self-defense because of threats and aggression. Additionally, women in prisons do not come from stable homes, often originating from families rife with violence, particularly from males. We see this in both Claudette and Doggett, who experience abuse and rape at the hands of males and economic constraints developed directly from patriarchal culture.

Conclusion

In the end, it is a patriarchal society that sends women to prison, as this is the society that defines what crimes are and are not. Once women become incarcerated, they are at the mercy of an institution and a product of said system. As a legacy born of reformatories, supposed "moral offenses," and the infantilization and reinforcement of gender norms are woven in the fabric of current prisons and criminal institutions. Further, increasingly, prisons are institutions that operate to generate income and profit, and focus on punishment rather than treatment and rehabilitation. As scholars have noted, prisons reflect the broader culture in which they exist. These characters, and others, are paying the price of a patriarchy, and as marginalized "others" in a patriarchy they end up in prison due to this masculine model of justice. It is not the men who suffer the consequences of said mistakes, however, within Litchfield; it is the women. It is always the women.

References

Covington, S. S., & Bloom, B. E. (2003). Gendered justice: Women in the criminal justice system. In B. E. Bloom (Ed.), *Gendered Justice: Addressing female offenders* (pp. 1–18). Durham, NC: Carolina Academic Press.

Johnson, A. G. (2014). *The gender knot: Unraveling our patriarchal legacy.* Philadelphia, PA: Temple University Press.

Kurshan, N. (n.d.). Women and imprisonment in the U.S.: History and current reality. In *Prison Activist Resource Center.* Retrieved from http://www.prisonactivist.org

Reviere, R., & Young, V. D. (2005). Women in US prisons: Behind the bars of the patriarchy. In R. Reviere, & V. D. Young (Eds.), *Women behind bars: Gender and race in US prisons* (pp. 1–13). N.p.: First Forum Press.

The Sentencing Project. (2015). *Incarcerated women and girls.* https://www.sentencingproject.org/publications/incarcerated-women-and-girls/

11

PRISON PRIVATIZATION THROUGH THE LENS OF *ORANGE IS THE NEW BLACK*

Piper Sells Dirty Panties

Tracy L. Hawkins

Prison Privatization

The frequency of state leaders signing contracts with for-profit, private prison management companies has been on the rise in recent years. According to a 2011 report from the American Civil Liberties Union (ACLU), prison management by private companies has increased 1600% between 1990 and 2009 and, "Today, for-profit companies are responsible for approximately 6% of state prisoners, 16% of federal prisoners, and, according to one report, nearly half of all immigrants detained by the federal government" (p. 5). This dramatic increase has come about at least partially because using private companies has been marketed as a way for states to save money. This is possible, advocates claim, because states are allowed to contract with private companies for maintenance, staffing, and over-seeing the daily function of prisons that it would normally run with taxpayer dollars.

Prison contracts guarantee that the state will pay the company a certain price per prisoner, and this more stable expenditure seems attractive to cash strapped states. However, as Vicky Pelaez, author of *The Prison Industry in the United States: Big Business or a New Form of Slavery?* notes, these contracts often include stipulations that the prisons must remain at least 90% full or the state will have to pay the company as if it is that full, even when it is not. This may result in minimal, if any, savings to the state, but, more importantly, it changes prison management because it allows profit to be a guiding principle for decision-making. Because the price per prisoner and minimum number of prisoners is set in advance, the company is motivated to lower costs so as to keep more of the payment from the state as profit. The biggest winner in this arrangement is Correction Corporation of America (CCA), the largest private prison management company in the United

States. According to CCA's (2016) corporate profile, they own and/or manage 77 correctional or detention facilities in 20 states plus the District of Columbia. Those facilities have a combined capacity of 89,000 inmates. Additionally in the fourth quarter of 2015, CCA reported revenue of $447.8 million, which is an increase of 5.8% over the prior quarter.

Since, under this arrangement, prison management is subject to the same economic motivations as other for-profit institutions, corporate leaders are motivated to implement "cost saving improvements" such as competition among food vendors which they claim will result in lower prices, reorganization of space so that the number of inmates per prison unit can be as much as doubled, and the hiring of part-time, instead of full time, correctional officers who will not be required to be provided with health insurance. While these "improvements" may be attractive to those looking to make money, studies now suggest that, in addition to being far less financially promising than they sound, these measures may actually compromise the health and safety of inmates, guards, and the community.

Side-by-side comparisons of public prison management and private prison management leave much to be desired in terms of conclusions. Many studies have sample sizes that are far too small, include unsatisfactory definitions of "adequate" medical care and living conditions, or are funded by invested parties. With these limitations, perhaps one of the most honest conclusions that can be drawn comes from a study conducted by Brad Lundahl and colleagues at the University of Utah in 2009 which compared publicly managed and privately managed prisons. That study concluded, "Cost savings from privatizing prisons are not guaranteed and appear minimal. Quality of confinement is similar across privately and publicly managed systems, with publicly managed prisons delivering slightly better skills training and having slightly fewer inmate grievances" (p. 383). Despite a lack of conclusive data that proves that abuse and exploitation have frequently occurred, we can imagine that injustices are possible because, as mentioned above, a major guiding principle for prison management decision-making is shifted from correction and rehabilitation to profit making. Because of the responsibility to shareholders, in a private prison decisions will necessarily be made with more concern for profit than would be the case in a public prison where profit is not an option. Though the concern for profit is not by its very nature at odds with inmate care, we can easily imagine cases where better food, better job training, or better healthcare would benefit inmates but hurt the bottom line, and as a result, those improvements are not implemented.

Because private for-profit prison management might open spaces for abuse and exploitation, it is important for voters and activists to be knowledgeable about such possibilities. Without an informed public, prison management companies would have little motivation to spend down their profits to make prison living conditions more humane. Without an informed public, management corporations would have few people to hold them accountable for avoiding abuse and exploitation. The problem is that the public is currently uninformed. There are large segments of voters who have little knowledge of the conditions of prison life or the trend toward privatization. Many voters and taxpayers may not visit prisons or know inmates or correctional officers who live and work in them, and this lack of information leads to low voter involvement in these issues and, in the end, this low involvement amounts to tacit acceptance of this trend's continuance.

To combat this, I argue that entertainment media, when carefully produced and consumed, might actually be a medium that could help fill in some of this gap in information. Entertainment media can inform viewers about issues unfamiliar to them and use viewer sympathies to motivate conversation and action. For example, Season 3 of Netflix's original series *Orange is the New Black* (*OITNB*) gives those who would otherwise be unaware of the changes brought about by prison privatization a powerful glimpse at its impact. As will be discussed below, the series depicts compromises in the healthcare, education, food quality, and safety of inmates, as well as the lack of training and concern for inmate rehabilitation that results from privatization. By depicting the way that these compromises hurt beloved characters, viewers become aware of the ways that these abuses and injustices are undermining inmate's chances of living a successful life after prison. Importantly, *OITNB* also helps viewers see that while prison leaders may want to help inmates, their efforts can easily be thwarted by economic incentives. The show depicts "good people" transforming into profit driven monsters with little concern for those around them, and this depiction calls viewers to interrogate their own complicity with the prison industrial complex.

Juxtaposition as Meaning Making

OITNB is known for its juxtapositions, a storytelling strategy wherein events inside prison are depicted alongside past events outside prison or events at the systemic level are depicted alongside events at an individual level. *OITNB* has used this method through all its seasons to highlight injustice and/or bias. For example, in Season 1, Episode 2 the in-prison experience of Piper (White middle class inmate) being starved by Red is juxtaposed with the out-of-prison experience of Piper going on a juice fast. This juxtaposition is used to highlight the absurdity of Piper's privilege, demonstrating that it is only from a position of privilege that one would voluntarily starve oneself. As another example, in Season 1, Episode 7 viewers see Fig (prison supervisor) drinking coffee through a straw so as not to stain her teeth in juxtaposition with Pennsatucky (White working class inmate) wanting desperately to get new teeth since hers were ruined by drug use. Here the creators demonstrate that those who possess class markers will protect them for themselves while denying them to others. Television critic Scott Kaufman (2014) writes, "The advantage of juxtaposing meaningfully related scenes is that it allows the audience to create connections, resulting in an episode that is less like a lecture than a lively discussion session."

Continuing that method of message-by-juxtaposition, Season 3 of *OITNB* asks viewers to have a lively discussion about the impact of private for-profit prison management. The overarching plot of Season 3 focuses on the transition of the Litchfield women's prison to management by a company called Management & Correction Corporation (MCC). As MCC takes over, the decline in quality of life experienced by the inmates and correctional officers is depicted through poor quality food and healthcare, and loss of the library books for job training, as well as the establishment of what amounts to a panty sweatshop, an abundance of untrained correctional officers who allow and even perpetrate violence against inmates, and the transformation of Joe Caputo's character (the prison supervisor) from sympathetic to antagonistic toward correctional officers and inmates alike. This structural change, and the overall decline in quality of life that comes with it, is juxtaposed with Piper's individual transformation from opportunistic entrepreneur to prison gang mob boss through her dirty panty business.

Declining Quality of Life: Food, Healthcare, and Resources

As MCC takes over management of *OITNB*'s Litchfield Penitentiary (a fictionalized version of the minimum-security women's prison in which Piper Kerman, author of the book *Orange is the New Black: My Year in a Women's Prison* on which the series is based, was housed) one of the major changes noticed by inmates is the declining quality of food. Prior to MCC's management, inmates worked in the kitchen to prepare fresh food. The kitchen staff was responsible for setting menus, ordering supplies from vendors (which had previously resulted in smuggled-in drugs), and preparing meals each day. After MCC begins managing the prison, however, all of the food is prepared offsite and brought onto the prison campus in plastic bags that only require heating. Danny Pearson, the only person MCC sends to work on Litchfield's campus, and Caputo discuss in Season 3, Episode 4 that this new food supply system is meant to keep meal costs below $2.00 per inmate. Inmates find the new food uneatable, however, and begin requesting Kosher meals as an alternative. The increase in requests for Kosher meals eventually leads to a dramatic increase in food costs, and when questioned by Pearson about the possibility of denying the inmates Kosher meals, Caputo notes that to deny inmates their ability to claim Jewish identity would surely result in an expensive lawsuit. Compromising, they decide to bring in a Rabbi to distinguish who is legitimately Jewish from who simply wants better food.

Off screen, while the data on quality of confinement measurements is mixed, we can easily imagine decisions about food quality, or even quantity and frequency, being made on the basis of "cost saving measures." For example, according to the website of Sheriff Joe Arpaio, who oversees the eight jails (7,500–10,000 inmates) of Maricopa County in Phoenix, Arizona, "The average meal costs between 15 and 40 cents, and inmates are fed only twice daily, to cut the labor costs of meal delivery. He even stopped serving them salt and pepper to save taxpayers $20,000 a year" (Maricopa County Sheriff's Office, 2015). These measures are obviously not in the best interest of the inmates and their nutritional needs.

At Litchfield, healthcare also suffers with privatization. MCC is concerned that healthcare costs will be more expensive at Litchfield than at the other prisons they manage because, as one representative points out, "Men don't have uteruses" (Season 3, Episode 4). Under MCC's management, the doctor who had been at Litchfield, and had seemed to really care about the wellbeing of the inmates, is replaced by an inexperienced doctor who does not understand safety protocols in a prison setting. As a result, in Season 3, Episode 12, the new doctor leaves medicine out on a counter, and Soso, an inmate suffering from depression, steals it and tries to commit suicide via overdose.

Additionally, just before MCC took over, there was an outbreak of bedbugs, which resulted in having to burn all the mattresses and most of the books in the prison's library. While the mattresses are eventually replaced, MCC does not want to spend money on getting more books, even though those books help the inmates work on their cases and learn skills for success after prison. Danny Pearson's father, the CEO of MCC who never sets foot on Litchfield's campus, suggests that the next company to own the prison can take care of that issue. This and other comments make it clear that MCC leadership only wants to own Litchfield long enough to turn a profit and then sell it to move on to other investments. As such, they are not interested in long-term investments for the wellbeing of the inmates.

Sweatshops

Alongside the controversy of privatizing prisons, prison labor has long been a contested issue. Though slavery was ended in the United States with the passage of the 13th Amendment in 1865, slavery and involuntary servitude have been and continue to be allowed as punishment after a criminal conviction. Diverse arguments have been put forward to support prison labor, but, according to political scientist Susan Kang, the main ones are the assertion that labor gives inmates job skills that will help them when they are released and the belief that prisoners should be required to pay for their own incarceration. While those arguments are at least somewhat focused on the good of the inmate or the sustainability of the prison itself, a third prominent argument is that the prison population is simply an untapped labor market that can be used by companies to increase their profits.

While it is the case that most prison labor supports the function of the prison itself, Sarah Shemkus explains in her article "Beyond Cheap Labor" that about 4% of prison labor is known as "correctional industries" which produce products sold to consumers outside the prison. Companies may employ prisoners to manufacture textile goods, process foods, or work in call centers. For example, companies as diverse as Whole Foods, McDonald's, Wendy's, Walmart, Starbucks,

Sprint, Verizon Wireless, Victoria's Secret, JC Penney, Kmart, American Airlines, and Avis have all been accused of using prison labor. The National Institute of Justice confirmed that in the early 1990s, a garment manufacturer called Third Generation used labor from a women's prison in South Carolina to sew $1.5 million worth of clothing that was sold to consumers through the Victoria's Secret and JC Penney brand names (see Yahr, 2015). Though Third Generation ended its use of that labor in the mid-1990s, the practice continues in other places. For example, until April 2016, Whole Foods sold dairy products from Haystack Mountain Goat Cheese, which uses prison labor in Colorado in part of its processing (Aubrey, 2015).

Importantly, in cases of "correctional industries", Kang notes that, "The production needs of the employer are prioritized and there are few opportunities for recourse against employers that abuse, fire or lay off prison workers" (2009, p. 148), and this is seen clearly in *OITNB*. As MCC takes over, inmates are offered the "opportunity" to apply for a new work assignment where they can earn a dollar an hour, much more than all of the other work assignment jobs. Inmates must apply and take a test for the new job, although Pearson later explains that the test results are irrelevant and that the test was a ruse to make the inmates blame themselves if they were not chosen for the new job. After a group of women is chosen randomly for the new job, it is revealed that they will be working for a lingerie company called "Whispers." Following strict guidelines from the company, the inmates are required to cut fabric and sew panties, which, they learn, are sold for $90 each. As such, the inmates basically become sweatshop workers.

As Piper works at cutting the patterns, she realizes that some fabric is being wasted. She offers her observation as an improvement to the company, but they do not care and simply ignore her. As a result, Piper begins stealing leftover fabric to make extra panties. As the season progresses, Piper realizes she can have women in the prison wear these extra panties for a few days and then, with her brother Cal's help, sell them online to people with dirty panty fetishes. Thus Piper's dirty panty business takes off.

Undertrained Officers and Lack of Safety

More imminently dangerous than declining food, healthcare, and resources and more infuriating than becoming sweatshop workers, the safety of inmates is likewise in decline. According to a 2011 report on prison privatization from the ACLU of Ohio, a 1999 study conducted by the University of Minnesota Law School's Institute of Criminal Justice concluded that, "Prison for profit inmates consistently reported living in a more dangerous and poorly supervised environment than public prison inmates. Many inmates used words like 'unstable' and 'disorganized' when describing their living conditions." Moreover, a case study of the Lake Erie Correctional Institution (LAECI) in Conneaut, Ohio is telling. LAECI had previously been publicly funded and operated, but management was taken over by CCA on December 31, 2011. A study prepared by a Correctional Institution Inspection Committee in 2013 then reports, "Inmate on inmate assaults increased by 187.5 percent between 2010 and 2012," and "Inmate on staff assaults increased by 305.9 percent between 2010 and 2012." The study concludes:

> LAECI's primary issue is safety and security. Staff interviews, inmate focus groups, the inmate survey, and institutional data all indicate that personal safety is at risk at LAECI. Assaults, fights, disturbances, and uses of force have all increased in comparison to prior years. There is a high presence of gang activity and illegal substance use. Inmates reported frequent extortion and theft. Incident reports indicate that staff hesitate to use force even when appropriate and at times fail to deploy chemical agents prior to physical force, risking greater injury to both inmates and staff.
>
> *(Geisler, 2013)*

These statistics play out on *OITNB* as well, and viewers see the way that these policies harm characters with whom they have come to identify. Since MCC is incentivized to cut costs, they pursue a policy of making all their officers part-time, so that the company is not required to provide health insurance to them. This, of course, results in cut hours for current officers, which lowers morale and makes them less motivated to be fully focused on their jobs, and the need to hire new inexperienced officers. The advertisements for new officers state that the only required qualifications are a GED and no felonies, which Caputo, a supervisor, feels is not sufficient to ensure that officers will be able to keep the inmates safe or to ensure that the hiring process will keep out criminals who would want access to the inmates.

As the newly hired part-time correctional officers start work, MCC will not pay them to go through the more rigorous 40-hour training that Caputo suggests. Instead, they are given minimal training and are asked to read a manual. Because of this lack of training, the new correctional officers begin doing dangerous and unethical things around the inmates. In Episode 7, a new correctional officer uses pepper spray on inmates and himself. In response to this incident, Pearson offers to pay for six hours of training for the correctional officers. Additionally, although officer training had previously included a sexual harassment seminar, without that training or any understanding of the responsibilities of being a correctional officer, another new officer develops an inappropriate relationship with Pennsatucky and eventually rapes her. Also due to the untrained correctional officers who do not care to learn the inmates' names and a computer error, which should have been caught by any number of human officers, the wrong inmate is released and only later returned to the prison because Caputo knew where to find her.

Inmate violence is also an issue that the new correctional officers are not equipped to handle and when the untrained officers walk in on Sophia being beat up, they do nothing to protect her and instead run away to get help. As a result, Sophia is seriously injured and asks that the officers receive more training. In response, Caputo says that MCC will not pay for more training but does have lawyers who can "crush" Sophia's case. Lastly, Caputo's fears do come to fruition and, because of the lack of thorough background checks for new officers, Alex is attacked, in the garden shed by Kubra's henchman Aydin, who has now apparently been hired as an officer. Throughout the season, the impact of the undertrained officers escalates from pepper spraying, to rape, to assault, to murder of inmates who are supposed to be under the protection of the state.

Overcrowding

Adding to the problems of declining living conditions and increasing violence, prison population growth has also been dramatically increasing in the last 30 years. For example, according to Alex Friedmann, associate editor of *Prison Legal News*, in 1983 the US housed 648,000 prisoners and by 2010 that number had increased to 2.3 million. This increase was fuelled in the 1980s and 1990s by the "War on Drugs" which instituted harsh penalties and long prison terms for drug related crimes. Lobby groups who stood to make a profit from prison management also contributed to political campaigns that promised to bring even harsher sentencing.

While this overcrowding is more commonly reported in the news, some voters may not realize the impact this has on inmates' lives. *OITNB* Season 4 may change that though because when MCC takes over Litchfield, they buy the inmates new beds and mattresses. This, at first, looks like a helpful improvement for the inmates, but in one of the last scenes in the last episode of Season 3, we see that the beds are being replaced with bunkbeds so that the population of Litchfield can be doubled. While we have not yet witnessed the impact of this change, it will undoubtedly be negative.

Pursuit of Profit Leads to Abuse and Exploitation

OITNB makes it abundantly clear that prison privatization is bad for all parties involved. Health, safety, and living/working conditions are all in decline. The only winner in this season is the CEO who cares about a short-term profit and never has to see the impact of his decisions on these women's lives. While this depiction is powerful enough to make viewers see the corporate overlords as heartless monsters, I argue that the creators have put something more powerful into the season – an interrogation of the idea that profit-driven motivations are harmless and unobjectionable. I argue that *OITNB* encourages viewers to identify the pursuit of profits as the underlying problem that leads to the abuse and exploitation of all of our favorite characters.

While Netflix keeps its viewer data secret, due to the protagonist's character-istics and the book that inspired the series, it is safe to assume that *OITNB* is aimed at a middle class, largely White and female audience. Since Season 1, we (the middle class White people who have Netflix subscriptions and identify with Piper) have entered the Litchfield prison through and as Piper. This has, of course, led to many types of critique, including that she is the White suburban tour guide who leads us to view exhibits of exotic trans, Black, Hispanic, and butch women. While these critiques are certainly valid, I think the viewer-as-Piper approach is somewhat redeemed in Season 3 because it is the mechanism through which we are able to see our own complicity in this system of injustice. By valuing profits, we also perpetuate, or at least problematically tolerate, abuse and exploitation. This is achieved, once again, through juxtaposing the systemic with the individual.

In Episode 11, Flaca, one of Piper's panty wearers, suggests that the "panty girls" unionize so that they can get money, not merely Ramen flavor packets, as payment from Piper for their work. Not yet hardened by her business pursuits, Piper goes to Red to ask for advice. Red wants a cut of the profits but suggests that Piper could put money in the women's commissary accounts using a phone based pay system. Piper talks to Alex about this, but Alex is concerned that with money involved, this business is becoming more like a prison gang. Piper ignores Alex's concerns and settles on paying the women $8 per pair of panties, plus their choice of panty style and flavor packets. However, in the meeting where she announces these changes, she rather ruthlessly humiliates and fires Flaca. Piper uses this speech to scare the other women into being happy with the arrangement she has proposed. Alex tells Piper that her management of these women is becoming cruel, but Piper responds that she is only doing with this business what Alex did with drugs.

As the final step in Piper's transformation to heartless panty CEO, toward the end of Season 3 after dating Stella for a while, Piper learns that Stella has stolen Piper's panty business profits because she is getting out of prison soon and will have no money or place to live. To Stella's face, Piper makes it seem like she understands Stella's predicament and actions, but behind her back, Piper hides several pieces of contraband in Stella's bunk and then calls the correctional officers to do a search. As a result of the found contraband, only two days before she was scheduled to be released, Stella is taken to maximum security for an extended sentence. Piper takes credit for Stella's misfortune, and the other women become terrified of Piper's heartlessness.

Following a similar pattern of transformation from sympathetic character to callous boss, as the correctional officers attempt to unionize to protect themselves from MCC's cuts, they ask Caputo to lead them because they trust that he understands the processes and has their best interests at heart. However, MCC offers Caputo an irresistible raise so that he will stop helping the officers organize, and he takes the offer, abandoning the officers to figure out how to protect themselves.

Summarizing the message of Season 3, TV Writer Kayla Hawkins (2015) writes about this parallel,

But, I found the most interesting permutation of the corporate plot to come in Season 3, Episode 11, "We Can Be Heroes," which mirrored the prison guards' attempt to unionize with Flaca's attempt to do the same thing with Piper's panty girls. In both cases, the fight was uphill against an uncaring CEO who aimed to cut them down. Caputo ultimately chickened out, choosing to take a promotion over sticking up for his coworkers, while Flaca was cut down but ultimately given the choice to rejoin her coworkers. That doesn't mean that Piper didn't get her own corporate ruthlessness, though, striking back with a downright MCC attitude of valuing the bottom line over humanity. When Piper sent Stella to max over the loss of her panty money, I was horrified at the cruelty, yet curious what Jenji Kohan and the rest of the staff wanted the audience to think. In my opinion, it was setting up Piper and MCC as equally evil villains for Season 4, pushing how both enterprises are dehumanizing their staffs and recklessly underestimating what the consequences will be. Continuing to show the fallout from the very real inspiration of the horrors of for-profit prisons will make future *Orange Is the New Black* seasons harder to watch, but ultimately should make those real abuses harder to ignore.

This gets to the heart of the issue. By juxtaposing the decline of the prison and Caputo's fall from "good guy" status with Piper's transformation into cruel dirty panty selling mob boss, the nefariousness of the profit-above-all mentality is revealed. At the macro level, Caputo and MCC shirk their responsibilities as caregivers to the inmates and the correctional officers for profit and promotion. At the micro level, Piper gives up any trust or genuine friendship she had gained, even with Stella and Alex, in order to establish herself as a boss whom workers fear. In both cases, the entity started out with good intentions but because each experienced a shift in their guiding principles for decision-making (from correction/rehabilitation and friendship to profit making) they quickly become "evil villains" who perpetuate, or at least tolerate, abuse and exploitation.

The Conversation Continues

At the beginning of Season 3, Piper has made peace with her role as an inmate and built some (somewhat) caring relationships with her peers. Likewise, at the beginning of Season 3, Caputo is working to make the prison a more caring place. By the end of the season, however, Piper's originally benign, if opportunistic, entrepreneurial spirit has led to her transformation into an uncaring dictator who is completely willing to exploit, intimidate, and threaten her "employees" if they do not follow her wishes completely. Likewise, Caputo and MCC have forsaken whatever good intentions and ability to improve the inmates' lives they may have had in order to earn more money. Importantly, as these transformations are happening, both Piper and MCC squash resistance by any means necessary. In the end then, this juxtaposition asks us to think about how the pursuit of profit, at both the individual and structural levels, so easily results in exploitation and injustice.

As we think about this question, we must connect what we see on screen to the off screen world of prison experiences. By watching *OITNB*, viewers who might otherwise ignore these issues are educated about the plight of inmates whose living conditions are managed by companies focused on profits over rehabilitation. By watching *OITNB*, viewers are encouraged to question the very underpinnings of capitalism and the concept of privatization. Does desire for profit persuade people, even people with good intentions, to make decisions that result in injustice or exploitation for others? Does allowing prison management to enter the realm of profit-making undermine the very idea of prison as a place for the rehabilitation of inmates? Do we have a responsibility, as voters or activists, to resist measures that make the management of already at-risk lives fall into the realm of profit making? *OITNB* guides us to this conversation and asks us to consider whether the answer to all three of these questions is a resounding yes. Moreover, *OITNB* guides us to ask, as Alex does, "So, I'm just a fly in the web of the prison industrial complex?"

References

Aubrey, A. (2015, October 1). Whole Foods says it will stop selling foods made with prison labor. *National Public Radio*. Retrieved from http://www.npr.org/sections/thesalt/2015/09/30/444797169/whole-foods-says-it-will-stop-selling-foods-made-by-prisoners

American Civil Liberties Union. (2011, November 2). Banking on bondage: private prisons and mass incarceration. Retrieved from: https://www.aclu.org/sites/default/files/field_document/bankingonbondage_20111102.pdf

Corrections Corporation of America. (2016, February 10). CCA reports fourth quarter and full year 2015 financial results. Retrieved from http://ir.correctionscorp.com/phoenix.zhtml?c=117983&p=irol-newsArticle&id=2137326

Friedmann, A. (2012, January 15). The societal impact of the prison industrial complex, or incarceration for fun and profit – mostly profit. *Prison Legal News*. Retrieved from: https://www.prisonlegalnews.org/news/2012/jan/15/the-societal-impact-of-the-prison-industrial-complex-or-incarceration-for-fun-and-profitmostly-profit/

Geisler, G., Report Coordinator. (2013, January 22–23). *Correctional Institution Inspection Committee Report on the Inspection and Evaluation of the Lake Erie Correctional Institution.* Retrieved from http://big.assets.huffingtonpost.com/lakeeriereport.pdf

Hawkins, K. (2015, July 14). 'Orange is the New Black' puts for-profit prisons in the spotlight & makes some interesting points about corporate negligence. Retrieved from http://www.bustle.com/articles/92012-orange-is-the-new-black-puts-for-profit-prisons-in-the-spotlight-makes-some-interesting-points

Kang, S. (2009). Forcing Prison Labor: International Labor Standards, Human Rights and the privatization of prison labor in the contemporary United States. *New Political Science*, 31(2), 137–161.

Lundahl, B.W., Kunz, C., Brownell, C., Harris, N., & Van Vleet, T. (2009). Prison privatization: A meta-analysis of cost and quality of confinement indicators. *Research on Social Work Practice*, 19(4), 383–394.

Maricopa County Sheriff's Office. (2015). Retrieved from http://www.mcso.org/About/Sheriff.aspx

Pelaez, V. (2008, March 10). *The Prison Industry in the United States: Big Business or a New Form of Slavery?* El Diario-La Prensa, New York and Global Research. Retrieved from: http://www.globalresearch.ca/the-prison-industry-in-the-united-states-big-busi ness-or-a-new-form-of-slavery/8289

Shemkus, S. (2015, December 9). Beyond cheap labor: Can prison work programs benefit inmates? *The Guardian.* Retrieved from http://www.theguardian.com/sustainable-busi ness/2015/dec/09/prison-work-program-ohsa-whole-foods-inmate-labor-incarceration

Yahr, E. (2015). Yes, prisoners used to sew lingerie for Victoria's Secret—just like in 'Orange is the New Black' Season 3. *The Washington Post.* Retrieved from https://www.washing tonpost.com/news/arts-and-entertainment/wp/2015/06/17/yes-prisoners-used-to-sew-lingerie-for-victorias-secret-just-like-in-orange-is-the-new-black-season-3/

12

EXECUTING WOMEN

Media Explanations of Female Criminality

Sarah Lazzeroni

Introduction

The use of the death penalty has been hotly contested in recent years as more states have repealed death penalty laws and controversies about how we enact death sentences have arisen. While consensus is growing that the death penalty (especially as currently administered) may not be consistent with American ideals of liberty and equality, often ignored are the experiences of women on death row. In an analysis of women sentenced to death between 1973 and 2011, Victor Streib (2012) found that women constituted only 6.6% of all persons sentenced to death. Multiple theories have emerged in an attempt to explain why so few women are sentenced to death, including chivalry/paternalism, the Evil Woman hypothesis, and gendered patterns of offending. As legal scholar Elizabeth Rapaport (1990) argues theories like the chivalry/paternalism framework and the Evil Woman hypothesis invoke dominant understandings of gender, including but not limited to the inherent passivity of women juxtaposed with the inherent violence of men and gendered expectations of women as spouses and mothers. On the other hand, other scholars explain these gender discrepancies by pointing to differences in the types of crimes women commit and experiences with hardships like sexual abuse and domestic violence.

This chapter looks at gendered behavioral assumptions through a feminist lens in order to critically analyze media narratives about women sentenced to death. Special attention will be paid to how these narratives are shaped by and reinforce dominant ideas about gender, sexuality, and rationality. Scholar Judith Baxter (2008) outlined feminist post-structuralist discourse analysis (FPDA). FPDA will be used as the primary theoretical framework in this chapter in an attempt to illuminate how gendered power dynamics are perpetuated through the media's discussion of women on death row. Based in post-structuralism and Michel Foucault's work on language and power in his books *The Archaeology of Knowledge* and *Power/Knowledge: Selected Interviews and Other Writings 1972–1977*, FDPA is aimed at uncovering the relationship between discourse, knowledge, and power – specifically, gendered power dynamics – through an analysis of language.

Discourse, Knowledge and Power

The aim of the present chapter is to examine discursive practices, or uses of language, within newspaper articles that serve to create and maintain narratives about gender and criminality. Feminist scholar Michelle Lazar (2007), outlines discursive practices as those which shape our understandings of social reality – they are taken for granted assumptions that influence our social, economic, and political circumstances in material ways. Essentially, discursive practices shape how we talk about social phenomena and are capable of producing, reinforcing, and resisting dominant narratives about said phenomena.

In her article "Feminist postructuralism and discourse analysis," Nicola Gavey (1989) discusses how these assumptions constitute knowledge, which "is understood to be not neutral – it is closely associated with power". Therefore, knowledge is created with the specific intention of defining subjects in a certain way that upholds existing power structures. Foucault argues in *Power/Knowledge* that power is "diffuse" through the "web" of social relations in ways that force us to intentionally and unintentionally enact and reinforce power dynamics. He explains in *The Archaeology of Knowledge* that "discourses operate as practices that systematically form the objects of which they speak" (p. 49), meaning that those who are able to define knowledge (often taken as truth) are able to maintain power. Therefore, the construction of our identities as they relate to the embodiments of gender, sexuality, race, disability, etc. are all beholden in some way (and often in intersecting, sometimes conflicting ways) to the ways in which these issues are talked about in the public realm. However, as scholars note, this does not mean that individuals are entirely without recourse, as they may use their agency in ways that resist dominant narratives and actively create new ones.

Media Discourse

The media represents one such producer of discourse, or language, that serves to define knowledge and maintain power, although the increasing diversification of media through technology like social media has increased the resistive possibilities of media. Ireland linguist Anne O'Keeffe (2011), makes the point that media is a "form of institutional talk" that can be analyzed in order to understand how media upholds or denies dominant narratives through a critical examination of texts (e.g., newspaper articles). As mentioned above, discursive practices shape our social position in material ways. Comprised of television, movies, radio, newspapers, and, increasingly, social media, American media both describes and reinforces dominant narratives about both crime and femininity.

When viewed as one part of larger discursive practices associated with maintaining power structures (in addition to institutions such as law and science), it makes sense that the media must navigate a tenuous relationship between informing the public while also selling a product to the public. While dominant narratives about gender and criminality are inarguably entrenched in American society, this does not mean that they are static. Through media discourse, we can also begin to deconstruct these lessons and create new ones that disrupt existing power structures. However, the public nature of the media decreases individual agency in combating dominant narratives, a restraint that will become apparent later in this chapter when specific representations of women on death row are closely examined.

Media and Crime

Television, newspapers, and movies all serve as important influencers of public thinking about crime, formulating specific and intentional narratives that often have social and political consequences. Previous research supports the idea that conceptions of criminality are both reflected in and reinforced by the media, painting stereotypical portraits of offenders. For example, researcher Rachel Lyon (2009) found that the media tends to focus on aspects of cases that also promote the fear of crime and relies heavily on gender stereotypes. Women are often presented as passive and men as violent, with Black men being represented as the most predatory. Legal scholar Chimene Keitner, argues that "societal expectations and understandings of the use of violence play a key role in the structure and outcomes of criminal trials" (2010, p. 39), as criminal justice actors (such as police, judges, and jury members) are not immune to the influences of dominant media narratives about crime. Additionally, as scholars have found, the American media greatly informs public opinion about crime and criminals that can make some outcomes (like the sustained use of the death penalty) seem inevitable. There is a large market for this type of "sensationalized crime coverage." Scholars have demonstrated that promoting mass fear of crime and "criminals" is an effective business strategy for media organizations who want to attract large audiences, even if doing so results in the stereotyping and stigmatization of individuals who commit crimes.

Historically, cases considered most extreme (and often rare) by the criminal justice system also receive the most media attention. Professor and documentary filmmaker Rachel Lyon found that homicide cases and cases involving female defendants receive the most attention, especially cases of murder involving strangers, otherwise known as random murders. Similarly, even though women do not often commit these random murders, media scholar Barbara Barnett posits that cases involving female defendants in murder cases often draw a large amount of media attention because they are a rarity. Often, representations of "violent women" in media stories, whether on television or in newspapers, focus on details that are legally irrelevant, yet salacious enough to drive sales, including past relationships, appearance, demeanor, and sexuality. Barbara Barnett found that examples of the chivalry and evil woman frameworks are therefore evident in media narratives about female offenders, illustrating the interplay between the criminal justice system and the media.

According to research, popular media narratives serve as the main source of information about criminal justice for the American public. Many of these narratives not only highlight the most newsworthy criminal activity (often according to rationales related to the extreme nature of certain crimes and the quest for higher sales), but also attempt to explain the reasons *why* crimes were committed. In researching media coverage of social problems, scholar Mira Sotirovic (2006) found that, when explaining why crimes were committed, both television shows and newspaper stories often highlight individualistic explanations over ones based in social and historical context, although newspapers have been shown to do a better job of giving details about the backgrounds of defendants. Such explanations are in line with Western models of rational choice and free will.

In researching media coverage of the death penalty, social scientist Chris Haney notes that the media perpetuates the idea that "individuals alone are responsible for violent crime, and that their behavior stems entirely from deep-seated personal traits like depravity, narcissism, and psychopathology" (2009, p. 727). These individualistic explanations often ignore the more complex realities of criminal behavior and serve to justify the punitive nature of the criminal justice system. As newspapers attempt to explain both the details *and* motivations behind criminal activity, it is important to understand the explanations provided by newspapers to the public. Mira Sotirovic concludes that "conservatives are more likely to explain both crime and welfare in individualistic terms" (2006, p. 131), which could potentially explain the prevalence of executions and the high levels of public support for the death penalty in the South, which tends to be more conservative.

These individualistic versus contextual explanations matter because research shows that journalists' accounts of criminal activity often focus on the individual characteristics of the individual perpetrator. A lack of context can be damaging by painting perpetrators into stereotyped corners, with women killers specifically being portrayed as either "mad" or "bad." In both scenarios, scholars argue, women are punished for failing to comply with expectations of femininity. Both of these explanations for criminal activity are individualistic and gendered, leaving little room for context that may serve to enhance our understanding of why women kill or even better yet, our understanding of how to more effectively support women.

Instead of providing context, Jeanine Kraybill's (2009) research on newspaper articles about women facing the death penalty found that the papers often focused on extralegal factors such as their past relationships, sexual promiscuity, physical appearance, demeanor, and non-traditional roles as females in society. Processes of defeminization result in dehumanization, and when these processes are promoted by the press, both law and gender are reinforced as legitimate systems of power. The violation of both the law *and* norms of femininity therefore leads to extreme punishments, as well as increased media attention.

Femininity and Crime

As media outlets often attempt to explain the details of a crime as well as its motivation (the "*why?*"), a few dominant narratives have emerged concerning the relationship between femininity and crime. A comprehensive analysis of criminal activity conducted by Jennifer Schwartz and Darrell Steffensmeier (2012) found that, although women have historically not committed crimes at the same rate as men, the gap in rates of offending has decreased, with more and more women being imprisoned in recent years. They found a large increase in the number of arrests of women for violent crimes which have not been mirrored in arrest numbers for men. Yet, women still constitute a tiny proportion of individuals sentenced to death, even though they account for around ten percent of murders. These gaps in offending not only illustrate the material consequences of narratives about crime and gender, but they also provide the impetus for narratives used to explain why women commit crimes.

One dominant narrative is the chivalry thesis, also known as the paternalism framework, which asserts that female offenders evoke sympathy amongst jurors, judges, and the general public simply because they are women. In explaining the gender gap in offending, this narrative supports the idea that women are given lesser sentences than men for equal crimes because of their gender. As legal scholar Jessica Salvucci (2011) notes, this theory views American society as inherently patriarchal, with men acting as the protectors of "weak" and "feeble" women. These narratives diminish women's personal agency and blameworthiness because women are assumed to be passive and cooperative in contrast to men's aggressiveness and competitiveness.

Of course, for women to have access to the "benefits" of their gender, they must also adequately comply with the expectations of femininity. According to the Evil Woman hypothesis, outlined by Jessica Salvucci, women are more likely to receive death sentences if they violate traditional expectations for female behavior, thereby defeminizing themselves and forfeiting the sympathy women allegedly receive. According to feminist scholars Meda Chesney-Lind and Michele Eliason, any process of defeminization inevitably results in "masculinization," which creates "standards that will permit the demonization of some girls and women if they stray from the path of true (passive) womanhood" (2006, p. 32).

The accepted image of femininity is not only passive and controlled, but it is also historically White, chaste, heterosexual, and beautiful according to Western standards. Women who fall outside of this description (e.g., women of color, LGBTQ women, women who have sex with more than one partner, etc.) are defeminized because of characteristics including, but not limited to, their gender. Because our conceptions of femininity are shaped by things like race and sexuality, it is important to consider the interactions of these subjectivities in creating an individual's social position. For example, legal scholar Joey Mogul, contends that queer women on death row are put there "because they…do not conform to sexist notions society has proscribed for women. Consequently, they are not afforded the protectionist notions accompanying these sexist stereotypes" (2005, p. 490). For queer women, their sexuality represents a violation of femininity that promotes their dehumanization and, in turn, harsher punishments.

The conceptions of truth also play into the narrative of victimhood that is present in many representations. Numerous studies have found that female offenders have unique pathways to crime that often involve abuse (both in childhood and adulthood), trauma, substance abuse, and mental illness more than the pathways to crime for men. The American Civil Liberties Union surveyed current death row inmates and found that 50% of the women had been abused, illustrating the importance of understanding the role of abuse in the lives of women sentenced to death. The individualized nature of many representations of offenders removes the actions of female offenders from important context, such as the research findings listed above. These findings suggest that women's victimization is presented either in sensationalized (often extralegal) details used to defeminize them or written off as untrue, thereby portraying them as vindictive liars.

Discourse Analysis

Resting on post-structuralist assumptions that social reality and truth are constructed, discourse analysis provides a conceptual framework through which to analyze cultural artifacts that give us insight into discursive practices. According to feminist scholar Nicola Gavey,

> Discourse analysis involves the careful reading of texts, with a view to discerning discursive patterns of meaning, contradictions, and inconsistencies. It is an approach that identifies and names language processes people use to constitute their own and others' understanding of personal and social phenomena. These processes are related to the reproduction of or challenge to the distribution of power between social groups and within institutions.
>
> *(1989, p. 466)*

As such statements become ingrained into the social fabric of life (via institutions like education and the media), they come to represent a "discursive field" that manifests itself in power relations. Objects and practices become "visible and knowable" when they are presented as problematic. It also allows for the potential for counter-narratives to develop once dominant narratives have been deconstructed.

Feminist Post-Structuralist Discourse Analysis

In order to understand how gendered power dynamics are reinforced in discourses about female criminality, feminist post-structuralist discourse analysis (FPDA) was used to understand how women are portrayed as both powerful and powerless and how these portrayals were related to individualized or contextualized discourses. Developed by Judith Baxter in the early 2000s, FPDA is typically used to examine spoken language (for example, as Baxter did in her 2002 examination of gendered classroom dynamics), but in this case it is used to analyze written texts. FPDA is distinct from critical discourse analysis (CDA) because it goes one step further in assessing subjectivities by recognizing that individuals' social positions are continuously in flux based on the context of the situation.

Additionally, in line with other feminist orientations, Baxter's conceptualization of FPDA prioritizes gender difference as a "dominant discourse" that interacts with other discourses (e.g., discourses about race and sexuality) to shape the power dynamics of specific situations. Others argue that a more intersectional approach should be adopted in feminist discourse analysis in order to understand how "systems of power" interact with one another. Both Baxter and intersectional feminists operate on two similar assumptions: that individuals experience both privilege (power) and oppression (powerlessness) at the same time and that individuals' privilege and oppression are predicated on their position relative to other individuals. Therefore, the content of the articles were interpreted with an eye towards this complexity in that instances of contradictions and inconsistencies were scrutinized for meaning.

Case Studies

In order to explore dominant narratives related to women sentenced to death, I examined newspaper articles about the sixteen women who have been executed in the post-Furman era (since 1976). I focused on this specific subset of women sentenced to death because executing women is rare and, as outlined above, previous research has shown that violent crimes receive a large amount of media attention. It could be expected, then, that women who were actually executed would receive the most media attention of women convicted of murder.

Using the Alliance for Audited Media's list of the top 25 newspapers with the highest circulations (both paper and digital), newspapers with circulations (both paper and digital) over 450,000 were included in the sample in order to examine how the women in question were represented in the most popular publications (Media Intelligence Center, 2015). Of the seven newspapers with circulations over 450,000, both *The Wall Street Journal* and *The Los Angeles Times* were removed from consideration because searches through LexisNexis did not return any results from these publications. LexisNexis was used to search for each woman's name, with multiple searches completed for each woman – one including middle names and the other including only first and last names, amounting to 429 articles in the original sample. However, after duplicate articles and irrelevant articles (e.g., obituaries or announcements referencing people who happened to have the same name as one of the executed women) were removed from the sample, there were 377 articles in the final sample.

Searches for two of the women (Karla Faye Tucker and Aileen Wuornos) produced the majority of articles analyzed, with 170 articles for Tucker and 56 articles for Wuornos. Articles about Tucker, and Wuornos were selected for closer examination because the majority of the articles were about these two women. Tucker was executed in 2002 for killing a man she was attempting to steal from. Wuornos was executed in 2002 for killing a man along the Florida interstate, and admitted to killing six other men.

Aileen and Karla: Discourse in Action

Tucker was described as having "cascading curls, piercing eyes, and [a] sugary demeanor." Termed "death row's first poster-girl," Tucker fulfilled gendered expectations in terms of her appearance, yet fell short of meeting them in other respects. Depictions of Tucker's sexual past ("a former rock band groupie and drug-addicted prostitute") and the well-reported detail that she "bragged" she was "sexually aroused by wielding the pickax" used to kill her victims were used to portray her as hypersexual, thereby violating norms of femininity that demand women be chaste. Phrases like "she bragged" imbue Tucker with a sense of power that is tied into competitiveness and therefore predominantly granted to men. Additionally, descriptions of her assumed hypersexuality serve to masculinize Tucker in ways consistent with dominant narratives about men being more sexual than women. In these ways, Tucker was portrayed as a "bad," evil woman.

Just as with Wuornos, attempts at contextualizing Tucker's actions were made in some articles, as were attempts at rehabilitating her femininity. For example, one journalist noted that Tucker's upbringing constituted a "lurid tale of growing up with a mother who shared tricks and needles with her daughters." Meant to convey background information about how Tucker ended up where she did, this information instead serves as a reminder of the "dangers" of violating conventions of femininity. The message is that Tucker's mother was a hypersexual drug abuser, and so her daughter followed suit, with even worse outcomes. Again, these depictions of the path to criminality remain individualized, with no mention of the relationship between drug abuse and criminality placed in a larger social context (e.g., any mention of gendered pathways of criminality).

Conversely, Tucker was also depicted as powerless, although this led to different results than Wuornos' powerlessness. Tucker's execution was protested by hundreds of people, including evangelists Bill Graham and Pat Robertson, and almost half of the articles examined were about Tucker (170 out of 377). Many articles noted that Tucker received so much support because she became a born-again Christian in prison, renouncing her crimes and asking for forgiveness. Her newfound religion acted as evidence of purity, bolstering her image of femininity, especially when paired with her "winning smile." Tucker effectively reclaimed her femininity, positioning her as someone in need of protection – and the public tried to come to her rescue. So, while her hypersexuality condemned her to death, her salvation was rooted in her subsequent adherence to feminine ideals while imprisoned. Even though she was eventually executed, the different reactions to the execution of a woman with some feminine qualities (Tucker) and the execution of a woman like Wuornos, whose only claim to femininity was her victimhood, illustrate how conceptions of femininity have material consequences.

Although Tucker's supporters were unable to stop her execution, the varied reactions to her case and the other women's cases illustrates the benefits of adhering to conventions of femininity for death row inmates. An interesting part of Tucker's case highlighted by the media was the public debate over her execution that included many references to whether or not then-Governor George W. Bush would grant her clemency. Bush was quoted as saying that Tucker "put a face on the death penalty" for him, even though she was not the first woman executed in the post-Furman era (Velma Barfield was). Analyzing this statement within the context of paternalistic views about protecting women who conform to ideals of femininity, it becomes clear that Tucker was the "face" of death row at least partially because her appearance was in line with traditional conceptions of femininity.

Additionally, Bush said that choosing to execute Tucker was "the hardest thing he did as governor," yet most journalists who discussed his decision claimed it was difficult because of political considerations, not because Tucker was a woman. This context betrays the dominant narrative about chivalry and paternalism exempting feminine women from harsh punishments, as it appears that political concerns trumped the leniency Tucker may have been otherwise granted. Namely, Bush's need to be "tough on crime" and appeal to conservative voters during the presidential campaign conflicted with his need to appeal to Christian televangelists like Billy Graham and Pat Robertson, both of whom supported granting clemency for Tucker. Mentions of this political context were the only substantive references to the social forces at play during the executions, and it led to an interesting diversion from the assumed outcome.

In comparison to Tucker, Aileen Wuornos had little chance to use her femininity to her advantage. It becomes obvious that Wuornos violated expectations of femininity in numerous ways that led to her eventual masculinization and blameworthiness. Wuornos was termed a "man-hating lesbian" and "hitchhiking prostitute" who killed men "for revenge." Many references to her appearance were also noted, usually similar to statements like "this woman was beastly in looks and deeds" and "a stocky, straggly-haired woman with desperate eyes and a foul mouth." A few articles described Wuornos as the main provider for herself and her girlfriend at the time of the murders, claiming that she stole from the men she murdered for this purpose. Such depictions of Wuornos serve to defeminize and masculinize her, as journalists mention not only that she is a lesbian, but also that she fulfills the "male role" within that relationship.

One news article noted that Wuornos was classified as America's first female serial killer by the Federal Bureau of Investigation, a designation that implies she was a cold, calculated murderer, consistent with the narrative of "bad," evil women. Her actions are entirely incompatible with conceptions of femininity, and the articles illustrate strategies of defeminization that aid in explaining Wuornos' actions. Additionally, they are all individualized descriptions of her case, thereby reflecting and feeding the discourses about autonomy and rational choice that frame the majority of representations of criminality in America. The more masculine Wuornos was assumed to be, the more culpable she was for her crimes.

While Wuornos was at once presented as an "Evil Woman," she was also presented as powerless. Many references were made to the abuse and hardships Wuornos suffered, painting her as a victim. Although details about past sexual abuse and rape experienced by Wuornos could be interpreted as contextual information by some, these details serve to support individualized explanations for her crimes. For example, multiple articles noted that Wuornos contended that she only became violent with her victim after he raped her. True contextual information would have highlighted the prevalence of sexual abuse and rape, and even incorporated the voices of women who have suffered such assaults. Instead, her victimhood is repurposed as an explanation for her crimes, because the emotional and psychological repercussions of the abuse she suffered are presented as the catalyst for her seeking revenge against men, painting her as a "mad" woman. Whereas defeminizing Wuornos serves to increase perceptions of her (masculine) agency, painting her as a victim could potentially serve to re-feminize her. However, because dominant narratives about femininity imply women are "childlike" and "naïve," her femininity in the guise of victimhood only serves to compromise the veracity of her story.

Over half of the articles about Wuornos were either explicitly or at least partially about movies about Wuornos' case. Two documentaries and the movie "Monster," starring Charlize Theron, were mentioned repeatedly. The dominance of these media representations of Wuornos highlights the importance of television and movies in shaping our perceptions and attitudes about crime. It also illustrates how interactions between media discourses (in this case, movies and newspaper articles) can reinforce dominant narratives concerning gender and criminality. However, much more interesting are the different ways Theron and Wuornos were discussed, especially in relation to one another. For example, an article in the *St. Cloud Times* noted the physical transformation Theron endured to portray

Wuornos: "Her bombshell beauty buried under a mop of greasy, bleach-damaged hair; freckled, blemished and badly windburnt skin; a severe overbite; a reported 30-pound weight gain; and eyebrows plucked into oblivion." Wuornos' lack of femininity is juxtaposed with Theron's extreme femininity; whereas Wuornos was executed for her crimes, Theron was rewarded for her portrayal of Wuornos' crimes.

Conclusion

Stories about the cases of Aileen Wuornos and Karla Faye Tucker promoted individualized, rather than contextualized, discourses about criminality, while also reinforcing stereotypes about femininity, albeit in varied ways. For example, Tucker, the woman who received most media attention, fit appearance standards of femininity, but was portrayed negatively as violating norms in other ways (namely, sexuality). Such examples illustrate how multiple discourses (related to concepts including but not limited to sexuality and victimhood) interact with one another to shape individuals' specific social locations in relation to one another. While dominant narratives about criminality often forgo contextual information, there were instances in which historical or political context was included in the articles. For example, there were discussions of all three women in relation to larger political events (such as the election of George W. Bush). Still, the context provided often focused more on the politician than the woman up for execution, with many articles mentioning the execution of women in passing. In future examinations of discursive practices relating to criminality and gender, it is important to explore the implications of intersectionality in more detail. Both of the women examined in detail were White, so future works could pay attention to the ways in which racial and gendered systems of power intersect to inform the social location of women sentenced to death.

The inclusion of historical and political context, even if it was done so in a flawed manner, highlights the utility of feminist post-structuralist discourse analysis. Although discursive practices reinforcing gendered power differences are still popular within the media, there is the potential for changes to be made in the depiction of women offenders, especially violent women offenders. Attempts were made at contextualizing the experiences of these women, but too often journalists opted to explain crime in individualized terms that only serve to further "other" the object that is the violent female in American society. Hopefully, by bringing attention to the multiplicities and interdependence of these discursive practices, counter-narratives rich with context can start to develop in the pursuit of meaningful, balanced portrayals of women offenders.

References

American Civil Liberties Union. (2004, December). The forgotten population: A look at death row in the United States through the experiences of women. Retrieved from https://www.aclu.org/sites/default/files/FilesPDFs/womenondeathrow.pdf

Barnett, B. (2006). Medea in the media: Narrative and myth in newspaper coverage of women who kill their children. *Journalism*, 7(4), 411–432.

Baxter, J.A. (2008). Feminist post-structuralist discourse analysis: A new theoretical and methodological approach? In K. Harrington, L. Litosseliti, H. Sauntson, & J. Sunderland (Eds.), *Gender and Language Research Methodologies* (pp. 243–256). Basingstoke: Palgrave Macmillan.

Chesney-Lind, M., & Eliason, M. (2006). From invisible to incorrigible: The demonization of marginalized women and girls. *Crime, Media, and Culture*, 2(1), 29–47.

Foucault, M. (1972). *The Archaeology of Knowledge*. New York: Random House Books.

Foucault, M. (1980). *Power/Knowledge: Selected Interviews and Other Writings 1972–1977*. New York: Random House Books.

Gavey, N. (1989). Feminist poststructuralism and discourse analysis. *Psychology of Women Quarterly*, 13, 459–475.

Haney, C. (2009). Media criminology and the death penalty. *DePaul Law Review*, 58(3), 689–740.

Keitner, C.I. (2010). Victim or vamp? Images of violent women in the criminal justice system. *Columbia Journal of Gender and Law*, 11(1), 38–87.

Kraybill, J.E. (2009). Death penalty: How newspaper coverage has perpetuated negative stereotypes about female violence and gender roles. Thinking Gender Papers as part of the UCLA Center for the Study of Women. Retrieved from: http://escholarship.org/uc/item/8rm5m2dq

Lazar, M.M. (2007). Feminist critical discourse analysis: Articulating a feminist discourse praxis. *Critical Discourse Studies*, 4(2), 141–164.

Lyon, R. (2009). Media, race, crime and the punishment: Re-framing stereotypes in crime and Human rights issues. *DePaul Law Review*, 58(3), 741–758.

Media Intelligence Center. (2015). Alliance for Audited Media. Retrieved from http://abcas3.auditedmedia.com/MICenter/Home/Index?s=68b1fc41-6f16-4689-9ed012a6c3940f47&v=NO#0

Mogul, J.L. (2005). The dykier, the butcher, the better: The state's use of homophobia and sexism to execute women in the United States. *New York City Law Review*, 8, 473–493.

O'Keeffe, A. (2011). Media and discourse analysis. In J. Gee, & M. Handford (Eds.), *The Routledge Handbook of Discourse Analysis* (pp. 441–454). London: Routledge.

Rapaport, E. (1990). Some questions about gender and the death penalty. *Golden Gate University Law Review*, 20, 501–565.

Salvucci, J. (2011). Femininity and the electric chair: An equal protection challenge to Texas's death penalty statute. *Boston College Third World Law Journal*, 2010–2011.

Schwartz, J., & Steffensmeier, D. (2012). Stability and change in girls' delinquency and the gender gap: Trends in violence and alcohol offending across multiple sources of evidence. In S. Miller, L.D. Leve, & P.K. Kerig (Eds.), *Delinquent Girls: Contexts, Relationships, and Adaptations* (pp. 3–24). New York, NY: Springer.

Sotirovic, M. (2006). How individuals explain social problems: The influences of media use. *Journal of Communication*, 53(1), 122–137.

St. Cloud Times. (2004, January 29) Theron humanizes 'Monster' character. St. Cloud, Minnesota.

Streib, V. (2012). Death penalty for female offenders: January 1, 1973, through December 31, 2011. Accessed via Death Penalty Information Center.

PART 5

Prisoners and Policies

Diane M. Daane

Correctional policy has traditionally been written for men's prisons and tailored to the needs of male inmates. As the number of women incarcerated in correctional facilities began to increase, there was finally recognition that women's prisons and female inmates have different issues and needs than their male counterparts. Change has been slow and significant modifications are still needed, in part because women still make up a small minority of the United States jail and prison population. Public policy, including prison policy, is often driven by public interest. Women in prison have not had the interest or attention of the public, but that may be changing. *Orange is the New Black* (*OITNB*) has drawn attention to the plight of female inmates and, though fictional and not a completely accurate portrayal of women's prisons or women in prison, has the potential to educate the public and influence changes to correctional policy that address the needs of this growing population.

Policy regulates, or at least tries to regulate, all aspects of life in prison. Prison movies and television shows generally focus on the hardships of prison life, and are told from the perspective of an inmate, although other inmates are often portrayed as violent and menacing. The entertainment industry pays little attention, if any, to rehabilitative programs or prison policy other than security policy. *OITNB* is no different in this regard, but there is a new twist in that the focus is on women in prison rather than men. The difficulties of living in prison are numerous and make compelling viewing. Perhaps the classic description of the pains of imprisonment written by sociologist Gresham Sykes best explains the deprivations experienced by inmates that have widespread appeal to audiences. Sykes described the difficulty of separation from family, the lack of personal property, the inability to continue sexual relationships, a sense of loss of security, loss of freedom, and living by rules that govern almost all aspects of life including what to wear, what to eat, and when to sleep. These hardships offer the entertainment industry compelling drama to entice viewers.

In Part 5 of this book, the authors address prison policy as it relates to inmates in segregation and the need for educational programming. *OITNB* does depict women in segregation and the consequences of this isolation as well as the impact of the mere threat of being placed in solitary confinement. It is not surprising that the show depicts solitary confinement. It reaches the audience at an emotional level because the deplorable conditions are disturbing. It is not uncommon for "lock-up" to be depicted in prison movies and television programs because of the ability to engage the audience. However, educational programs are rarely mentioned in *OITNB*. Educational programs are not as likely to captivate the show's audience the way grittier topics like solitary confinement do. Miltonette Craig provides information on the importance of educational programming in prisons in an effort to fill the void left by the show.

In "The Prison within the Prison: Solitary Confinement in *Orange is the New Black*," Edith Kinney concludes that despite creative license, *OITNB* raises awareness about the use, abuse, and risks of solitary confinement, and provides the opportunity for celebrity activism to influence a social movement that can bring about needed correctional reform. Kinney briefly addresses the inadequacies of law and policy regulating the use of segregation in correctional institutions and highlights practices by some prison staff members who use segregation for corrupt and vindictive purposes. Since a large percentage of women in prison have been physically, emotionally, or sexually abused, and because a large percentage of women in prison were the primary or sole caregiver for their children before incarceration, segregation and the accompanying loss of visitation and communication privileges has a profound effect on the women. The effects of isolation, particularly in harsh conditions for an extended period of time, can have physical, psychological, and emotional consequences for inmates. These effects of isolation can also have a negative impact on the inmates' families and family ties, thus potentially creating problems within the institution and obstacles for the women's successful reintegration back into the community upon release.

Kinney identifies the reasons inmates in *OITNB* are placed in segregation, referred to as secured housing units (SHU). It should be noted that in real-life practice, SHU may also be used as protective custody for other situations where an inmate needs protection from other inmates. Kinney argues that the show exposes the use of solitary confinement as being at odds with law and policy and as an arbitrary, corrupt, and devoid of due process means to control and punish inmates who do not conform with the demands of correctional officers.

In "Education behind Bars: What *Orange is the New Black* Neglects" Craig concludes that while *OITNB* has explored many social justice issues for female inmates, it has not dealt with the need for literacy and education programs in women's correctional institutions. Craig argues that educational programs in correctional settings are an essential part of rehabilitative programming designed to aid prisoner reintegration and reduce recidivism, in part because incarcerated offenders are less educated than the general population. Correctional education programs reduce the risk of recidivism by improving literacy, communication skills, job skills, and self-esteem. The positive results of education increase the likelihood of finding and maintaining employment and decrease the likelihood of reoffending. Craig also notes the difficulty of reintegrating back into society, especially for those returning to the community with little social support and an obligation to care for and support children. These issues are reflected by the offender population depicted in *OITNB* since female inmates are more likely than male inmates to have responsibility for minor children and many are drug offenders.

While all federal correctional facilities have some form of educational programs, *OITNB* does not reflect that reality. There are only limited references to education and they are shown for the first time during Season 4. Craig suggests *OITNB* does not depict educational programs because they are less exciting to audiences and because prominent characters in the show have an educational level well beyond the level of most actual prisoners. Craig argues that failure to include scenes depicting education is a major shortcoming of the series and that *OITNB* misses an opportunity to inform viewers, particularly when it comes to educational programs tailored specifically for women.

Kinney and Craig analyze two important issues and the corresponding policies that affect women in prison namely, correctional policy as it relates to solitary confinement and educational programs. Unfortunately, *OITNB* has only a limited portrayal of educational policies. While the fictional nature and creative license of the show must not be overlooked, *OITNB* can bring awareness about the issues and needs of women in prison and the policies that control their lives and access to programs.

Reference

Sykes, G. M. (1958). *The Society of Captives: A Study of a Maximum Security Prison*. Princeton, NJ: Princeton University Press.

13

THE PRISON WITHIN THE PRISON

Solitary Confinement in *Orange is the New Black*

Edith Kinney

The original Netflix series *Orange is the New Black* (*OITNB*) has played a remarkable role in raising public awareness about dysfunction in our criminal justice and prison systems. The show challenges conventional wisdom and Law and Order oriented media representations of the prison system that sensationalize and over-simplify crime and punishment. *OITNB* offers a unique exploration of what criminologist and sociologist Gresham Sykes refers to as the "pains of imprison-ment" for women prisoners as well as their loved ones. This chapter examines *OITNB*'s portrayal of solitary confinement, and how the series serves as a platform for awareness-raising and celebrity activism against the practice.

OITNB is based on the memoir of Piper Chapman, a White, blonde, privileged women serving fifteen months in federal prison. Piper's fish-out-of-water story serves as a "Trojan horse," entertaining the audience while educating them about the injustices of mass incarceration and inviting viewers to identify with impri-soned people. The show's diverse cast and flashbacks to complicated life histories, families, children, lovers, and traumas humanize incarcerated women, under-scoring the importance of community and social connection to survive life inside and outside the system.

OITNB's stories of imprisoned women expose poor prison conditions and abusive practices common in correctional facilities across the United States, including solitary confinement. Throughout the first four seasons of *OITNB*, multiple characters are sent to the "Hole" – isolation in solitary confinement in the SHU ("secure housing unit"). Prisoners in the SHU are locked in small, cramped cells "23/7," in some cases for decades, deprived of opportunities for social contact, education, programming, and time outdoors.

Challenging public understandings of solitary confinement as a punishment reserved for the "worst of the worst," *OITNB* brings viewers through the prison gates and into "the Hole," portraying solitary confinement as a torturous form of punishment misused in American prisons. The plot of *OITNB* exposes the multitude of reasons that individuals may be sent to the SHU, many of which have little to do with prison security. Correctional facilities use solitary confinement for a variety of reasons: as punishment for violence against staff or other inmates; as discipline for both major and minor infractions; to "treat" and control mentally ill inmates; and to isolate individuals in "protective custody," as is the case for many transgender prisoners according to researchers Jennifer Sumner and Lori Sexton.

Whether for punishment, protection, or prison management, the threat of solitary confinement looms large throughout the *OITNB* series. Symbolizing the prison within the prison, the portrayal of SHU in *OITNB* viscerally represents the traumatizing mental, physical, and emotional effects of isolation and its mis/ use by prison officials. The show further reveals the negative impact of solitary on the families and loved ones of inmates in isolation when visitation and/or communication is prohibited. Finally, *OITNB* also reflects how gender, sexual orientation, and mental health interface with SHU as a form of punishment, protection, and power within women's prisons. *OITNB* reveals the diverse and often arbitrary reasons prisoners are sent to solitary, and the Kafkaesque lack of due process that limits prisoners' ability to challenge their detention. This chapter examines how *OITNB* represents the manifold functions of solitary confinement as a tool of punishment, "protection" for vulnerable inmates, and prison order. Drawing on critical criminology and socio-legal studies, the following sections explore the unique role of *OITNB* as both a tool to raise public awareness about the prison system and a vehicle for celebrity activism regarding prison and criminal justice reform.

Solitary Confinement in Law, Policy, Practice, and Perception

> Solitary confinement is a prison within a prison. But unlike the hivelike communities of people that exist behind prison walls, which have conflicts but also opportunities for redemption, 24-hour lockdown leaves you completely alone in a six-by-eight-foot cell for weeks, sometimes months and even years. Here, the terror and the lasting damage of incarceration may be increased a thousand-fold. This is unproductive for individuals, the institutions and the outside communities, to which the vast majority of prisoners will return.
>
> *(Congressional testimony of* OITNB *author Piper Kerman)*

Solitary confinement was first employed in U.S. prisons over two centuries ago; "separate and silent" isolation was a "penal experiment" intended to "prevent moral contagion" and increase penitence to reform prisoners say criminologist K. Alexa Reiter and legal scholar Keramet Koenig (2015). By 1890, the U.S. Supreme Court decision *In re Medley*, 134 U.S. 160, 168 (1890) observed of solitary confinement that

[a] considerable number of the prisoners fell, after even a short confinement, into a semi-fatuous condition, from which it was next to impossible to arouse them, and others became violently insane, others, still, committed suicide, while those who stood the ordeal better were not generally reformed, and in most cases did not recover sufficient mental activity to be of any subsequent service to the community.

Despite the U.S. Supreme Court's early recognition of the harmful effects of solitary, no court has held the practice to be *per se* unconstitutional, and its use has evolved to serve a variety of institutional purposes in the era of mass incarceration. The "supermax" facilities designed in the late 1980s to isolate the "worst of the worst" prisoners were architecturally designed, according to Jewkes (2015, pp. 20–21) to "instill total psychic and bodily control over prisoners designated 'threatening', 'non-compliant', or 'high-risk'" through "both sensory deprivation and sensory overload."

Solitary confinement is defined as the physical and social isolation of individuals who are confined to their cells for more than 22 hours a day. Though isolation for over fifteen days in solitary confinement is considered torture under international law, some individuals in the U.S. have been held in solitary for years to decades. In response to international criticism, the U.S. government's recent periodic report to the UN Committee Against Torture (2014) claims that there is "no systematic use of solitary confinement in the United States," despite evidence of the "extensive use of solitary confinement and other forms of isolation in United States prisons, jails and other detention cent[er]s, for purposes of punishment, discipline and protection, as well as for health-related reasons.

Despite the euphemistic designations of "secured housing units" (SHU), "administrative segregation," and even "protective custody," solitary confinement is practiced in U.S. correctional and detention facilities and adopts a variety of forms. This extreme punishment is not reserved for the "worst of the worst" violent criminals in state and federal prisons; it is also used in local jails to punish, isolate, and/or "protect" some pre-trial detainees, juveniles, transgender individuals, mentally ill people. Indeed, recent studies surveying the Federal Bureau of Prisons and 45 states show that over 67,400 individuals were subjected to solitary confinement in U.S. facilities in 2016; this estimate does not include those isolated in jails, juvenile, military, or immigration facilities, meaning that approximately 100,000 people are held in isolation for months to years in the U.S. according to the Association of State Correctional Administrators and the Liman Center for Public Interest Law.

Legal challenges to solitary confinement are grounded in the Eighth Amendment prohibitions against cruel and unusual punishment and Fourteenth Amendment due process guarantees. Two factors must be satisfied to establish an Eighth Amendment violation: first, the condition or action complained of must be "objectively sufficiently serious," and second, prison officials must be "deliberately indifferent" to the harm or injury caused by the condition or action (*Farmer v. Brennan*, 511 U.S. 825, 834 (1994)). The high legal standard of "deliberate indifference," courts' deference to correctional officials, and the practical challenges prisoners face in documenting abuse or inhumane conditions limits formal legal oversight of solitary. A byzantine complaint and grievance process make it difficult for inmates to challenge their placement in SHU, or to be released from SHU once isolated there say Kitty Calavita and Valerie Jenness, authors of *Appealing to Justice: Prisoner grievances, rights, and carceral logic*. Litigation regarding solitary confinement addresses a variety of violations including excessive use of force, mistreatment, and constitutionally inadequate physical and mental health care. Although some courts have held that the use of solitary in SHU was unconstitutional as applied to particular inmates, such as those with pre-existing mental health conditions, solitary itself has survived legal challenges, and until recently, few laws regulated or prohibited the practice.

Solitary confinement is uniquely harmful for incarcerated women. As the *Orange is the New Black* author, Piper Kerman, explained in her Congressional testimony, women make up the fastest growing population in the criminal justice system, and over 60% are imprisoned for nonviolent offenses. Many are victims of sexual abuse and/or intimate partner violence before incarceration; many suffer physical or sexual abuse while incarcerated; and nearly three out of four incarcerated women are diagnosed with mental illness according to Bureau of Justice statisticians Doris James and Lauren Glaze. These experiences can lead to what Piper Kerman refers to as "cycles of infractions and punishment" as women struggle to cope with prison life and conform behavior to prison rules.

Long-term isolation is also used to "protect" prisoners, including juveniles and transgender individuals, who are vulnerable to exploitation and abuse by other inmates. However, solitary can be used in discriminatory ways. Research by the Silvia Rivera Law Project, a transgender rights organization, and interviews with trans people in both men's and women's prisons found that trans prisoners are "subjected to disproportionate isolation and solitary confinement where they experience regular physical and sexual assault, harassment, and the denial of food and urgent medical services by correctional officers" for common offenses as well as those specifically related to gender expression (SRLP 2007, p. 22).

The stories of imprisoned women in *OITNB* illustrate the diverse ways in which solitary impacts the prison experience. Challenging conventional portrayals of prison that situate the viewer as the potential victim of crime, focusing on prisoners as dangerous criminals, *OITNB* instead humanizes "convicts" as mothers, spouses, friends, or lovers, enabling viewers to sympathize with the complex reasons women are incarcerated and the injustices they suffer in prison. As such, the narrative structure and perspective of *OITNB* exposes viewers to the sights, sounds, and indignities of imprisonment, making the show an effective advocacy tool to raise public awareness about the injustices of mass incarceration and extreme punishment in our prisons. Although some portrayals of prison life in

OITNB employ artistic license, the sights, sounds, and injustices of the SHU depicted in *OITNB* reflect the realities for many incarcerated people held in "the Hole." The next section analyzes the representation of "the prison within the prison" in *OITNB*.

Solitary Confinement in *Orange is the New Black*

Solitary confinement plays a central, organizing role in the plot of *OITNB* over the first four seasons of the series. The specter of solitary confinement is woven throughout *OITNB*, taking the viewer through the prison gates, past the overcrowded dormitories of general population, and into the extreme isolation of the SHU. The show's increasingly critical portrayal of the SHU exposes viewers to both its torturous conditions and the multifaceted uses of solitary confinement as it is practiced in today's correctional facilities.

The following analysis examines *OITNB*'s illustration of the mis/use of solitary confinement in three main ways: solitary as *punishment* for rule infractions or violence against correctional officers or other inmates; solitary as *"protection"* for vulnerable inmates; and solitary as an exercise of *power*, a threatened punishment that can be leveraged by both correctional officials (COs) and inmates for control and retaliation in the prison.

In *OITNB*'s first episode, Piper is warned about the extreme punishment of solitary confinement in the SHU. Characters sent there disappear for several episodes, sometimes for trivial or nonexistent violations of prison rules; those who emerge are traumatized, while others are held in indefinite isolation. To be sure, the SHU depicted in *OITNB* reflects the extreme conditions of solitary confinement: montages depict women suffering the terror of isolation in cramped, windowless, dirty concrete cells. Indifferent correctional officers ignore cries for help, and the viewer is overwhelmed with the screams of tortured inmates denied food, clothing, medical treatment, sleep, and outside communication. But where *OITNB* is unique is that it also reveals the varied uses of solitary confinement in contemporary prisons beyond punishment for the "worst of the worst" prisoners.

The disciplinary function of solitary confinement for cases of actual violence against correctional officers or other prisoners is juxtaposed with warnings that correctional officers may send inmates to SHU on a whim, like having extra stamps or mouthing off contends Human Rights Watch. Correctional officials can exercise their discretion arbitrarily to send prisoners to SHU for minor rule violations, like having an extra blanket or wearing makeup. Solitary is also used as a tool for prison management, for example, placing transgender individuals in solitary to "protect" them say scholars Jennifer Sumner and Lori Sexton. Correctional officials also leverage the threat of SHU as a mechanism of control, for example, by threatening to place a prisoner in solitary to dissuade reporting and cover up misconduct, such as sexual assault. Finally, the risk of isolation in SHU for infractions or fighting can also create a powerful tool that prisoners may use to threaten rivals, to settle disputes, or to induce conformity with prison hierarchies and informal codes of conduct among imprisoned people.

Several stories of SHU solitary confinement in *OITNB* illustrate the use of solitary as a punishment for violence and rule infractions. Piper – and the viewer – soon realize the potentially dire consequences of solitary confinement for unintentional violations of prison rules or resisting the authority of COs. When Piper is assigned to work in the electrical shop, the alcoholic lackadaisical correctional officer, Luschek, introduces the new inmates to their work, and the harsh consequences for even simple mistakes: "Lose a tool, go to SHU." When a screwdriver is discovered missing at the end of the day due to Luschek's incompetent supervision, all the women are threatened with SHU. Before ordering a search, lead correctional officer Caputo warns them that a screwdriver is considered a deadly weapon, possession of which risks automatic solitary and five years added to their sentence.

When none of the women admit to taking the tool, Luschek blames one prisoner, Watson, for improperly organizing the tools. Watson adamantly refuses to be patted-down by the male correctional officer, demanding a female officer instead: "I don't know about these other bitches, but no man guard is patting me down and copping a feel." In response, a CO ominously replies, "Of course, as is your right. [Officer], take her down to SHU – let her wait there until we can find a female officer to conduct a thorough, *thorough* search." As Watson is dragged away, Caputo asks, "Anyone else have a problem with a male officer? If you cooperate, it tells me you have nothing to hide." The other women, including Piper, fearfully submit to the search, which an abusive male correctional officer nicknamed "Pornstache" uses as an opportunity to grope their breasts and bodies. *OITNB* viewers learn that SHU is so harsh that it may lead prisoners to suffer humiliating searches that violate their rights, including strip and body cavity searches, and that prisoners who try to enforce their rights or challenge COs' power may be sent to isolation for resisting authority.

Later, Piper discovers she inadvertently put the screwdriver in her sweatshirt pocket. Worried for Watson as well as herself, Piper consults a woman recently released from the SHU after spending weeks there for telling a CO to "kiss her ass." Piper asks if SHU was "really that bad." Dead-eyed, the woman responds, "It's just like the Hamptons, only fuckin' horrible…A lady next door to me in there ate a rat. A *live* rat. Because it bit her, she bit it back. And back, and back, and…." The traumatizing psychological effects of solitary confinement are evident when Watson is released from SHU after two weeks: she is antisocial and has difficulties sleeping and interacting with others.

The power of COs to send individuals to solitary confinement for arbitrary infractions at their discretion is further evidenced by Piper's own first exposure to SHU. Although the real Piper Kerman was never sent to solitary confinement, *OITNB*'s protagonist brings the viewer inside the SHU. While Piper's homophobic counselor Officer Healy initially cautioned Piper to "protect" her from predatory lesbians, he became enraged and vindictive after learning of Piper's history with women. When Piper's enemy informs Healy that Piper and another woman are "lesbianing together" by dancing, he flies into a rage: "Think it's appropriate to violate your fellow inmate?…That looked like attempted rape to me," he tells another correctional officer, "Take her to SHU!" When Piper protests, "You can't do that!" and the correctional officer agrees, Healy pulls rank and orders, "You put her in the goddamn Box, or I will…write you up, too."

Piper's experience in SHU gives the viewer a first-person perspective on the terrifying conditions of indefinite, long-term solitary confinement. As a correctional officer walks Piper, shackled, into the SHU, the audience glimpses flashes of haunted, screaming women locked in concrete boxes. When Piper is thrown in a cell, she fearfully asks, "How long am I gonna be in here?" the correctional officer gruffly responds, "Till we let you out," slamming the cell door shut. Feces appears to be smeared on the wall, fingernail scratches mark the floor and walls, and "kill me now" is etched on the cell door. The only human contact she has is when the correctional officer wordlessly shoves a tray of moldy baloney through a small slot on the door, and later a "nutraloaf" common to SHU units in real prisons, providing the bare minimum of calories and nutrients required to sustain prisoners, and intended to punish those in solitary confinement with further deprivation.

Not only does Piper's time in SHU reveal the physical deprivations of solitary, it also illustrates the traumatizing psychological effects of even short periods of isolation. In less than 48 hours in the SHU, Piper suffers intense fear, disorientation, and mental distress, alternatively pacing and screaming and huddling in the fetal position. As Piper begins to break down, she hears a disembodied voice:

You can rage, but they always win. They're the ones with the keys.
PIPER: How long have you been down here?
I lost track. I dunno, nine months? A year?
PIPER: A year? That's insane.
…They keep the lights on so you lose all sense of time. It's not living. I mean, yeah, you're breathing, but you ain't no person no more. It's bad….[Y]ou start to see shit that ain't there, you start to hear voices. They keep you here until they break you.

When Healy finally checks on Piper, he tells her he sent her to SHU for a "timeout" because she was dancing with another female inmate "provocatively. Sexually. *Gay* sexually!," and he was protecting her from "sick" lesbians. Piper protests that it is illegal for Healy to put her in SHU for this reason, and angrily rejects Healy in a defiant screaming rant, mocking his advances and homophobia. However, facing the terrifying prospect of indefinite, long-term confinement, she soon pledges to behave and follow Healy's orders if she is ever let out.

As in real prisons, correctional officers must document infraction/s to place individuals in SHU. Piper is released from solitary after less than 48 hours when an administrator reviews Healy's rash decision to send her to SHU and discovers Piper's fiancé has been calling prison authorities and threatening lawsuits:

> I don't even know what the hell she's doing in seg in the first place! Christ, even Mendez said it was uncalled for – and that guy lives to throw people in the Box....I don't have the write-ups or paperwork to support it. She got under your skin – this is personal. These liberal, wealthy offenders, they're connected. And if we review this, the paper trail is going to be sweaty.

While Piper is released in *OITNB*, the rapid review and processing of her case is atypical for most individuals placed in SHU. Not only is it rare for SHU placements or grievances to be so quickly reviewed by superiors, it is unlikely that most prisoners have allies like Piper's on the outside with ready access to resources, lawyers, and advocacy organizations with the ability to threaten public relations problems for prison administrators by drawing attention to mistreatment or abuse. These resources are unavailable to the vast majority of incarcerated women and their families, particularly given that the median annual income of imprisoned women is less than $14,000 according to Prison Policy Initiative researchers Bernadette Rabuy and Daniel Kopf. This limitation hinders efforts to identify and expose mistreatment in solitary confinement, and to galvanize campaigns for reform. This is especially problematic for those prisoners in long-term, indefinite isolation in solitary, as is the case for those who assault others – even in self-defense.

The punishment of solitary is particularly harrowing when there is no foreseeable end to isolation. Solitary is used to punish acts of violence against both COs and other prisoners, even those committed in self-defense. At the end of Season 1, Piper is forced to fight another inmate who threatened her with a shiv. After Healy refuses to intervene and leaves the two to fight it out, Piper defends herself, violently and repeatedly punching the woman who attacked her. The first season ends as if Piper has knocked the viewer, in the perspective of Piper's combatant, unconscious. The cliffhanger left fans who had "binge-watched" the series with the dread of knowing that Piper was headed to SHU – perhaps indefinitely, if she had killed her attacker. As *OITNB* viewers waited to learn her fate, the 11 months that passed before the next season's release created a sense of the slow passage of time for those in solitary.

The second season of *OITNB* opens in a SHU cell: Piper is finger-painting a bird on the cell wall with her breakfast. After a few weeks isolated in a cell the size of a parking spot, Piper has deteriorated mentally: she hears voices, loses time, and struggles to retain her grasp on reality, much like prisoners isolated in real solitary units. Unlike some *OITNB* characters who are sent to SHU never to return, like her roommate who attacked a correctional officer, Piper was isolated for 30 days for the fight. Nevertheless, Piper's hostility, fear, and withdrawn nature as she attempts to reenter general population and interact with others reflects many of the harmful mental effects of solitary confinement, difficulties that can prime individuals to commit other violations and end up back in SHU.

A second major function of solitary in *OITNB* is the use of isolation to "protect" individuals vulnerable to abuse by other prisoners. Viewers learn that simply "following the rules" in prison may not be sufficient to avoid being sent to solitary, given the power, discretion, and lack of accountability for correctional officials and the priorities of prison administrators. The story of transwoman Sophia Burset in *OITNB* illustrates the Kafkaesque nature of using solitary confinement as "protective" segregation – especially for trans prisoners – and becomes a central issue in the later seasons of the show.

The potential for violence against trans prisoners and prison administrators' legal duties to ensure their security makes trans people uniquely vulnerable to isolation in prison. In Season 3 of *OITNB*, Sophia is attacked by a group of women who accuse her of pretending to be a transwoman so she would be placed in women's prison; they assault Sophia, trying to grab her genitals to determine whether she was "really" a woman. Though one CO observes the fight, she does not intervene, and runs away to find a superior.

Although Sophia was the victim of an attack and potential hate crime, prison administrators direct the correctional officers to move Sophia to solitary because isolation is necessary for her safety and institutional order: "We can't weed out all the bullies – it's for her own protection." Sophia adamantly declines this protection, to no avail; the potential liability to the prison if she is attacked again is too great a risk for administrators. Isolated, unable to contact her wife or prison administrators, denied her medications and suffering withdrawal, Sophia fears she has been forgotten in SHU. Sophia refuses to eat, floods her cell, and lights her mattress on fire in her attempts to gain the attention of authorities. Like many inmates in solitary, her despair in solitary drives her to self-harm. When the Warden returns to find that the correctional officers left her wet and freezing in the flooded cell, the Warden finally orders them to move her to a dry cell: "This isn't Guantánamo. Get her a fucking shirt."

Sophia's story reflects the logics of solitary as protection, and her plight in SHU is a central plotline of Season 4. As reflected by the debates between prison administrators in *OITNB*, placing trans individuals in solitary confinement can serve as a cost- and liability-management strategy. Incarcerated trans people are commonly placed in isolation in "protective custody" under the auspices of ensuring their safety and preventing violence against them. This simultaneously supports the interests of prison administrators anxious to avoid potentially costly lawsuits from trans people and their advocates for failure to protect them under the Prison Rape Elimination Act (PREA) and other laws.

While some prison administrators were sympathetic to Sophia's plight and worried about the potential litigation in the long term, *OITNB* exposes how the short-term economic interests of the private prison industry can lead to a tolerance of poor conditions and abusive practices. When the Warden appeals to the private prison company's CEO to allow Sophia's release from SHU, he argues "What about when she gets out? Think about the long term," to which the CEO replies, "Nobody cares about the long term…the important thing is that we [succeed] this quarter…so that everyone can collect their bonuses." The extreme measures to which Sophia must resort to gain the attention of prison officials and the lack of care she received illustrates how difficult it can be for trans people in solitary to access needed medical and mental health care or legal representation, even when they are isolated for their own "protection."

Finally, the third function of solitary in *OITNB* shows how the threat of SHU can operate as an instrument of power, as fear of isolation makes the SHU a powerful disciplinary force for both formal and informal control within the prison. Several storylines in *OITNB* reveal how corrupt or indifferent correctional officers can selectively enforce prison regulations – backed by the threat of SHU – to control and coerce prisoners, to regulate prison economies, and to retaliate against those who may report misconduct. For example, one corrupt CO, "Pornstache," threatened to send prisoners to the SHU if they did not help him smuggle or sell drugs in prison, and he sexually abuses prisoners with impunity. Another inmate is raped by a CO, but is reluctant to report the abuse for fear of punishment and isolation.

As the most extreme punishment in the prison, the penalty of SHU also creates opportunities for inmates to leverage the threat of solitary against other inmates by inciting violence or reporting illicit behavior or rule violations. Exposing other inmates to SHU may be used as a tool of informal control, to settle disputes, or to punish rivals, and *OITNB* provides several examples of this tactic. For example, one woman set up her ex-girlfriend, arranging for another inmate to attack her. Because she had been growing out her fingernails in anticipation of her release, she mauled the girl and "got two more years down the hill" in SHU. Other inmates can also subject rivals to SHU, as when Piper snitched on an inmate she had befriended after finding out she had stolen Piper's money, or when Piper's enemy informed COs of her unauthorized "lesbian activity." The wide range of reasons that individuals might be sent to SHU, then, creates a threat of punishment that can be manipulated by correctional officers and prisoners alike for diverse ends, with little recourse for those sent to isolation.

In sum, *OITNB*'s portrayal of the SHU illustrates many of the ways in which solitary confinement is used and abused in U.S. correctional facilities. By exposing rights violations through the experiences of its imprisoned characters, *OITNB* raises public awareness about solitary, while also creating a platform for celebrity activism to campaign for reforms.

Mobilizing Reform by Exposing Rights Violations: Law and Society Lessons from *OITNB*

The immense popularity of *OITNB*, its accessibility to a wide range of people (Netflix subscribers), and the entertaining "fish-out-of-water" narrative of prison life make the show a fascinating case study for scholars of Law and Society and cultural criminologists. *OITNB* reveals how popular media representations of crime and punishment can create a platform to educate viewers about the pains of imprisonment while mobilizing public awareness of and support for prison reform efforts. The "mainstreaming" of prison reform movements into popular culture through *OITNB* reveals several lessons for scholars and advocates regarding the mutually constitutive relationship between law, popular culture, and social change.

Popular culture plays an important role in shaping public understandings of crime and the criminal justice system. Movies and television shows about crime and punishment not only identify victims and villains, they can also raise awareness about social issues and mobilize campaigns for criminal justice reforms, like campaigns to assist victims of human trafficking punished for prostitution offenses. Challenging stereotypes about incarcerated people and highlighting the discriminatory, disproportionate effects of mass incarceration on racial minorities, the prison "dramedy" *OITNB* illustrates how entertainment media can contribute to public awareness campaigns and celebrity activism addressing the injustices of mass incarceration. One key reform advanced both within the *OITNB* series and in celebrity advocacy building on the show's success is the need to reform the use of solitary confinement.

OITNB's portrayal of solitary confinement through several women's stories exposes the gap between "law on the books" and "law in action" in the prison context. Despite written prison regulations and a host of laws protecting prisoners' rights, *OITNB* reveals how dynamics of race, trans- and homophobia, corruption, drug dealing, and sex between COs and inmates shapes the enforcement and meaning of law in action. This gap is most evident when *OITNB* illustrates prison officials' discretionary power to send inmates to SHU with minimal accountability or due process for seemingly trivial reasons unrelated to prison security. Litigation on behalf of individuals in solitary reveals the continued gap between legal protections on the books and current prison practices, as reformers push to ensure that prisoners have the right to adequate food, sleep, and healthcare; that mentally ill prisoners are not isolated and can access constitutionally adequate care in prisons; and challenges to prison regulations that condemn individuals to indefinite, long-term solitary confinement on the basis of vaguely identified gang affiliations.

The popularity of *OITNB* and the media attention commanded by actors in the show reveal how influential celebrities and popular media can be in shaping public discussions about crime and corrections. *OITNB* mainstreamed many key themes in prisoners' rights and prison reform movements, illustrating the lived impact of mass incarceration: overcrowded, deteriorating, and inhumane prison conditions, discrimination and abuse against queer prisoners, inadequate programming and mental health services, prison privatization and profiteering, and the limited accountability of correctional officials for harms suffered by those under their care. As the women in *OITNB* suffer not only the "pains of imprisonment" but also the injustices of imprisonment in an era of mass incarceration, the show both informs and challenges public understandings of law, punishment, and due process in our correctional systems.

For example, in 2014, Piper Kerman testified in a hearing on "Reassessing Solitary Confinement: The Human Rights, Fiscal, and Public Safety Consequences" before the Senate Judiciary Subcommittee on the Constitution, Civil Rights, and Human Rights. Although Kerman herself did not spend time in solitary during her prison experience, fear of the SHU was common amongst prisoners in general. Kerman's testimony emphasized the traumatizing mental effects of solitary, its negative impact on prisoners and their children when visitation is revoked, and how "solitary is…misused as a threat to intimidate and silence women who are being sexually abused by staff.…The terrible threat of isolation makes women afraid to report abuse and serves as a powerful disincentive to ask for help or justice." Piper Kerman's testimony included references to case law, prison policy, and recent studies of the effects of solitary on inmates, and quoted extensively from individuals who shared their experiences of solitary confinement, including the narrative of one woman who described the continuing trauma she suffers from spending a year of her six-year sentence in the SHU:

When you have no one to talk to inside a grey, dingy cell with its blacked-out window, you start talking to yourself, then you think your inner self at least deserves an answer, so I began answering myself. I asked myself what if I got swallowed into this black hole in my cell and just disappeared. I asked myself if it would be better off for my family if this thorn in their side went away for them so they can truly forget me. The best way I can describe being in this small box when life is going on without you is you are dead and the cell is your coffin. Everything goes on without and around you. But you stay the same…stagnant.

Reformers and advocates have begun to emphasize how the SHU can negatively affect the families and children of people in solitary confinement. Revocations and limitations on visitations impact not only the prisoner, but also her loved ones. Many prisons are sited far away from urban centers, with limited, if any, public transit options, making it difficult and prohibitively costly for families to visit loved ones in prison. Restrictive visitation hours and a host of rules subject visitors to oftentimes humiliating searches, and visits may be cut short or cancelled for no reason. When an inmate is sent to SHU, families are rarely notified. The efforts of both Piper's fiancé and Sophia's wife to locate their loved one and confirm their wellbeing reveal the difficulty of maintaining contact with individuals placed in solitary. It also reflects the key role that family members of incarcerated individuals can play in collecting, disseminating, and generating attention to the conditions in solitary confinement, and the possibilities for reforms when families connect with advocacy organizations, as has been the case in recent efforts by the California Families to Abolish Solitary Confinement.

OITNB has also been instrumental in raising the public and political profile of the transgender rights movement. Sophia Burset's character is played by Laverne Cox, a transwoman who has parlayed her newfound fame into activism to raise public awareness of discrimination and abuse against trans people, particularly trans women in prison. Cox used media interviews about *OITNB* to discuss Sophia's plight in SHU, highlighting how the show demonstrates the realities of transgender prisoners' experiences whereby they are in solitary confinement allegedly as a safety measure for their own protection. Advocacy groups like the Silvia Rivera Law Project investigating the experience of trans individuals in both men's and women's prisons report that they are commonly harassed and subject to "exaggerated punishments" as compared with cis prisoners, as well as "disproportionate isolation and solitary confinement where they experience regular physical and sexual assault, harassment, and the denial of food and urgent medical services by correctional officers" (SRLP, 2007, p. 22). Cox leverages her *OITNB* celebrity and interviews with mainstream media like *People* and *TIME* magazines to raise awareness about the trans community and advocate on behalf of currently incarcerated trans people, for example, by producing *Free CeCe*, a 2016 documentary highlighting the case of an African-American transwoman sent to a men's prison after defending herself from a transphobic attack.

These efforts demonstrate how *OITNB* has raised the profile of prison issues and amplified demands for reform, particularly regarding use of solitary confinement in our prison system. The "binge-worthy" popularity of *OITNB* and the media attention commanded by actors in the show reveal how influential celebrity activism can be in stimulating public discussions about often-controversial issues, such as prisoner's rights and transgender rights. By raising awareness about abuse in prison, humanizing incarcerated people, and mainstreaming critiques of the prison industrial complex, *OITNB* has contributed to changing the conversation about mass incarceration, making prison reform "the new black."

In the years since Kerman's 2014 testimony, prison reform movements have gained momentum, with notable successes in efforts to curb the use of solitary confinement in both federal and state correctional systems. Political pressure for reform is growing in the wake of widespread prisoner hunger strikes, class action lawsuits, and increased media coverage and public awareness of neglect, abuses, and suicides in as well as after solitary confinement. A recent wave of reforms reflects an emerging trend in the U.S. to end the use of extreme isolation in prison through the use of solitary confinement. Several states have begun to reform their approach to solitary confinement, banning solitary for individuals under 21 years of age. Reforms in New York came after the tragic suicide of Kalief Browder, a teenager accused of stealing a backpack who was incarcerated in Rikers Island, often in solitary, for three years without trial. Other states, like California, are reviewing the files of individuals who have been in SHU for over a decade, allowing individuals to rejoin the general population (California Families Against Solitary Confinement, 2016). Finally, many state facilities are reducing reliance on solitary, ending the isolation of minors and mentally ill inmates, adding "step-down" programs to allow long-term SHU inmates to return to the general population; limiting solitary is also reducing the incidence of violence against correctional officers.

In January 2016, President Obama announced a series of executive actions limiting solitary confinement in the federal prison system that aimed to serve as a model for states to revise their own regulation of solitary, including banning solitary confinement for juvenile offenders and prohibiting officials from using solitary confinement to punish prisoners for "low-level infractions." As President Obama asked in his *Washington Post* op-ed describing these reforms, "How can we subject prisoners to unnecessary solitary confinement, knowing its effects, and then expect them to return to our communities as whole people? It doesn't make us safer. It's an affront to our common humanity." The proposed model laws impose limits on the use of solitary as well as length of time an individual can spend in solitary: a limit of 60 days for a first offense, versus the current maximum of 365 days. While still far longer the 15 days tolerated under the unanimously adopted United Nations Standard Minimum Rules for the Treatment of Prisoners, these reforms represent incremental progress in efforts to end long-term isolation and bring the U.S. in line with its international human rights commitments. It remains to be seen whether this momentum of reform will be sustained in the coming years.

Conclusion

OITNB offers teachers, researchers, and the general public an opportunity to reflect on the interplay between social movements, celebrity activism, and criminal justice reform movements in the U.S. By revealing the ways in which our prison system fails to rehabilitate incarcerated people, creates risks for imprisoned people and staff alike, *OITNB* serves as vehicle both to reveal the torture that is solitary confinement and to direct public attention to a wide range of prison and criminal justice reform issues. The popularity of the series has created new opportunities for both the author of *OITNB* and cast members to engage in celebrity activism, amplifying the awareness-raising and potential mobilizing effects of the show. The humanizing effects of *OITNB*'s narrative style, its attention to issues of trauma, discrimination, mental health, and power in prison complicate the conventional wisdom that solitary confinement is a punishment of last resort reserved for the "worst of the worst." *OITNB* exposes the manifold ways in which solitary confinement is deployed to punish, "protect," and exercise disciplinary power over imprisoned women in ways that often have little connection to prison security.

OITNB challenges the traditional positioning of the viewer in crime and prison dramas as the potential *victim of crime*, instead inviting the viewer to identify with the imprisoned "criminals." It is this invitation that has made *OITNB* such a popular series, and that helps the show translate entertainment into advocacy efforts. By showing viewers what happens inside the prison and providing a platform for celebrity activism, *OITNB* illustrates how popular media can generate attention to efforts to reform the use and abuse of solitary confinement in U.S. prisons.

References

Association of State Correctional Administrators and the Liman Center for Public Interest Law. (2016). *Aiming to Reduce Time-in-cell: Reports from Correctional Systems on the Numbers of Prisoners in Restricted Housing and on the Potential of Policy Changes to Bring about Reforms* (Association of State Correctional Administrators (ASCA) and The Arthur Liman Public Interest Program, Yale Law School). New Haven, CT. Retrieved from https://www.law.yale.edu/system/files/area/center/liman/document/aimingtoreducetic.pdf

Calavita, K., & Jenness, V. (2015). *Appealing to Justice: Prisoner Grievances, Rights, and Carceral Logic.* Oakland, CA: University of California Press.

California Families Against Solitary Confinement. (2016, March 31). "Stop the torture" – UN official receives formal complaint from solitary prisoners' family members and advocates. Retrieved from https://prisonerhungerstrikesolidarity.wordpress.com/tag/california-families-against-solitary-confinement-cfasc/

Committee Against Torture. (2014). Concluding observations on the combined third to fifth periodic reports of the United States of America (No. CAT/C/USA/CO/3-5). United Nations.

Human Rights Watch World Report. (2014). *World Report 2014: The United States. Events of 2013.* Retrieved from https://www.hrw.org/world-report/2014/country-chapters/united-states

James, D. J., & Glaze, L. E. (2006). *Mental Health Problems of Prison and Jail Inmates.* Bureau of Justice Statistics.

Jewkes, Y. (2015). Fear suffused hell-holes: The architecture of extreme punishment. In K. Reiter, & A. Koenig (Eds.), *Extreme Punishment: Comparative Studies in Detention, Incarceration and Solitary Confinement* (pp. 14–31). London: Palgrave Macmillan.

Kerman, P. (2014). Reassessing solitary confinement II: The human rights, fiscal, and public safety consequences. Senate Committee on the Judiciary Subcommittee on the Constitution, Civil Rights and Human Rights, Washington, D.C.

Obama, B. (2016, January 25). Why we must rethink solitary confinement. *The Washington Post.* Retrieved from https://www.washingtonpost.com/opinions/barack-obama-why-we-must-rethink-solitary-confinement/2016/01/25/29a361f2-c384-11e5-8965-0607e0e265ce_story.html?tid=a_inl&utm_term=.58f440d59538

Rabuy, B., & Kopf, D. (2015). *Prisons of Poverty: Uncovering the Pre-incarceration Incomes of the Imprisoned.* Prison Policy Initiative. Retrieved from https://www.prisonpolicy.org/reports/income.html

Reiter, K., & Koenig, A. (Eds.). (2015). *Extreme Punishment: Comparative Studies in Detention, Incarceration and Solitary Confinement*. Palgrave. Retrieved from http://www.palgraveconnect.com/doifinder/10.1057/9781137441157

SRLP. (2007). *"It's war in here": A Report on the Treatment of Transgender and Intersex People in New York State Men's Prisons*. New York: The Silvia Rivera Law Project.

Sykes, G. M. (2007). *The Society of Captives: A Study of a Maximum Security Prison* (1st Princeton classic edition). Princeton, NJ: Princeton University Press.

Sumner, J., & Sexton, L. (2016). Same difference: The "dilemma of difference" and the incarceration of transgender prisoners: Incarceration of transgender prisoners. *Law & Social Inquiry*, 41(3), 616–642.

U.S. Supreme Court decision (1890) *In re Medley*, 134 U.S. 160, 168. Retrieved from http://caselaw.findlaw.com/us-supreme-court/134/160.html

14

EDUCATION BEHIND BARS

The Vital Issue that *Orange is the New Black* Neglects

Miltonette Olivia Craig

Introduction: America's Fascination with Glimpses "Behind the Barbed Wire"

For the past few decades, American television has offered viewers the chance to see what (purportedly) goes on inside of our prisons, and such programming is consistently popular. *Oz*, a gritty drama first airing in 1997 and addressing life inside the fictional Oswald State Correctional Facility, received critical acclaim and ran for six seasons on HBO. *Prison Break*, a 2005 series detailing the unjust imprisonment of one brother at the fictional Fox River State Penitentiary and the elaborate escape plan orchestrated by the other, ran for four seasons on Fox and had such a devout fan base that a reboot has recently debuted.

Netflix's *Orange is the New Black* (*OITNB*), first airing in 2013, provides a similar glimpse "behind the barbed wire" of the fictitious Litchfield Penitentiary while focusing on an oft-neglected segment of the U.S. prison population: women. Capitalizing on the success of Piper Kerman's book of the same name, which chronicles her year-long incarceration in the federal prison system, the Netflix series intends to entertain while simultaneously informing viewers about the myriad social justice issues facing female inmates. Like its predecessors, the show has received many accolades and has millions of enthusiasts. As proposed by feminist scholar Jane Caputi (2015), the series has even surpassed other prison-themed television programming with its broader emphasis on race/ethnicity, class, gender, sexuality, and the victim–offender overlap, among other salient issues facing incarcerated women. Suzanne Enck and Megan Morrissey (2015) argue that while the series features characters from traditionally underrepresented segments of society, such as women of color and economically disadvantaged women, a key limitation is that the show often reifies existing stereotypes via its dependence on narration through the lenses of its White, educated, upper-class protagonist.

Although *OITNB* has nobly tackled many important topics, the series has yet to substantially highlight the issues of education and literacy (or lack thereof) among the female prison population. This chapter attempts to fill that void by discussing the importance of education within the prison system as well as its relationship to crime and re-offending.

The "Incarceration Boom": America's Dramatic Increase in Imprisonment

The wide-ranging appeal of television narratives about the prison experience is undoubtedly a consequence of America's alarming rise in the number of imprisoned individuals. Due to changes in criminal justice policies and practices (e.g., tough-on-crime era initiatives), criminological scholars have examined an estimated fivefold increase in the incarceration rate within the past forty years. In terms of raw numbers, this signifies that approximately 1.5 million people are confined within American prisons at the state and federal levels. Another 800,000 people are detained within jails while they await trial, await sentencing, or serve short-term incarcerative sentences of less than one year. As criminologist Travis Pratt notes, "[o]ur incarcerated population is larger than China's (a nation that dwarfs us in overall population size), and our rate of incarceration is higher than for nations such as South Africa and Iran (nations where one can earn a stint in incarceration for merely holding certain political views)" (2009, p. xiii).

This exponential growth in the American prison population receives (and is deserving of) so much consideration simply because it is in stark contrast to our nation's prior imprisonment trends. Policy researchers Alfred Blumstein and Allen Beck noted that between 1925 and 1975 the U.S. incarceration rate held steady with 110 sentenced prisoners for every 100,000 U.S. residents, a historical pattern referred to as the "theory of the stability of punishment" (1999). However, at the height of mass incarceration (circa 2008), the U.S. had an imprisonment rate of 750 per 100,000. The increase in the number of incarcerated individuals is also notable because it has not been uniform across crime types or demographics.

The dominant factor for overall population growth has been arrests for drug offending. Researchers from the U.S. Bureau of Justice Statistics note that such offenders comprise more than 50 percent of the federal prison population and over 15 percent of state prison populations. These figures were even higher during the mid-1990s; at that time, drug offenders constituted 60 percent of the federal prison population and 23 percent of state prison populations (Carson, 2015). Additionally, the impact of America's "War on Drugs" was experienced most intensely by historically marginalized groups. Scholars such as Michelle Alexander (2010) as well as Stephanie Bush-Baskette and Vivian Smith (2012) discuss how incarceration rates based on drug offenses rose much faster for women and minorities, particularly African Americans and the socially–economically disadvantaged. Once incarceration becomes an "expected" event in the life course for particular groups – for instance, the research of criminologist Elaine Doherty and colleagues (2015) indicates that an estimated 1 in 18 African American women and 1 in 3 African American men will be imprisoned during their lifetime – the phenomenon indeed warrants continued attention by both academics and popular culture.

Mass Incarceration's Unavoidable Byproduct: Prisoner Reentry

Though death penalty and life-without-parole cases often generate the leading news headlines, prisoners serving such interminable sentences constitute a small portion of the U.S. incarcerated population. Most imprisoned individuals, approximately 95 percent, will eventually be released. Generally, prison inmates are either released discretionarily via parole – early release under a period of supervision, which is contingent upon adhering to certain conditions – or mandatorily as a result of "maxing out" – serving the entire sentence and often having no post-release supervision. In other instances, prisoners may be released due to overcrowding. (See also the U.S. Supreme Court decision in *Brown v. Plata* related to California's prison overcrowding crisis and legal scholar Jonathan Simon's analysis of the ruling.) As estimated by statisticians and sociologists, approximately 700,000 individuals leave prison every year. What's more is that each and every ex-prisoner is expected to successfully reintegrate back into her/his community despite the considerable obstacles they face.

The process of societal reintegration is known as prisoner reentry, and it entails a complex transition and reacclimatization to the various norms and expectations of "free" society. Reentry is difficult for formerly incarcerated individuals for several reasons. One reason relates to their physical/physiological condition post-imprisonment. As criminologists Joan Petersilia (2005) and Jeremy Travis (2005) note in their research, formerly incarcerated individuals often exit the prison environment with a broad range of health complications including substance abuse problems, mental illness, and infectious diseases such as HIV/AIDS, among other conditions.

Another explanation relates to the level of social support that ex-prisoners receive as well as the social obligations that they have post-imprisonment. As scholar Todd Clear (2007) discusses, familial and intimate relationships are strained and frequently deteriorate as a result of incarceration, and many reentering offenders lack the solid social networks necessary for an effective transition. The majority of formerly incarcerated individuals also have some level of caretaking responsibility for their families. For instance, researchers from the U.S. Bureau of Justice Statistics found that approximately 55 percent of men and 65 percent of women in state prisons, as well as 63 percent of all federal prisoners, have minor children (Mumola, 2000). The difficulties associated with parenting obligations during and following imprisonment are even more pronounced for women. Other researchers have reported that over half of the female federal prison population are parents of minor children and most had primary financial responsibility for their children prior to incarceration.

Furthermore, following release, many reentering offenders are subjected to collateral consequences or invisible punishments (e.g., disenfranchisement, professional license revocation, ineligibility for jury service, etc.), which function to exclude formerly incarcerated persons from full civic participation. Moreover, and as noted by Joan Petersilia, these individuals re-enter society with "the added stigma of a prison record and the distrust and fear that it inevitably elicits" (2003, p. 3), which is a formidable obstacle on their path to successful reintegration.

The Prison System's Revolving Door: America's Recidivism Problem

Understanding and addressing the complexities of prisoner reentry are important because of their relationship to post-release reoffending, which is also known as recidivism. One of the principal rationales of formal punishment via imprisonment is to specifically deter most or all individuals from reoffending. Criminologists Ray Paternoster and Alex Piquero explain that specific deterrence is said to occur once offenders who have been exposed to formal punishment "cease offending, commit less serious offenses, or offend at a lower rate because of the fear of some future sanction" (1995, p. 251).

However, punitive justice system policies have not been fruitful toward this aim, as U.S. recidivism rates have remained alarmingly high – even considering that empirical research varies in its measure of recidivism, as researchers utilize any one, or a combination of two or more, of the following officially recorded indicators: rearrest, reconviction, reincarceration, and parole or probation revocation for technical violations. As an example of the disconcertingly elevated re-offending rates, a study by criminologist Richard Rosenfeld and colleagues (2005) indicated that released prisoners' arrest frequencies for violent, property, and drug offenses amount to average annual rates that are between 30 and 45 times higher than those for the general population. In addition, researcher Matthew Durose and colleagues (2014) found that among a cohort of over 400,000 released prisoners, 67.8 percent were rearrested for a new offense within three years, and 76.6 percent were rearrested within five years. Even when using a more conservative methodology, a study conducted by the Pew Center on the States and the Association of State Correctional Administrators found that the three-year recidivism rate was 45.4 percent for prisoners released in 1999 from 33 states, and 43.3 percent for prisoners released in 2004 from 41 states. Although these data indicate stability in national reoffending trends over time, it is nevertheless extremely problematic that at least "four in 10 prisoners [return] to prison with three years of release" (2011, p. 12).

Research has also indicated that recidivism rates are often higher for drug offenders, who comprise the bulk of the federal prison population as well as the offender group to which *OITNB*'s protagonist and other main characters belong. In a study that followed 272,111 offenders released from prison in 1994 (of which more than 88,000 had served sentences for drug offenses), statisticians Patrick Langan and David Levin (2002) found that 66.7 percent of drug offenders were rearrested within three years of release. Additionally, results of a study conducted by criminologists Cassia Spohn and David Holleran indicated that "drug offenders who were sentenced to prison had the highest rate of recidivism and recidivated at the fastest rate" (2002, p. 350).

To its credit, *OITNB* does tackle the issue of recidivism among drug offenders – albeit briefly. Its most poignant example is told through Tasha "Taystee" Jefferson's story. Taystee, a drug offender, was granted parole in Season 1. Unfortunately, she experienced an array of difficulties that prevented a smooth societal reintegration. Taystee was unable to obtain adequate housing, and had no alternative other than to sleep on the floor of a relative's crowded apartment. She was subjected to stringent parole conditions including a nightly curfew, being required to secure a minimum number of job interviews each week (to which she received no call-backs), and frequent meetings with her parole officer. Due to a lack of social support and the general hopelessness she felt toward her daunting responsibilities in "free" society, Taystee returned to Litchfield soon after her release.

What Can Be Done?

As discussed in the preceding sections, America's "incarceration binge" has created a huge influx of offenders returning to their communities, and these individuals are tasked with becoming productive members of society even while facing significant obstacles. Since the reversion to criminal behavior seems virtually inescapable for many formerly incarcerated individuals, sound public and social policy demand the implementation of strategies that will lower the likelihood of recidivism. One such strategy is the expanded use of community supervision (namely, surveillance) to be carried out by parole or probation agents after offenders are released.

Supporters maintain that community supervision diminishes the risk to public safety that formerly incarcerated persons pose because it serves as a necessary "step-down function [and] proactive risk management" approach according to Michael Ostermann and colleagues in their work on different operationalizations of recidivism. Furthermore, Richard Rosenfeld asserts that his research on reoffending supports the expanded use of discretionary parole supervision in the community to reduce the risk to public safety posed by released prisoners – especially property offenders, younger offenders, and those with longer criminal records. In addition, psychologist David Farabee (2005) argues that closer surveillance of released offenders (specifically parolees) via indeterminate community supervision, rather than rehabilitative programs, is more likely to produce reductions in recidivism rates.

The increased use of intensive supervision also has detractors. First, critics contend that too many offenders are forced to return to prison for noncriminal rule infractions – also referred to as "technical violations" (e.g., missed meetings, broken curfews, failed drug tests, etc.) – which impedes and/or halts the reintegration process and further contributes to prison overcrowding problems. For instance, researchers from the U.S. Bureau of Justice Statistics report that nearly 35 percent of state and federal prison admissions in 2012 were due to parole violations rather than new offenses, and other research has demonstrated that recidivism is not lowered for offenders who are confined for a technical violation. The second major argument against intensive supervision is aimed at the effectiveness of this strategy. For example, in their research, scholars Amy Solomon, Vera Kachnowski, and Avinash Bhati (2005) found that offenders under supervision only had minimal increases in post-release performance when compared with those released unconditionally. Furthermore, the results of a study by sociologists Doris MacKenzie and Robert Brame (2001) indicated that the direct effects of supervision intensity on released offenders' involvement in new criminal activities were weak and inconsistent.

In light of the conflicting arguments and mixed empirical findings about the efficacy of intensive post-release supervision and other similar measures – as well as their potential unintended social and economic consequences for returning offenders – many scholars and correctional experts insist that the American criminal justice system should respond to the "*What Can Be Done?*" question by restoring the rehabilitative ideal that was once the prevailing principle of formal punishment. As explained by sociologist Michelle Phelps (2011), in the 1950s and 1960s, America's "correctional philosophy [was] deeply rooted in the idea that prison inmates could be reformed and returned to the free world as law-abiding citizens." Yet, by the 1970s, the criminal justice system experienced a severity-oriented paradigm shift. This dramatic change in the penal landscape is often attributed to a systematic evaluation of rehabilitative programming conducted by researchers Douglas Lipton, Robert Martinson, and Judith Wilks published in 1975 (and its abbreviated version, published a year earlier and referred to as the "*Nothing Works*" article). In this meta-analysis, the authors concluded that the rehabilitative programming then in existence was not effective at reducing recidivism. The movement away from rehabilitation-oriented practices has also been ascribed to the strength of public opinion and partisan political arguments at the time. Criminologist Francis Cullen describes the growing sentiment that prompted the shift – "rehabilitation was infected with the worst aspects of the social welfare state: the willingness to give human services to a population that was undeserving and would only learn from this generosity that waywardness is rewarded" (2005, p. 6).

Despite the shunning of the rehabilitative ideal at the height of the punitiveness era, the current penal landscape has begun to shift back to less retributive measures. Present-day recommendations demand that the ideal be reaffirmed and that the focus be placed on recidivism prevention for offenders *before* they are released. Educational programming within the correctional environment is one vital preventive approach.

Recidivism Prevention via Education

Although the topic of education within the prison system may not be as fascinating for television audiences as are other social justice issues, it is nevertheless exceedingly important due to its strong relationship to both offending and reoffending. Statistics indicate that correctional populations are considerably less educated than the general public. Researchers have found that approximately 40 percent of state prisoners, 27 percent of federal prisoners, and 47 percent of inmates in local jails had not completed high school or its equivalent at time of admission, compared to 18 percent of the general population. Lack of education among correctional populations is intensified when examining racial/ethnic differences. Statistician Caroline Harlow (2003) reported that minority prisoners in state institutions were less educated than their White counterparts – 44 percent of African Americans and 53 percent of Hispanics had not graduated from high school or its equivalent, compared to 27 percent of Whites. Additionally, the 2003 National Assessment of Adult Literacy evaluated the literacy of the U.S. adult prison population and compared prisoners' scores to a sample of non-incarcerated adults (Greenberg et al., 2007). This assessment found that prisoners had lower literacy levels, on average, in comparison to their non-incarcerated counterparts. Lower educational attainment among incarcerated offenders, while disconcerting, is not surprising. Research, for instance by economists Lance Lochner and Enrico Moretti (2004), consistently reports that schooling significantly reduces the probability of arrest and incarceration.

Education is also linked to offenders' post-release outcomes. The theoretical relationship between in-prison educational programming and recidivism is explained as follows: participation in educational programming improves offenders' literacy, communication skills, and other job-related competencies, which then increases their likelihood of finding employment and also decreases their likelihood of reoffending following reentry (Hall, 2015).

Another important benefit of in-prison educational programming is worth noting. Christopher Zoukis (2011), a federal prisoner and dedicated education advocate, notes that in addition to improving employability, such opportunities help to restore dignity and self-esteem to prisoners. This theoretical model indeed has merit, as educational programming has reliably been shown to reduce reoffending among formerly incarcerated persons in various parts of the country. For example, authors Lisa Burke and James Vivian (2001) conducted a recidivism study related to college programming within the correctional setting. Among a sample of offenders in Massachusetts (separated into two comparison groups, similar in demographic characteristics such as age, gender, and ethnicity as well as sentence length), results indicated that offenders who completed at least one college course were almost 22 percent less likely to be reincarcerated within five years of release. Also, prison administrator John Nuttall and colleagues (2003) examined recidivism rates of offenders formerly confined in New York. Findings from their study demonstrated that offenders who passed the General Education Development (GED) test while incarcerated recidivated at a significantly lower rate than offenders who did not pass.

Using a sample of offenders from Maryland, Minnesota, and Ohio to study recidivism, researchers Stephen Steurer and Linda Smith (2003) found that those who participated in correctional education had substantially lower rates of rearrest, reconviction, and reincarceration when compared to the group of offenders who did not participate. Additionally, sociologist Mary Ellen Batiuk and colleagues (2005) sought to separate the effects of different types of correctional education programs (college versus non-college) on recidivism outcomes. Among a group of released offenders in Ohio, the authors found that not only did educational programming reduce reoffending generally, but also that participation in college programs was even more effective at decreasing offenders' recidivism risk in comparison to other types of education such as GED and vocational programs. Similarly, researchers Grant Duwe and Valerie Clark assessed the effects of obtaining education on recidivism and post-release employment among offenders released from Minnesota prisons. When focusing on those who entered prison without a high school diploma or its equivalent, the researchers found that passing the GED in prison significantly increased the likelihood of securing employment after release. Such effects were even more pronounced for those offenders who participated in post-secondary prison education (e.g., associate's degree, vocational program certificate), which was associated with higher overall wages and less recidivism after their release.

Since there is a wide range of existing empirical studies on the education-and-reoffending link, several teams of researchers have synthesized the literature in order to reveal comprehensive conclusions regarding the effectiveness of correctional education on recidivism. One such meta-analysis was conducted by researchers David Wilson, Catherine Gallagher, and Doris MacKenzie in 2000, and it examined the effects of 33 recidivism studies published between 1976 and 1997. Their findings showed that inmates who participated in corrections-based education were not only employed at a higher rate, but also reoffended at a lower rate – a decrease of approximately 11 percent, on average – than their nonparticipant peers. (To further support this conclusion, MacKenzie updated the meta-analysis six years later in 2006 to include several newer and more methodologically rigorous studies, and found that the likelihood of *not* reoffending was 16 percent higher among academic program participants than nonparticipants.) Another valuable meta-analysis was conducted by researchers Steve Aos, Marna Miller, and Elizabeth Drake in 2006, and it reviewed the results of 30 studies on the efficacy of educational and vocational programs for adult offenders. Their findings indicated that among studies assessing adult education classes in particular, "[o]n average, these programs reduce the recidivism rates of program participants" (p. xv) – a reduction of more than 5 percent. Most recently, a team of researchers at the RAND Corporation conducted a meta-analysis in 2014, which examined 50 studies published between 1980 and 2011. Results demonstrated that

> correctional education for incarcerated adults reduces the risk of post-release reincarceration (by 13 percentage points) and does so cost-effectively (a savings of five dollars on reincarceration costs for every dollar spent on correctional education). And when it comes to postrelease employment for adults – another outcome key to successful reentry – researchers find that correctional education may increase such employment.
>
> *(Davis et al. 2014, p. xv)*

Recognition of this important association has prompted many corrections departments to begin, reinstate, or expand education-based programs. A notable example is the Federal Bureau of Prisons (BOP), which initiated mandatory education beginning in the 1980s. Thus, all federal correctional institutions provide some form of programming, which may include adult basic education classes, GED preparation classes, college courses, vocational training, and/or life skills classes. The U.S. government has also taken notice of the essential link between education and post-release outcomes by enacting important legislation. The Second Chance Act of 2007 has provided additional funding for correctional education, among other resources, and also signifies a notable step forward and a tangible acknowledgment of the difficulties that ex-prisoners encounter when they reenter "free" society.

Orange is the New Omission: The Missed Opportunity to Address the Importance of Education

With the breadth of information about the salience of education to correctional populations, *OITNB* neglects to tackle the issue in a substantive fashion. Not a single scene in the first three seasons of the series has taken place in an academic classroom setting. (Although Season 3 depicts the characters in a drama class, this is not an educational setting in the traditional meaning.) In fact, the few references to education-related issues in the first three seasons center on the atypically high literacy of certain characters rather than addressing the lack of education among many of the other women at Litchfield. Those with high educational attainment – and who occupy most of the screen time – include Piper Chapman (the protagonist and college graduate who "does not belong" in the prison environment), Poussey Washington (an avid reader who worked in the exceptionally understocked prison library and was fluent in English, French, and

German), and Suzanne "Crazy Eyes" Warren (who has at least a high school education and is also a newly minted author of science fiction erotica). In contrast, little is mentioned about the low educational attainment (and its consequences) of other characters, such as Marisol "Flaca" Gonzales who was incarcerated before completing high school.

A notable missed opportunity to focus on education involves programming that is specifically tailored toward female inmates. A variant of life skills education is the prison nursery program, available within some institutions, for incarcerated offenders who are pregnant. These nursery programs are designed to increase attachment between the mother and child as well as improve parenting efficacy, and are usually coupled with formal education requirements such as GED classes. Most importantly, prison nursery programs have been shown to reduce recidivism among participants as noted by nursing scholars Lorie Smith Goshin and Mary Woods Byrne (2009). Although the issue of pregnancy within the prison setting was depicted at length through plotlines associated with characters Maria Ruiz and Dayanara "Daya" Diaz, it would have been beneficial to address nursery-based educational programming within this context, such as the Mothers and Infants Nurturing Together (MINT) program offered by the Federal Bureau of Prisons. Although the MINT program is limited to low-risk female prisoners and is available to just a small number of women who would greatly benefit (only seven MINT centers are in operation nationwide), shining a spotlight on its existence to the legions of the show's fans could potentially broaden the program's impact.

Again, to its credit, *OITNB* does attempt to bring educational programming into the storyline in Season 4, after three seasons of silence on the issue. However, the few, brief references do not fully encapsulate how significant prison-based education can be as a component of successful reentry and as a barrier to recidivism. The Season 4 narrative of Litchfield inmate Aleida Diaz, a drug offender, serves as one example of this shortcoming.

Aleida decides to earn a GED once she is faced with an unexpected early release date and a realization of her lack of lawful job-related skills. Even though she is aware of the benefits that education can have post-release (e.g., improving her job prospects so she can earn enough money to provide a stable living environment for her four minor children and newborn grandchild), and begins studying for the test on her own, the material is particularly daunting for her. Aleida becomes increasingly discouraged and eventually gives up on test preparation. In a particularly powerful diatribe, Aleida passionately justifies why she is so discouraged: "They tell you to get the GED like it's gonna change anything. How's a GED gonna make me *not* a felon? ... The GED only exists to make me feel like it's my fault when I fail when the game is fucking rigged!" (Jones, et al., 2016). Her feelings of dejection are valid, as having a criminal record does decrease employment prospects despite educational achievement.

As discussed by researchers Grant Duwe and Valerie Clark, "[c]ompared with the population in general, released prisoners are generally at a disadvantage due not only to the educational and employment history deficits they often have, but also to the harmful effects that prior criminal history has on obtaining employment." Nevertheless, reentering society without acquiring legitimate job-related skills, whether via educational or vocational programming, will make the reintegration process more difficult. If the link between education and employment stability is as strong as much of the existing research suggests, then an offender's chances of recidivism can be substantially reduced by participation in correctional education (e.g., gainfully employed individuals are too busy with work to commit crime or have too great of a "stake in conformity" to risk jeopardizing their employment status by breaking the law). Therefore, Aleida's storyline would have benefited from having another character present a sensible counterargument to her assertions. As described in the preceding section, there are empirically substantiated desistance- and earnings-related benefits of completing the GED and other types of educational programs. And although a felonious past will not disappear simply due to participation in correctional education, the secondary consequences of such a past can be assuaged with educational programming.

Another limited reference to in-prison education in Season 4 of the series occurs via a non-inmate lens – specifically, through the ultimately futile efforts of Litchfield's warden, Joe Caputo. Following the privatization of the facility, which transferred its operations from the state of New York to the for-profit Management & Correction Corporation (MCC), Caputo is visibly overwhelmed by the hardline and cost-obsessive changes that have been implemented. He is particularly distressed by inmate overcrowding coupled with undertrained correctional staff, which are both driven by MCC's profit motive: more prisoners plus lower labor costs equal higher financial gain. After attending CorrectiCon (a highly objectionable corrections industry conference with such session titles as "Immigration Violations: The Next Gold Mine") and being inspired by the keynote address that urged administrators to make prisoners' lives "feel full," Caputo develops and submits a proposal for the (re)implementation of literacy-oriented educational programming. Even though he included information regarding the strength of empirical research on the benefits of education and post-prison outcomes (e.g., employment, recidivism), his original proposal is heavily modified before approval. MCC replaced the proposed educational programming with free labor disguised as coursework, such as substituting language arts classes with "Concrete 101." While viewers can understand and empathize with Caputo's sense of disillusionment with MCC's greed at the expense of prisoners' current and future well-being, this captivating narrative unfortunately never gains traction again. Once more, the series misses an opportunity to facilitate an in-depth discussion of the impact that disinvestment in educational programming can have on offenders' post-release outcomes.

Despite the scant attention to this issue within the show, it is important to note that educational programming actually does take precedence in most federal prisoners' experiences. With very few exceptions, all inmates with less than a high school education must attend literacy classes for 240 instructional hours or until all sections of the GED test are passed. Furthermore, educational achievement in prison yields "good time" credits that translate into earlier release dates for many inmates, which keep education and literacy classes in extremely high demand. Offenders held in federal detention centers as they await sentencing also have access to educational programming, and achievement may translate into reduced sentence severity, which again keeps classes in high demand. As a volunteer GED instructor at a federal women's prison, I witness firsthand how integral education and literacy programs are to the prison experience – particularly in the minimum-security context, as sentences are shorter and reentry prospects are far more imminent. These programs are also important to offenders' post-prison lives, as successful societal reintegration by way of education "offers a path to increased employment, reduced recidivism, and improved quality of life" say Diana Brazell and colleagues at the Urban Institute's Justice Policy Center and John Jay College of Criminal Justice (2009, p. 2) – factors that are especially relevant to women in this environment. Consequently, I find that *OITNB*'s failure to centrally depict the education issue in depth is a major shortcoming of the series.

Conclusion

The correctional environment and its administrators, which are primarily tasked with ensuring the safety of the general public as well as the inmate population, also "have a broader social obligation to prepare [their] prisoners for the inevitable return home" says Jeremy Travis, author of *But They all Come Back: Facing the challenges of prisoner reentry*. Since correctional education is an evidence-based strategy that can help attenuate the many challenges that offenders face upon their release, such programs should be supported and expanded. To that end, in 2012, the U.S. Department of Education developed a reentry education model intended to solidify and restructure this type of programming within all branches of the corrections field. This model takes efforts to improve offenders' education and employability a commendable step further by planning to place offenders on an education continuum. The Department's continuum includes the following stages: (a) assessment of skills at admission to determine appropriate in-prison programming; (b) provision of education services while incarcerated; (c) re-assessment of skills at pre-release to determine appropriate post-prison programming; and (d) provision of education services under the direction and supervision of parole/probation officers and/or case managers. By integrating in-prison and community-based programs, the Department of Education asserts "offenders can gain the knowledge and skills needed to obtain long-term, living-wage employment, and transition successfully out of the corrections system" (2012, p. 3).

Hopefully, the popular Netflix series will follow the lead of scholars and policymakers by turning its focus to a more profound illumination of correctional education during upcoming seasons. Doing so will ensure that the show's viewers are exposed to multiple facets of the true prison experience and that they have the opportunity to learn about the vital role education plays in the reentry and reintegration processes.

Acknowledgements

I am extremely grateful to Drs Laurie L. Gordy and Shirley A. Jackson for the opportunity to contribute to this anthology. I would like to thank Jenna Cronin, Literacy Teacher, and Beth Nichols, Reentry Affairs Coordinator, for the opportunity to serve as a volunteer instructor and mock job fair interviewer at FCI Tallahassee. I would also like to thank Kaleena Burkes, Ileen Williams, and Tracey Woodard for comments on previous drafts of this chapter.

References

Alexander, M. (2010). *The New Jim Crow: Mass Incarceration in the Age of Colorblindness*. New York, NY: The New Press.

Aos, S., Miller, M., & Drake, E. (2006). *Evidence-based Adult Corrections Programs: What Works and What Does Not?*Olympia, WA: Washington State Institute for Public Policy.

Batiuk, M. E., Lahm, K. F., McKeever, M., Wilcox, N., & Wilcox, P. (2005). Disentangling the effects of correctional education: Are current policies misguided? An event history analysis. *Criminology and Criminal Justice*, 5(1), 55–74.

Blumstein, A., & Beck, A. J. (1999). Population growth in U.S. prisons, 1980–1996. In M. Tonry & J. Petersilia (Eds.), *Prisons* (pp. 17–62). Chicago, IL: The University of Chicago Press.

Brazzell, D., Crayton, A., Mukamal, D., Solomon, A., & Lindahl, N. (2009). From the classroom to the community: Exploring the role of education during incarceration and reentry. Washington, D.C.: Urban Institute, Justice Policy Center.

Burke, L. O., & Vivian, J. E. (2001). The effect of college programming on recidivism rates at the Hampden County House of Correction: A 5-year Study. *Journal of Correctional Education*, 52(4), 160–162.

Bush-Baskette, S. R., & Smith, V. C. (2012). Is meth the new crack for women in the War on Drugs? Factors affecting sentencing outcomes for women and parallels between meth and crack. *Feminist Criminology*, 7(1), 48–69.

Caputi, J. (2015). The color orange? Social justice issues in the first season of Orange is the New Black. *The Journal of Popular Culture*, 48(6), 1130–1150.

Carson, E. A. (2015). *Prisoners in 2014. Bureau of Justice Statistics Report no. NCJ-248955*. Washington, D.C.: U.S. Department of Justice.

Clear, T. (2007). *Imprisoning Communities: How Mass Incarceration makes Disadvantaged Neighborhoods Worse*. New York, NY: Oxford University Press.

Cullen, F. T. (2005). The twelve people who saved rehabilitation: How the science of criminology made a difference. *Criminology*, 43(1), 1–42.

Davis, L. M., Steele, J. L., Bozick, R., Williams, M. V., Turner, S., Miles, J. N. V. et al. (2014). *How Effective is Correctional Education, and where do we go from here? The Results of a Comprehensive Evaluation*. Santa Monica, CA: RAND Corporation.

Doherty, E., Cwick, J., Green, K., & Ensminger, M. (2015). Examining the consequences of the "prevalent life events" of arrest and incarceration among an urban African-American cohort. *Justice Quarterly*, doi:10.1080/07418825.2015.1016089

Durose, M. R., Cooper, A. D., & Snyder, H. N. (2014). *Recidivism of Prisoners Released in 30 States in 2005: Patterns from 2005 to 2010*. Bureau of Justice Statistics Report no. NCJ-244205. Washington, D.C.: U.S. Department of Justice.

Duwe, G., & Clark, V. (2014). The effects of prison-based educational programming on recidivism and employment. *The Prison Journal*, 94(4), 454–478.

Enck, S. M., & Morrissey, M. E. (2015). If orange is the new black, I must be color blind: Comic framings of post-racism in the prison-industrial complex. *Critical Studies in Media Communication*, 32(5), 303–317.

Farabee, D. (2005). *Rethinking Rehabilitation: Why Can't we Reform our Criminals?* Washington, D.C.: American Enterprise Institute for Public Policy Research.

Goshin, L. S., & Byrne, M. W. (2009). Converging streams of opportunity for prison nursery programs in the United States. *Journal of Offender Rehabilitation*, 48(4), 271–295.

Greenberg, E., Dunleavy, E., & Kutner, M. (2007). *Literacy behind bars: Results from the 2003 National Assessment of Adult Literacy Prison Survey*. Washington, D.C.: U.S. Department of Education, National Center for Education Statistics.

Hall, L. L. (2015). Correctional education and recidivism: Toward a tool for reduction. *Journal of Correctional Education*, 66(2), 4–29.

Harlow, C. W. (2003). *Education and Correctional Populations*. Bureau of Justice Statistics Report no. NCJ-195670. Washington, D.C.: U.S. Department of Justice.

Jones, N., Kohan, J. (Writers), & Burley, M. A. (Director). (2016). It sounded nicer in my head [Television series episode]. In L. Morelli (Producer), *Orange is the new black*. New York, NY: Kaufman Astoria Studios.

Langan, P. A., & Levin, D. J. (2002). *Recidivism of Prisoners Released in 1994*. Bureau of Justice Statistics Report no. NCJ-193427. Washington, D.C.: U.S. Department of Justice.

Lipton, D., Martinson, R., & Wilks, J. (1975). *The Effectiveness of Correctional Treatment: A Survey of Treatment Evaluation Studies*. New York, NY: Praeger.

Lochner, L., & Moretti, E. (2004). The effect of education on crime: Evidence from prison inmates, arrests, and self-reports. *American Economic Review*, 94(1), 155–189.

MacKenzie, D. (2006). *What Works in Corrections: Reducing the Criminal Activities of Offenders and Delinquents*. New York, NY: Cambridge University Press.

MacKenzie, D., & Brame, R. (2001). Community supervision, prosocial activities, and recidivism. *Justice Quarterly*, 18(2), 429–448.

Mumola, C. J. (2000). *Incarcerated Parents and their Children*. Bureau of Justice Statistics Report no. NCJ-182335. Washington, D.C.: U.S. Department of Justice.

Nuttall, J., Hollmen, L., & Staley, E. M. (2003). The effect of earning a GED on recidivism rates. *Journal of Correctional Education*, 54(3), 90–94.

Paternoster, R., & Piquero, A. (1995). Reconstructing deterrence: An empirical test of personal and vicarious experiences. *Journal of Research in Crime and Delinquency*, 32(3), 251–286.

Petersilia, J. (2003). *When Prisoners Come Home: Parole and Prisoner Reentry*. New York, NY: Oxford University Press.

Petersilia, J. (2005). From cell to society: Who is returning home? In J. Travis & C. Visher (Eds.), *Prisoner Reentry and Crime in America* (pp. 15–49). New York, NY: Cambridge Press.

Pew Center on the States. (2011). *State of Recidivism: The Revolving Door of America's Prisons*. Washington, DC: The Pew Charitable Trusts.

Phelps, M. S. (2011). Rehabilitation in the punitive era: The gap between rhetoric and reality in U.S. prison programs. *Law & Society Review*, 45(1), 33–68.

Pratt, T. C. (2009). *Addicted to Incarceration: Corrections Policy and the Politics of Misinformation in the United States*. Thousand Oaks, CA: Sage Publications.

Rosenfeld, R., Wallman, J., & Fornango, R. (2005). The contribution of ex-prisoners to crime rates. In J. Travis & C. Visher (Eds.), *Prisoner Reentry and Crime in America* (pp. 80–104). New York, NY: Cambridge University Press.

Solomon, A. L., Kachnowski, V., & Bhati, A. (2005). *Does Parole Work? Analyzing the Impact of Postprison Supervision on Rearrest Outcomes*. Washington, DC: Urban Institute Justice Policy Center.

Spohn, C., & Holleran, D. (2002). The effect of imprisonment on recidivism rates of felony offenders: A focus on drug offenders. *Criminology*, 40(2), 329–357.

Steurer, S. J., & Smith, L. G. (2003). *Education Reduces Crime: Three-state Recidivism Study*. Laurel, MD: Correctional Association of America.

Travis, J. (2005). *But They All Come Back: Facing the Challenges of Prisoner Reentry*. Washington, D.C.: Urban Institute Press.

U.S. Department of Education. (2012). *A Reentry Education Model: Supporting Education and Career Advancement for Low-skill Individuals in Corrections*. Washington, D.C.: U.S. Department of Education, Office of Vocational and Adult Education.

U.S. Supreme Court Decision. (2011). *Brown v. Plata*, 563 U.S.

Wilson, D. B., Gallagher, C. A., & MacKenzie, D. L. (2000). A meta-analysis of corrections-based education, vocation, and work programs for adult offenders. *Journal of Research in Crime & Delinquency*, 37(4), 347–368.

Zoukis, C. (2011). *Education behind Bars: A Win-Win Strategy for Maximum Security*. Mechanicsburg, PA: Sunbury Press.

PART 6

Prisons and Culture

Laurie L. Gordy

Prisons are considered a total institution. In his classic book, *Asylums,* sociologist Erving Goffman characterized total institutions as social arrangements in which all aspects of an individual's life are carried out in the same setting "under the same single authority" with a "tightly scheduled" daily routine that is "imposed from above." Individuals living in total institutions have little opportunity for privacy and for autonomy. There is limited choice since almost all of the day-to-day events are controlled by and for the institutional administration. Daily routines, such as when, how, and where to shower, are dictated by rules beyond an inmate's control. Behaviors, interactions, and objects take on new meanings (or purposes) within this total institution that shape individual's identity and the prison culture. In fact, the trailer for Season 1 of *Orange is the New Black* (*OITNB*) begins with the main character, Piper Chapman, explaining how showers and baths were her "happy place" until entering prison.

Given that inmates and staff are products of the external culture, total institutions operate as separate entities yet they are still shaped by the broader culture and society in which they exist. Within prisons, cultural perceptions and representations of social groups and social issues shape the interactions, rules, and relationships that develop. Throughout the four seasons of *OITNB*, the creator, Jenji Kohan produces images of prison culture and integrates current cultural events into the dialogue, characters, and setting. *OITNB* addresses important cultural and social issues for female inmates (such as: sexual assault, health issues, and religious freedom) yet for the purpose of entertainment, it often oversimplifies and dramatizes many of these as well. While these cultural representations are of course fictional they do provide an opportunity for us to examine the influence of cultural myths, norms, and stigmas on interactions, behaviors, and rules within the total institution of female prisons in the United States.

As a total institution, prisons regulate space, boundaries, and bodies that intentionally limit the amount of agency inmates can exercise. Female inmates cannot advocate for themselves particularly in areas of justice regarding sexual assault and health care. In this last part of the book, the authors analyze the relationship between social structure and human agency as female inmates try to maintain some sense of humanity and control over their lives within prisons. All three authors in this section provide a relational perspective on prison life as they examine the dynamics of relationships between inmates, and between inmates and correctional officers. The intensity and power dynamics of these relationships are exacerbated due to the characteristics of total institutions and broader cultural stereotypes. Specifically, the authors examine how female prisons and the portrayal of a female prison in *OITNB* reflects and challenges cultural attitudes about sexual assault, aging, and religion.

In "Consent Behind Bars: Changing Depictions of Sexual Assault on *Orange is the New Black*", Amber Lopez describes the challenges female inmates face in combatting sexual assault given the cultural myths as well as the structural barriers within a total institution. Given the characteristics of total institutions, it is difficult for female inmates to resist any demands for sexual actions and all sexual relations between inmates and prison staff are illegal. Furthermore, Lopez concludes that *OITNB*'s presentation of sexual assaults between inmates and correctional officers changed over the first three seasons and moved away from reinforcing rape myths to provide a more critical view of consent. Media portrayals of social issues both affect and reflect cultural attitudes, and thus it is increasingly important that cultural portrayals of sexual assault do not contribute to the myths surrounding sexual assault and survivors of sexual assaults. Lopez notes that female inmates are disproportionately affected by sexual assault in their lifetimes (within and outside of prison), are blamed more for the sexual assaults given the cultural stereotypes and rape myths and thus their concerns are neglected within prisons. Lopez's argument is that this change in *OITNB*'s portrayal of sexual assault reflected broader cultural changes to how U.S. culture, and particularly colleges and universities, were moving to a cultural standard of affirmative sexual consent. In the third season, *OITNB* allowed viewers to see the flaws in both the cultural myths surrounding sexual assault as well as the flaws in the legal system's ability to handle such cases, particularly where female inmates have been assaulted by correctional officers. Central to Lopez's argument is that in order for sexual assault to be reduced (both inside prison walls and outside of them), cultural myths surrounding rape need to be challenged and changed.

Within total institutions, inmates have limited control over their own bodies. Given the devaluation of women and the female body in patriarchal societies, female inmates have limited agency in protecting their bodies from exploitation and in advocating for treatment of their bodies when they have health issues. In "Gray is the New Orange: Older, Infirm Female Inmates and the Liminal Space between Human and Animal", Hadar Aviram analyzes how the cultural view of inmates as "fiscal subjects" and the higher risks and injuries female inmates face make it difficult for elderly female inmates to advocate their own health care needs. Inmates are viewed, as Aviram argues, as economic burdens and thus, health care needs are often neglected. This is particularly problematic for elderly inmates given the increased health issues that people face as they age, the negative cultural perceptions of the elderly, and the powerlessness inmates face in addressing their own health needs. *OITNB* highlights the serious health issues facing two elderly female inmate characters: cancer and dementia. As Aviram concludes, while *OITNB* informs the audience of the limits to health services elderly female inmates face, it does not critically address the cultural and structural constraints to effectively addressing these limits. The relationship between inmates and prison staff is fraught with tension such that inmates have to plead to have even the most basic of health issues addressed. Cultural attitudes that often dehumanize inmates and ignore women's health care needs contribute to both less informed health care policies for female inmates and less economic commitment to the welfare needs of inmates. These cultural stigmas combined with the power imbalances in prisons, as Aviram notes, result in limited voice for some of the most vulnerable female inmates, the elderly and the infirm.

One area where inmates do have some voice and agency is in religious faith. In "Broccoli, Love, and the Holy Toast: Cultural Depictions of Religion in *Orange is the New Black*", Terri Toles Patkin analyzes the autonomy religion can provide for inmates, the depiction of inmate's faith and religious practice in *OITNB*, and the religious symbolism in *OITNB*. Religion can provide hope, purpose, and meaningful relationships for inmates in a dehumanizing place such as prison. Inmates can connect and interact with other inmates based on shared values that remind them of their humanity and of their identity outside of prison. Presenting the role of religion in inmates' lives humanizes inmates and this is one way that *OITNB* invites its viewers to empathize with the female inmates. While *OITNB* does provide examples of religion and inmates practicing their faith, as Toles Patkin notes, it does so in a more superficial, and often stereotypical way. Viewers of *OITNB* are left with the impression that female inmates use religion to "work the system" and this is consistent with the cultural stereotypes of inmates as manipulative human beings. Additionally, Toles Patkin illustrates how *OITNB* portrays several stereotypes of religious groups, most significantly Jews. The intent and effect of these stereotypes is not clear. Religious stereotypes, symbolism and implicit religious references are embedded in the interactions, behaviors, and story lines of *OITNB*. These images reinforce that religion is central to prison culture. Within a total institution such as prison, religious rituals and religious identity provide inmates with some sense of control over their identity. As Toles Patkin demonstrates, *OITNB* represents the role of religion in prison culture and in relationships, religious identity as a way to humanize inmates, stereotypes of religious groups and inmates.

Prisons are structured as total institutions and inmates grapple with finding meaning and agency in a place where they are dehumanized and for the most part, powerless. Female inmates often encounter gender, race, and religious stereotypes that exacerbate the existing negative perceptions of inmates. These chapters demonstrate how female inmates' control over their own bodies and minds is shaped by broader cultural views and values as well as the structural position of inmates within the hierarchy of prison structure. Stereotypes of sexual assault survivors, the elderly and religious groups dehumanize female inmates and further limit the amount of agency female inmates have. Furthermore, the economic constraints facing prison administrators, in a culture that values a more punitive approach to prisons, shape the ability to effectively implement policies providing basic human rights to inmates. Given that the broader culture often blames women for sexual assault, views the elderly as non-productive members of society, and inmates as untrustworthy and manipulative, it is challenging for female inmates to adequately receive justice when sexual assault takes place, receive health care when facing a serious illness, and freely and fully practice their religion. *OITNB* draws our attention to these structural constraints and at the same time, reflects, challenges, and reinforces these cultural perceptions.

Reference

Goffman, E. (1961). *Asylums*. Garden City, New York: Anchor Books.

15

CONSENT BEHIND BARS

Changing Depictions of Sexual Assault in *Orange is the New Black*

Amber Lopez

Introduction

Orange is the New Black (*OITNB*) premiered in 2013, the same year that the sexual consent movement began to gain traction on college campuses across the country, making sexual assault and consent national issues. This chapter explores some of the ways that *OITNB* and the sexual consent movement have been in dialogue with each other over the course of the show's first three seasons (2013–2015). I use *OITNB* as a case study, and trace the ways that changes in its depiction of sexual assault may reflect broader shifts in public understanding of this crime and of sexual consent. I argue that *OITNB*'s depictions reflect updated understandings of sexual assault as the violation of consent, regardless of the identity of the victim or the circumstances of the crime. However, *OITNB*'s depictions of sexual assault are imperfect, and identifying where they falter may help us to understand the greatest obstacles for addressing sexual assault in a variety of contexts, from the ivory tower to prisons.

In 2003, Congress unanimously passed the Prison Rape Elimination Act (PREA), which created a commission to report on the state of prison rape and to draft recommendations to address this issue. Prisoners' rights activists considered the passage of PREA a triumph, but the execution of PREA has been a slow process – one that is still taking place today. Recently though, debate over sexual assault has focused on college campuses, and has reinvigorated national attention to these crimes. In 2013, students at colleges across the country started to organize and file federal Title IX complaints against their schools for failing to adequately respond to sexual assault claims. A new legal and social standard of affirmative sexual consent, requiring active affirmative consent at every stage of a sexual encounter, became activists' primary demand. Many colleges responded by implementing affirmative consent policies, and some states enacted new legislation. However, these new reforms often failed to address the underlying reason that sexual assault laws and policies fail: they are based on rape myths.

Rape myths are stereotypical ideas that essentially invalidate sexual assault victims and their claims. They encompass a broad range of beliefs about victims, perpetrators, and the circumstances of the crime itself. Examples of rape myths include the ideas that women lie about rape, and that they "ask for it" through the way they dress, their sexual history, or behavior like drinking. Rape myths are also related to demographic features like race and class. So, for example, women of color are often vilified through rape myths as hypersexual and therefore always consenting to sex. When assaults match up with rape myths, they are more likely to be reported, prosecuted, and result in serious sentences, but when assaults do not match up with these myths, consequences are far less likely. While rape myths have posed serious problems for all women making sexual assault claims, female inmates face compounded rape myths and structural obstacles to reporting and successfully prosecuting their attackers.

As of 2014, according to the Bureau of Justice Statistics, there were a total of 1,561,525 prisoners in state and federal prisons (Carson, 2015). Only 112,961 of these prisoners were women, but according to a 2015 report by *The Sentencing Project*, "women now comprise a larger proportion of the prison population than ever before." Though research shows that prison rape and sexual assault affect many more men than women, female inmates are disproportionately affected by these crimes. According to the Bureau of Justice Statistics, "between 2009 and 2011, females represented about 7% of all state and federal prison inmates, but accounted for 22% of inmate-on-inmate victims and 33% of staff-on-inmate victims" (Beck, et al., 2014). In addition, in their article "Bars to Justice: The Impact of Rape Myths On Women in Prison," legal scholars Hannah Brenner, Kathleen Darcy, Gina Fedock, and Sheryl Pimlott Kubiak, whose work I reference throughout this chapter, argue that female inmates have the most difficult time seeking justice for sexual assault because they face both common rape myths and prison-specific rape myths. For example, because inmates are all already convicted criminals, they are often seen as less trustworthy and more manipulative. However, the researchers argue that despite "a growing recognition of the complexity of sexual victimization, the problem of sexual violence in prison has attracted much less attention than campus rape" (2016, p. 523). So, it was unusual and important when a TV show as popular as *OITNB* took on issues of sexual assault in prison, and it drew attention from fans, critics, and academics.

Despite vast differences in how power and control operate in prisons and colleges, sexual assault regulation is similarly flawed in both, due to longstanding problems in how law and policy define rape and sexual assault, and how individuals interpret and execute these regulations. Brenner and colleagues argue that as important as PREA and other laws are to improving the circumstances of inmates, "informal internalization and perpetuation of rape myths bar their successful application" (2016, pp. 552–553). This means that even with improved laws and policies, rape myths can still derail the success of these measures. So, before we try to overhaul sexual assault laws, it is important to understand common cultural ideas, or norms, related to sexual assault.

Sexual Assault on Screen

OITNB's depiction of sexual assault is particularly interesting because in prisons, all sexual contact between staff and inmates is prohibited, whether it is consensual or not. This unusual circumstance sets the scenarios on the show apart from most other TV shows that address sexual assault. *OITNB* is therefore unique in its ability to challenge viewers to think critically about whether the sex depicted on the show is ethical, by exploring instances of assault in more depth, by removing normal benchmarks of consent, and by abandoning the idea of a purely innocent victim. The women that are assaulted in *OITNB* are criminals, yet audiences are pushed to see them as victims as well – breaking down rape myths that position women as either sinners or saints, but never both. By abandoning traditional representations of sexual assault from the beginning, each interaction must be evaluated, not in terms of a strict legal criteria, or stereotypes, but in all its complexity.

Conceptualizing Consent

Scholars and activists critique criminal law related to rape and sexual assault for being simplistic and out of date. Rape law was originally instituted to protect a man's claim over his wife. So, it is not surprising that rape myths underlie many of our current laws. According to legal scholar Deborah Tuerkheimer, in her 2014 article, "Slutwalking in the Shadow of the Law," in most parts of the United States, sexual assault law is based on the concept of "nonconsensual intercourse by force," meaning that non-consent alone typically is not enough to establish rape. Tuerkheimer asserts in another article that about half of all states at the time required that force must be used against a victim to classify a sexual encounter as rape. Affirmative sexual consent challenges this model by abandoning the force requirement and instead making ongoing affirmative consent the standard. Basically, "Yes Means Yes" replaces the former "No Means No" motto, effectively shifting the burden of proof from the victim to the alleged perpetrator of an assault, because a victim's silence can no longer be considered consent.

In 2014, California's S.B. 967 became the first legislation to establish a standard of affirmative sexual consent at colleges that receive state funds for student aid. The bill defines affirmative sexual consent as: "affirmative, conscious, and voluntary agreement to engage in sexual activity" that is "ongoing throughout." Since S.B. 967 passed, there have been widespread calls for similar affirmative consent standards across the country. However, research suggests that sexual assault legislation should be incremental for it to be effective, otherwise, legal scholar Dan Kahan argues, "As states adopt more severe laws, police grow more reluctant to arrest, prosecutors to charge, juries to convict, and judges to punish" (2000, pp. 607–608). Therefore, successful legislation must correspond with cultural norms for decision makers to enforce reformed legislation. According to Tuerkheimer, "Rape law reform can only be effective if it bears a close connection to social norms," otherwise, "legal transformation will do little to affect actors' decision-making throughout the criminal process" (2014, p. 1507). Rape myths are at the root of many harmful laws and policies related to sexual assault, or at the very least, they undermine the application of well-intentioned policies. So, unless rape myths are challenged, research suggests that enacting new affirmative consent legislation just will not work. Television and other forms of media, like *OITNB*, may play a role in the success of law and policy by challenging these rape myths and validating the experiences of victims.

Consent from the Ivory Tower to the Prison Cell

The fact that prisons and colleges have failed to adequately address sexual assault claims in recent years, is not so surprising. It is part of a nation-wide systemic failure in dealing with these crimes. The criminal justice system's treatment of rape and sexual assault cases has been criticized for its failure to provide justice to victims. In addition, many argue that the very structure of the process reinjures victims of assault by forcing them to recount their experiences in painful detail for police, prosecutors, and if they are lucky, for a judge and jury. They face harsh cross-examination, and until recently, had no protection from questioning about their sexual histories. According to Brenner and colleagues, Rape Shield laws were created, "due to lawmakers' recognition that evidence about a victim's past sexual history as a proxy for rape reflected myths about sexuality and was extremely damaging." However, they point out that "[n]o such formal protections exist in prison, and the informal permeation of rape myths creep into investigations" (Brenner at al., 2016, p. 566). So, while sexual assault laws and policies are failing at the broadest national level, female inmates face the greatest obstacles to seeking justice.

Though men still make up much of the prison population, there are now more women in prison than ever. According to *The Sentencing Project*, Black and Hispanic women are disproportionately imprisoned. Michelle Alexander, civil rights lawyer and acclaimed author of *The New Jim Crow: Mass Incarceration in the Age of Colorblindness*, describes inmates as disproportionately people of color, of low socioeconomic status, and in the case of felons, unable to vote, even after their release from prison. In addition, research by Ashley Blackburn, Janet Mullings, and James Marquart (2008) suggests that rates of lifetime sexual assault among incarcerated women are significantly higher than among the general population. Therefore, not only is sexual assault and harassment a problem for inmates inside prison walls, but it is also thought to be a contributing factor to women's criminality and imprisonment. Women who experienced abuse before entering prison are also more likely to experience continued abuse in prison. Therefore, inmates are likely to suffer from multiple stigmatized identities. This stigma, combined with tough structural and legal obstacles, make it extremely difficult for inmates to gain protection from and justice for sexual assault.

Nowhere is the issue of sexual consent more pressing than in the prison system, where women experience severely constrained agency. In his famous 1961 study, *Asylums: Essays on the Social Situation of Mental Patients and Other Inmates*, the preeminent sociologist Erving Goffman describes prisons as total institutions, in which the lives of prisoners are almost entirely regulated. According to Goffman, the inmates and staff are characterized by an antagonistic relationship in which each "conceive[s] of the other in terms of narrow hostile stereotypes," where, "Staff tends to feel superior and righteous; inmates tend, in some ways at least, to feel inferior, weak, blameworthy, and guilty" (1961, p. 6). This antagonistic relationship poses a problem for inmates reporting sexual assault, as they are forced to report these crimes to staff that are typically at odds with them, or at the very least, not their equals.

Modern American prisons are characterized by the highest rates of imprisonment in the world, privatization, and the prison industrial complex. In the 1980s, the prison population exploded with the implementation of the War on Drugs. This explosion in the prison population led to the privatization of prisons to reduce the costs associated with incarceration. According to legal scholar Patrice A. Fulcher, "the allocation of government resources to support the privatization of prisons led to the Prison Industrial Complex ("PIC") becoming a '*hustle*'; it altered the public function of incarceration from rehabilitation, custody, and control to private profiteering" (2012, p. 592). Even the National Prison Rape Elimination Commission (NPREC) report seems to acknowledge this fact to some extent, stating that outsourcing leads to a risk that, "contractors will fail to adhere to the agency's policies and meet the same standards" (2009, p. 164). Yet despite these risks, the practice of prison privatization continues. But this is not the only obstacle that inmates face in reporting sexual assaults.

According to the NPREC, "when prisoners are willing to report sexual abuse, their accounts are not necessarily taken seriously and communicated to appropriate officials within the facility" (2009, p. 11). Furthermore, the report states that victims face threats of retaliation if they, or witnesses, speak out about assaults. And though "in all 50 States, it is a crime for facility staff to engage in any sexual conduct with individuals in custody," regardless of an inmate's consent, successful prosecution of these cases is rare according to the report (p. 37). Therefore, the very structure of the prison makes it difficult to address issues of sexual assault. And with little institutional oversight, harmful prison practices can go unchecked.

Unlike college students, inmates do not have the option of seeking justice in the criminal court system, and the process that is available to them is highly flawed. According to Brenner and colleagues, the process for reporting a sexual assault in prison is complicated and includes little outside oversight. They describe the process as starting with an inmate writing and submitting a "grievance" to a "grievance coordinator" employed by the Department of Corrections. Then, "it may go to an internal investigator, again, employed by the correctional facility." From there, they write that, "If the allegation, if true, would constitute criminal sexual contact pursuant to statute, the internal investigator is tasked to inform state police," but unfortunately, "The policies for reporting are often extremely complicated; inmates and officers alike are often under educated on how to utilize reporting procedures" (Brenner et al., 2016, p. 556). Thus, according to scholars Kitty Calavita and Valerie Jenness in their article, "Inside the Pyramid of Disputes: Naming Problems and Filing Grievances in California Prisons," there are several obvious problems with this system, including its lack of transparency and its adversarial nature, which is similar to the courts in some significant ways: the process is difficult, there is little room for review, and the progression of a claim is out of the complainant's hands. But inmates who *do* successfully file grievances face an even greater set of obstacles.

Inmates must fight an uphill battle to achieve justice after filing a grievance. They are forced to report their assaults to officers and administrators within the prison, leaving them vulnerable to retaliation in the form of harassment and segregation, as well as violence. In addition, some states have unreasonably high evidentiary burdens. The scholars describe these burdens as so strict that, "evidence of corroborating witnesses, successful polygraphs, and DNA evidence are often insufficient to overcome [them]," reflecting an "assumption that the inmates are lying." The idea that women lie about rape is a common and powerful rape myth at the national level, but it is exponentially more powerful when it is used against inmate victims who have already been judged "guilty" in a court of law.

In contrast, when sexual assault cases are reviewed within the university, they are subject to a lower burden of proof than in criminal court. Here too, female victims are often accused of lying about rape, but college students are typically considered more credible than inmates. According to legal scholar Lavinia Weizel, under Title IX, the standard of proof is a "preponderance of evidence," or "more likely than not," rather than "beyond a reasonable doubt" in the criminal justice system (2012, p. 1617). However, even with this legal advantage, many colleges fail to properly carry out the law, and many victims do not find justice. In addition to increased legal barriers, and compounded rape myths, the low rates of success for grievances also deter inmates from reporting assaults. This can prevent inmates from accessing additional options for pursuing justice, because existing law "requires an inmate to 'exhaust all administrative remedies,' referring to formal grievance procedures, to preserve her right to sue civilly," according to Brenner and collaborators (2016, p. 561). Thus, to access civil justice, inmates are forced to first use all internal grievance procedures, though many inmates do not make it past this step, leaving them with only one option in terms of reporting sexual assaults.

In 2012, the Department of Justice (DOJ) issued its "National Standards to Prevent, Detect, and Respond to Prison Rape; Final Rule," in response to PREA. It includes directives for prevention planning, supervision and monitoring, cross-gender searches and viewing, training and education, reporting, grievances, and more. Though these standards are comprehensive, financial constraints and inequalities among prisons affect the standards' application. Therefore, the DOJ admittedly seeks to, "yield the maximum desired effect while minimizing the financial impact on jurisdictions," while it allows, "discretion and flexibility to agencies to the extent feasible." Consequently, while PREA supposedly aims to "eliminate" prison rape, it is worrisome that its recommendations only do so "to the extent feasible." This policy seems to quite literally put a price on inmates' safety.

Despite the problems with its recommendations, the DOJ does acknowledge the importance of culture to its proposed reforms, stating that, "The success of the PREA standards ... will depend on effective agency and facility leadership, and the development of an agency culture that prioritizes efforts to combat sexual abuse," though culture "cannot, of course, be directly mandated by rule." This position echoes legal scholars' argument that laws can only be successful when they match up with cultural norms. Therefore, while the PREA standards provide a helpful guide for prisons to improve their handling of sexual assault, just as new national laws can only be effective if they mirror norms, the same is true of laws specific to prisons. So, while popular culture is often trivialized, it can serve a vital role in perpetuating or challenging cultural norms. *OITNB* has done both.

Screening Assault in Orange is the New Black

Because my research is based on a content analysis of the first 39 episodes of *OITNB*, media coverage of the show, and broader coverage of sexual assault from 2013 to 2015, I cannot definitively prove that the writers of *OITNB* responded to issues of affirmative sexual consent raised by campus sexual assaults. However, at a 2014 panel on writing at the Austin Film Festival, *OITNB* writers Lauren Morelli and Stephen Falk described being free from any obligation to address audience criticism: "I think that's actually been an advantage of each season. We've already been working on the next season before the past season comes out. So, we can't respond to the audience at all ... we're sort of just on our own path." Therefore, under the guidance of *OITNB*'s creator and lead writer Jenji Kohan, the writers say they independently develop the themes included in each season of the show. Morelli also described the writers as trying to address political and social issues, particularly in the prison: "You know, we're trying to layer in issues underneath some of the humor, so that we're also making a statement, hopefully, about our prison system and the country." So, while

OITNB's writers have not explicitly stated their inspiration for addressing issues of sexual assault, interviews on the writers' process suggest that they are heavily influenced by social issues. This chapter demonstrates the thematic ties between real-world discussion of sexual assault and the fictional representations of assault on *OITNB*. In the following two cases of male correctional officers assaulting female inmates, I argue that *OITNB* changed as the consent movement redefined cultural norms.

Case 1: Daya, Bennett, and Mendez

OITNB's first season premiered in June of 2013, as federal Title IX complaints against universities were beginning to gain national attention. The first season seemed to reflect a nascent, but incomplete awareness of the changing discussion of sexual assault. In her article "TV Can Make America Better," for *Salon*, Jennifer Pozner (2014) argues that the romantic relationship between Daya and Bennett is *OITNB*'s "worst narrative failure," because of its lack of attention to the issue of sexual assault in women's prisons. Considering the real-world prevalence of sexual assault perpetrated by correctional officers, the romance between Daya and Bennett not only seems unrealistic, it also seems to reinforce stereotypes that frame female inmates as actively pursuing sex with correctional officers, even though correctional officers (COs) clearly hold power over inmates *in their custody*. This is not to say that inmates are without any agency, or that they cannot (and do not) have romantic relationships with correctional officers or administrators. But given the illegality of these relationships and their potentially abusive nature, this type of relationship constitutes a real threat to female inmates, and this threat is downplayed in the first season of *OITNB*.

The relationship between Daya, a young, Hispanic inmate whose mother is also incarcerated at Litchfield Penitentiary, and John Bennett, a young, White correctional officer at the prison, begins early in the season, as Daya initiates flirtatious conversations with Bennett. Things quickly escalate when Bennett passes Daya a note asking her to meet him in the utility closet, where they eventually have sex. Despite Bennett's position of authority over Daya, the two are portrayed basically as equals, with Daya taking an active role in flirting and pursuing sex with Bennett. Because Bennett never uses explicit force with Daya, the coercive elements of their relationship are largely invisible. The audience is encouraged to view the relationship as romantic through the editing and plot. Pozner points out that, "every time Daya and Bennett are on-screen together the soundtrack shifts to soft rom-com music, a classic tool of persuasion and a cinematic shortcut to create emotional buy-in from the audience." This is an issue because, "We're meant to see their furtive glances and secret courtship as inappropriate and somewhat uncomfortable, but ultimately as a mutual, consensual love story – not what it legally is: rape." Thus, the relationship between Daya and Bennett seems to resemble a story of forbidden love, rather than an illegal and potentially dangerous situation.

The purely romantic relationship between Daya and Bennett is soon challenged when Daya discovers that she is pregnant. Because sex between inmates and COs is illegal regardless of consent, Daya is left with few options, especially if she wants to protect Bennett. A small group of Daya's friends and family convince her that her only option is to frame another CO for her pregnancy. Ignoring her initial resistance to the plan, Daya begins a sexual relationship with CO Mendez, a corrupt and predatory male guard. As soon as their relationship begins though, Mendez is portrayed as morphing from a sexually aggressive, drug-dealing correctional officer, into a sort of lovesick teenager. By depicting Mendez as a largely innocent victim, framed for rape, *OITNB* positions Daya as the aggressor, despite her subordinate position and her legal inability to consent to sex with a correctional officer.

Salamishah Tillet, writing in 2013 for *The Nation*, argued that this depiction, "not only reproduces stereotypes that women in prison are untrustworthy and lie about sexual assault, but also cushions the real violence experienced by women in prison as romance." A 2010 study on "False Allegations of Sexual Assault: An Analysis of Ten Years of Reported Cases" by Lisak, Gardinier, Nicksa, and Cote, suggests that the prevalence of false sexual assault claims is between two and eight percent. But when we consider the number of unreported rapes, this rate could be significantly lower, according to another 2010 study by Belknap:

> Although false allegations are 5% of all rapes reported to the police, the fact that at least 90% of rapes are never reported to the police (not just including college samples, and this is a conservative estimate) suggests that of all rapes (those reported and not reported to the police), 0.005% are false allegations.

Thus, in its first season, before national discussion of sexual assault and consent had started to grow, *OITNB*'s main representation of sexual assault mostly upheld traditional rape myths about women.

Despite the unrealistic and stereotypical depiction of Daya's relationships with Bennett and Mendez, *OITNB* did take a more critical view of the prison's handling of sexual assault claims. This seemed to reflect growing distrust of colleges' sexual assault procedures during the year of *OITNB*'s Season 1 premiere. Anticipating the prison's unwillingness to address allegations of sexual assault by a CO, Daya's friends, Red and Nicky, advise Daya that she must have physical evidence of her rape for the prison to take her claim seriously:

R: You know he needs to –

N: Come inside you.

R: Or on you.

N: Right. At the very least you need to Lewinsky this shit. Get some splooge on your uniform. Anything that will be concrete proof.

R: After you're done, you go straight to the medic's office. Tell him you've been raped. Have him do an exam immediately. Don't stop to pee. Don't wash anything. Understand?

This exchange demonstrates an understanding of how difficult it is for inmates, and women in general, to seek justice for sexual assault. Without physical evidence, authorities often do not investigate assault claims. Even with DNA evidence, many grievances are found to be unsubstantiated. According to Brenner, Darcy, Fedock, and Kubiak, many perpetrators are also aware of the importance of DNA evidence to a successful claim, so they take steps to avoid leaving any behind. In Daya's case, even with the eyewitness account of an administrator, Mendez is not prosecuted – he is put on leave.

OITNB continues its criticism of the prison's handling of sexual assault claims in its second season, as Mendez is recalled from leave to support the prison when it is short on experienced correctional officers. Faced with Mendez, Daya finally reports her pregnancy to the prison administration in order to push them to press charges against Mendez. With this undeniable evidence, Fig is forced to take official action, but before she does so, she blames Daya for having "encouraged" Mendez to have sex with her (Season 2, Episode 10). Though in prison all sex between correctional officers and inmates is prohibited by law, authorities often favor rape myths over the laws and policies that they are obligated to uphold, as demonstrated by Fig's questioning of Daya's role in the assault.

Mendez's return also highlights one of the largest threats facing inmates today: prisons are increasingly run by private contractors that seek to increase profits by eliminating important prison resources, foregoing adequate training for correctional officers, and implementing the minimum requirements of the NPREC's suggested policies. The importance of the bottom line is clear in the reactions of prison administrators to the NPREC's findings. According to a 2013 study by Struckman-Johnson and Struckman-Johnson, because of the cost of reforms, administrators' reactions to the NPREC recommendations have been mixed, despite the seriousness of the study's findings. So, while *OITNB*'s first season depicted sexual assault and consent inconsistently, reinforcing rape myths that blame women for lying about rape while pointing out flaws in prison policies, Season 2 is characterized by increased attention to the effect that rape myths and budgetary constraints play in the way that the prison administration deals with sexual assault claims.

Case 2: Doggett and Coates

The third season of *OITNB* introduces a new plot line that fundamentally changes the way the show depicts sexual assault. Tiffany Doggett, a White female inmate from a lower-class background, is at the center of two rapes: one in the past (through a series of flashbacks), and one in the present. For her work detail,

Doggett drives correctional officers on prison errand runs. On one of these errand runs, she meets Coates, a White male correctional officer, new to the prison. They establish a friendly relationship, like the unrealistic one between Daya and Bennett in Season 1.

However, the relationship between Doggett and Coates quickly changes from the model laid out by Daya and Bennett when, walking back to the van, Coates grabs Doggett, pushes her against a tree, and kisses her. Doggett at first protests, but then is motionless, staring ahead. The tenth episode of the third season is dedicated almost entirely to Doggett's prior experience with sexual assault. It opens with Doggett's mother explaining to her, as an eleven-year-old girl, what it means for her to have started her period:

> Now that you're a tittin' and a hairin', boys are gonna see ya different. And
> pretty soon, they're gonna do ya different. Best thing is to go on and let em
> do their business, baby. If you're real lucky, most of em 'll be quick, like
> your daddy. It's like a bee sting – in and out, before you knew it was
> happening.

This flashback fades into Doggett's first encounter with Coates since his unwelcome kiss. He delivers a flawed apology: "I'm really sorry if I made you feel uncomfortable or did anything you didn't want to do, but maybe you also did want to?" Here, Coates' apology includes rape myths that frame women as desiring or enjoying rape and "playing hard to get." Despite this, Doggett forgives Coates. The progression of these scenes suggests that Doggett's decision to excuse Coates is influenced by her mother's early advice to "go on and let [men] do their business." Her personal history is therefore depicted as influencing her present choices, and her ability to consent to a relationship with Coates.

Doggett's rape by CO Coates is immediately preceded by a flashback to an earlier rape from her teen years. She's at a party, when an acquaintance of hers approaches her and rapes her. While the scene starts off with the teenage boy pleading for sex, he quickly becomes forceful. After a short struggle, Doggett winces, then her face falls, and she seems to stop resisting as he rapes her. Doggett's memory fades into the present. Coates is angry with her for supposedly making them late the day before and his anger quickly escalates. He grabs her and lifts her into the van as she says "No, no!" He replies, "This is what you're asking for. This is what you're beggin' for, isn't it? You just lay there and keep quiet. You keep quiet," as he begins to rape her. Doggett's face again drifts into a state of resignation and she stops fighting.

Doggett's two rapes reflect the lived experiences of many women in prison. Research by the NPREC (2009) states that "from 31 to 59 percent of incarcerated women reported being sexually abused as children, and 23 to 53 percent reported experiencing sexual abuse as adults." This prior abuse can "create a vulnerability to future abuse." The same report states that women are more likely than men to be sexually abused prior to entering prison. *OITNB* also depicts the scenario between Doggett and Coates in more detail than in prior seasons. The story encompasses Doggett's rape, as well as the psychological and physical consequences of it. This type of depth is rare in television portrayals of sexual assault, and commentators were quick to note that *OITNB* had finally delivered a more realistic depiction representation of this crime.

The complexity and emotional power of Doggett's rape stands out from the shallow depiction of Daya and Mendez in Season 1 of *OITNB*. Myles McNutt of *A.V Club* writes:

> Although *Orange is The New Black* has engaged with rape in the past, it commits to it here and does so with clarity and purpose ... it points to how quickly the power relationship between guard and inmate can escalate, and benefits from a clear disinterest in titillation ... This is a dark series of events that speaks to how horrifying rape is but also how easily it can happen, and how the emotional state of rape victims is compromised by the sheer weight of navigating life as a woman (especially when intersected with issues of class, as is the case with [Doggett]).
>
> *(2015)*

From a sociological standpoint, we might call this an intersectional depiction of Doggett – one that considers the many elements that limit her ability to consent to a relationship with Coates. The most significant of these identities is her role as an inmate. We are provided only limited information about Doggett, and some of that information plays on stereotypes of White trash bigotry and miseducation about sex. However, these White trash roots and her previous portrayal as an antagonist, are softened by the friendship that she develops with Boo, a butch lesbian inmate who is extremely critical of many of her views. Thus, both Doggett and her experiences are treated as complex, instead of being guided by shallow rape myths.

In a 2015 review for *Vulture* titled, "'Orange is the New Black' Is the Only TV Show that Understands Rape: Grab a notebook, *Game of Thrones*," Jada Yuan contrasts *OITNB* with other popular television shows that fail to recognize rape as a complex and emotional experience. She labels *OITNB* the only show that has produced such a strong depiction of rape and argues that rape is an important topic for television and other media to explore, if it is done thoughtfully:

> Our natural instinct is to look away when confronted with something that ugly – and that's why it's so important for our television shows to hold their gaze. What's most striking about *Orange is the New Black*'s treatment of rape, and what separates it from any other current TV show, is ... director Jesse Peretz's simple, bold decision to keep the camera close and steady on Manning's face ... As long as she has no escape, as long as she must endure

this horrible thing happening to her, we, the audience, will have no choice but to stay with her. She did not invite this. She did not deserve this. This is not her shame; it is ours.

Yuan's article is also important because of the intense conversation that it sparked among commenters. The article was shared 35.3 thousand times and spurred over a hundred comments, with many long, thoughtful responses to the article and to depictions of rape on other television shows – ones that might pass what Yuan calls, "a Pennsatucky Test for rape scenes much like the Bechdel Test," in which depictions of rape would involve background, consequences, and women discussing how to deal with these issues.

Doggett and Boo decide that to report her rape would be useless, as the grievance would ultimately pit Doggett's word against a CO's. As an inmate, they thought Doggett would automatically be viewed as less credible. This assumption is supported by the low rate of success of many inmate grievances. Despite the NPREC's call for "zero tolerance" of sexual abuse in prison, inmates' claims rarely result in prosecution. Brenner and colleagues argue that this failure acts "as a deterrent for inmates in seeking a formal report or investigation" (2016, p. 561) Also, without DNA evidence, and considering the previously friendly relationship between her and Coates, Doggett's case would face scrutiny because of its mis-alignment with rape myths that require rape to be committed by a criminal stranger. So, unfortunately, the decision that Doggett makes is a decision that many inmates make. In a prison setting, where inmates' lives are literally con-trolled in all respects by the total institution of the prison and its COs and administrators, there are few options for victims seeking justice, and inmates are at risk of being retaliated against for reporting assaults.

The relationship between Doggett and Coates challenges rape myths that require an innocent victim and an unknown criminal attacker. The plot follows a CO's forceful abuse of authority to sexually assault an inmate, at the same time that it depicts a bond forming between the two. This mix of assault with familiarity and friendship characterizes many acquaintance rape scenarios on college cam-puses, and broader society as well. The fact that a prior relationship between victim and attacker is so often used to invalidate assault claims, suggests that it is an especially difficult rape myth for inmates to overcome. Brenner and her associates assert that even in cases where inmates and correctional officers have no established relationship, just because they interact with each other within the confines of the prison, "society has a difficult time overcoming rape myths" (2016, p. 548). Therefore, acquaintance rape poses an especially significant pro-blem for inmates, who necessarily have some knowledge of, or interaction with the COs who attack them.

OITNB's third season was characterized both by complex depictions of sexual assault, and by strong criticism of law and policy. Rather than reporting her sexual assault, Doggett and her friend Boo take justice into their own hands.

They work together to extract Doggett from her job with CO Coates, and even carry out a plan to take revenge on him. However, in the moment of truth, when they have the opportunity to inflict pain on Coates, they both decide not to (Season 3, Episode 13). This scene may be one of the most progressive in *OITNB*, because it illustrates the central flaw of the prison system: retributive justice does not actually resolve victims' pain. Therefore, *OITNB* not only challenges rape myths in its third season, it challenges viewers' definitions of justice.

Conclusion

OITNB has provoked some of the most complex conversations about sexual assault and consent on television. In its first season, it was criticized for its portrayal of a romantic relationship between an inmate and a CO, as well as its perpetuation of a popular rape myth that frames women as lying about rape. However, in each following season, *OITNB* has increasingly produced thoughtful and provocative depictions of sexual assault, reflecting changing norms around affirmative sexual consent. The writers of the show translated national debates over campus rape to the prison, highlighting the danger that women in general face, as well as the increased threat that inmates face.

OITNB's prison setting, where all sexual relationships between inmates and correctional officers are illegal, regardless of consent, forced viewers to consider what really makes sex ethical and consensual. It is rarely as simple as "Yes Means Yes," as we see in the case of Doggett and Coates. Their case suggests that consent is the product of a variety of factors that affect an individual's agency. *OITNB* also illustrates the institutional and legal barriers that inmates face in seeking justice for their assaults: assumptions about victim credibility, administrators' acceptance of rape myths, structural barriers to reporting claims, and the unsatisfying punitive solutions offered by the criminal justice system.

However, while *OITNB* advances representations of sexual assault on television in many ways, it seems to reinforce some rape myths related to race. While Daya, a Latina woman, is portrayed as manipulative and actively pursuing sexual relationships with two correctional officers, Doggett, a White woman, is portrayed more sympathetically. Though she had been a largely antagonistic and even violent character in prior seasons of *OITNB*, in the third season, when she begins her relationship with C.O., Doggett, a white female character, is presented in a more sympathetic way and the assault is clearly presented as a rape. This reinforcement of racial rape myths seems to illustrate the difficulty of getting rid of such powerful stereotypes. Because rape myths are tied into ideas about race, gender essentialism, and patriarchy, they are difficult to untangle, especially for large institutions interested in addressing the outcomes, rather than the causes of sexual assault.

Our current sexual assault laws and policies are failing in many ways, but it is important to consider the process of changing these laws. First, to be successful, they must reflect cultural norms. Therefore, we have to challenge the harmful rape myths that underlie current laws. In addition, as activism has increasingly called for harsher sentencing for sexual assault and rape, we must consider the many ways that these future laws could be corrupted by bias. Mandatory minimum sentencing for sexual assault will likely disproportionately affect people of color, contributing to mass incarceration and continuing existing inequalities. Finally, and perhaps most importantly, we need to examine what justice means in cases of sexual assault. Can retributive justice create a less violent culture, or are we just trapped in a cycle of abuse?

References

Alexander, M. (2010). *The New Jim Crow: Mass Incarceration in the Age of Colorblindness.* New York, NY: The New Press.

Belknap, J. (2010). Rape: Too hard to report and too easy to discredit victims. *Violence Against Women*, 16(12): 1335–1344.

Blackburn, A. G., Mullings, J. L., & Marquart, J. W. (2008). Sexual assault in prison and beyond: Toward an understanding of lifetime sexual assault among incarcerated women. *The Prison Journal*, 88(3), 351–377. Retrieved from http://tpj.sagepub.com

Brenner, H., Darcy, K., Fedock, G., & Kubiak, S. (2016). Bars to justice: The impact of rape myths on women in prison. *Georgetown Journal of Gender and the Law* 17(2): 521–574. Retrieved from heinonline.org

Calavita, K. & Jenness, V. (2013). Inside the pyramid of disputes naming problems and filing grievances in California prisons. *Social Problems*, 60(1), 50–80. Retrieved from http://www.jstor.org/stable/10.1525/sp.2013.60.1.50

Carson, A. E. (2015, September). *Prisoners in 2014.* Retrieved from https://www.bjs.gov/content/pub/pdf/p14.pdf

Department of Justice. (2012). National Standards to prevent, detect, and respond to prison rape; Final Rule. *Federal Register*, 77(19), 37106–37232. Retrieved from https://www.regulations.gov/document?D=DOJ-OAG-2011-0002-0001

Fulcher, P. A. (2012). Hustle and flow: Prison privatization fueling the prison industrial complex. *Washburn Law Journal*, 51, 589–617. Retrieved from https://www.privateprisonnews.org/media/publications/fulcher_prison_privatization_fueling_prison_industrial_complex_june_2012.pdf

Goffman, E. (1961). *Asylums: Essays on the Social Situation of Mental Patients and other Inmates.* Garden City: Anchor Books.

Lisak, D., Gardinier, L., Nicksa, S. C., & Cote, A. M. (2010). False allegations of sexual assault: An analysis of ten years of reported cases. *Violence Against Women*, 16(12), 1318–1334.

McNutt, M. (2015, June 20). Orange *is the* New Black: 'A Tittin' And A Hairin'. Retrieved from http://www.avclub.com/tvclub/orange-new-black-tittin-and-hairin-221137

National Prison Rape Elimination Commission. (2009, June). *National Prison Rape Elimination Commission Report.* Retrieved from https://www.ncjrs.gov/pdffiles1/226680.pdf

Pozner, J. L. (2013, August 29). TV can make America better. *Salon.* Retrieved from http://www.salon.com/2013/08/29/tv_can_make_america_better/

Struckman-Johnson, C., & Struckman-Johnson, D. (2013). Stopping prison rape: The evolution of standards recommended by PREA's national prison rape elimination commission. *The Prison Journal*, 93(3), 335–354.

The Sentencing Project. (2015, November). *Incarcerated Women and Girls*. Retrieved from http://www.sentencingproject.org/wp-content/uploads/2016/02/Incarcerated-Women-and-Girls.pdf

Tillet, S. (2013, July 23). It's so not 'OZ': Netflix's 'Orange is the New Black.' *The Nation*. Retrieved from http://www.thenation.com/article/its-so-not-oz-netflixs-orange-new-black/

Tuerkheimer, D. (2014). Slutwalking in the shadow of the law. *Minnesota Law Review*, 98(4), 1453–1511. Retrieved from http://www.minnesotalawreview.org/wp-content/uploads/2014/04/Tuerkheimer_MLR.pdf

Tuerkheimer, D. (2015). Rape on and off campus. *Emory Law Journal*, 65(1), 1–45. Retrieved from http://law.emory.edu/elj/_documents/volumes/65/1/articles/tuerkheimer.pdf

Weizel, L. M. (2012). The process that is due: Preponderance of the evidence as the standard of proof for University adjudications of student-on-student sexual assault complaints. *Boston College Law Review*, 53(4), 1613–1655. Retrieved from http://lawdigitalcommons.bc.edu/bclr/vol53/iss4/10

Yuan, J. (2015, July 6). 'Orange is the New Black' is the only TV show that understands rape: Grab a notebook, Game of Thrones. *Vulture*. Retrieved from http://www.vulture.com/2015/07/orange-is-the-new-black-is-the-only-tv-show-that-understands-rape.html#

16

GRAY IS THE NEW ORANGE

Older, Infirm Female Inmates and the Liminal Space between Human and Animal

Hadar Aviram

Introduction

"The animals, the animals, trapped, trapped, trapped till the cage is full": Regina Spektor's theme song for *Orange is the New Black* calls attention to the liminal space between human and animal – an important theme in incarceration. As commentators such as sociologist Löic Wacquant (2009) and legal scholar Jonathan Simon (2007) contend, the era of mass incarceration is characterized by an over-arching warehousing project, which – rather than deterring or rehabilitating – is focused merely on incapacitation and control. The logic underscoring this carceral project is one of actuarial assessment of risk by which we "selectively incapacitate" people based on their presumed dangerousness according to law professors Malcolm Feeley and Jonathan Simon (1992), though in some places even risk distinctions are not made, and the system indiscriminately incapacitates everyone under its control. The rising costs and pressures of incarcerating an enormous population have led to a decline in standards and conditions, sometimes offering inmates little or nothing beyond what Giorgio Agamben (1998) calls "bare life."

This disturbing trend has undergone an interesting transformation in the aftermath of the 2008 financial crisis. As state and local governments responded to budgetary cuts, correctional budgets, which have been a considerable percentage of govern-mental expenses, have come under scrutiny. My own work argues for the first time in forty years, the overall United States correctional population began to decline, and great strides were made in struggles against the death penalty, solitary confinement, and the war on drugs, after decades of inaction. The effects of a bipartisan move to cut incarceration costs have been, however, mixed. The Great Recession and the discourse of austerity that surrounded it have highlighted the neoliberal transformation in our perception of inmates. Erving Goffman's classic analysis of the prison as a total institution, which encompasses all aspects of its inhabitants' lives calls for their perception as wards of the state, whose food, clothing and care is the responsibility of the state. The neoliberal retreat of the state from its welfare obligations has recast inmates as fiscal subjects, whose care is a burden on the prison economy, and who participate in the market by consuming prison services, albeit not by free choice. This perspective has been the foundation of various privatization efforts, as well as "pay-to-stay" schemes that require inmates to financially contribute to their own incarceration according to several legal scholars, including not only the author of this work but also that of Robert Weisberg (2007) and Kim Shayo Buchanan (2007) among others.

Elderly and Infirm Inmates

I posit this perspective on inmates as fiscal subjects has led to a new interest in categories of inmates that have been neglected for decades: the growing categories of the elderly and the infirm. While some of this interest might be humanitarian in nature, it largely stems from the fact that these categories consume the lion's share of prison healthcare expenses while not posing a serious reoffending risk – costs exacerbated by the growth of the elderly and infirm prison population itself, due both to lengthy sentences and to the commission of new crimes at an older age report Urban Institute researchers, KiDeuk Kim and Bryce Peterson (2014).

Studies in prison gerontology identify a pattern of ignorance and neglect regarding this population. Policy researcher Cyrus Ahalt and his colleagues (2013) find that, despite the decline in overall prison population, the share of inmates whose health care is costly rises, to nearly 10% of the prison population. With the rise in healthcare costs and state cuts in spending, many correctional agencies struggle to account for their needs. The lack of quality health care in prison affects this older population upon release, too, while the paucity of cost data has significantly hampered innovations in policy and practice to improve value in correctional health care (achieving desired health outcomes at sustainable costs). Geriatric researcher Tacara Soones and colleagues (2014) find that not only is data unavailable to the agencies at large, but knowledge deficits regarding the unique issues faced by the geriatric prison population were also found among legal professionals. A survey of legal professionals in the criminal justice system, which included judges, prosecutors, defense attorneys, and court-affiliated social workers, revealed knowledge deficits regarding age-related health, identification of cognitive impairment, assessment of safety risk, and optimization of services upon release from jail. These problems, compounded by the inmates' fragility and vulnerability and the unsuitability of prison facilities, inhibit the ability to effectively care for inmates, in matters ranging from pain alleviation to palliative care.

Even though these problems characterize all elderly and infirm inmates, they are uniquely perverse with regard to women. The literature on women and crime has long observed that female prison populations are much less frequently studied, an oversight often excused by the population's small size. This oversight extends to serious neglects in policymaking. An exploratory study of policies and programs specifically designed to address the needs of female inmates over 45 years old revealed a disturbing picture of what the authors refer to as "malign neglect" according to sociologists Monica Williams and Robert Vann Rikard (2014). Among the forty states surveyed, plus the Federal Bureau of Prisons, only two – Alabama and Ohio – specified policies and/or programs that focus on aging female inmates, by comparison to 23 states that had such programs for aging male inmates. As the authors observe, this is particularly problematic because, in general, female inmates require more medicinal and psychiatric services than males. As criminology professor Azrini Wahidin observes, gerontology as a field has been gender-blind, and has tended to ignore the fact that gender is not a homogenous category that remains static over the life course.

Ignoring aging and infirm women is particularly perverse given the unique health challenges they face. As John Linder and Frederick Meyers demonstrate, female inmates are at an even higher risk than male inmates and suffer more frequent and serious diseases, illnesses, and injuries than do male prisoners. Many women enter with chronic illness or are diagnosed with one. As many as 57% of female inmates have a history of sexual or physical abuse or both; according to the Bureau of Justice Statistics, one in four women in state prisons was physically or sexually abused before the age of 18. These tragic personal histories are associated with a higher incidence of high-risk sexual behaviors, and those carry risks of infections and psychiatric disorders. In addition, a disproportionately large number of female inmates suffer from chronic conditions such as diabetes, hypertension, cardiac disease, and cancer. Nutritional counseling is often neglected, and prisons typically offer meals that are high in calories, fat, and sugar, which exacerbate these conditions.

OITNB Images of Elderly and Infirm Female Inmates

Orange is the New Black (*OITNB*), a Netflix original series loosely based on Piper Kerman's memoir of the same name, depicts the lives of female inmates in a federal correctional facility. The series has been lauded for introducing mainstream audiences to various important prison-related issues, such as solitary confinement, the disciplinary apparatus, racial segregation, and reproductive justice. Indeed, the series should be lauded for presenting the struggles of old and infirm inmates through the stories of two strong and outspoken characters: Sister Jane Ingalls, a nun serving a prison term for her role in a protest against a nuclear site, and Rosa Cisneros, a terminally ill cancer patient serving a sentence for bank robbery. The two characters' stories touch upon the "malign neglect" surrounding the care of elderly and infirm women in prison. However, the narrative vehicle for these stories, through two vocal women possessing experience and skills of self-advocacy, obfuscates some of the most serious problems pertaining to these groups of inmates: deficiencies in medical literacy and the inability to have a voice in addressing their basic needs. Despite these shortcomings, the series succeeds in highlighting the liminal space of age and illness and the challenges of incarceration.

In *OITNB*, we are introduced to Sister Ingalls – an educated, White middle-aged inmate – early on in the series, and frequently see her in the company of other aging women, who refer to themselves as the "Golden Girls." Her story, however, comes to the forefront of the series after she witnesses the cruel fate of a fellow Golden Girl, a fellow inmate named Jimmy Cavanaugh. Jimmy suffers from advanced dementia; she is in her seventies but believes she is still in her twenties and that Lyndon Johnson is still president. Searching in vain for her long-dead husband, Jack, Jimmy repeatedly escapes from prison, and her final escape provokes panic at the institution. After a further episode, in which she breaks her arm in the chapel by mistaking the altar for a diving board atop a swimming pool, she is awarded so-called compassionate release. To the inmates' shock, a screaming Jimmy is merely transported to a bus station and, from then on, left to her own devices. The other inmates, who know that Jimmy has only one estranged daughter living abroad, are distressed at her situation.

Through Jimmy's character, the series introduces the contradictions inherent to compassionate release policies, which are designed to address the cost of keeping ill inmates behind bars but do not address their needs after release. In line with this rationale, in 2010, sixteen states and the District of Columbia had provisions for geriatric release. These provisions, however, were not used to the extent intended. In some states, such as Maryland, Virginia, and Wisconsin, the releases are contingent upon age, rather than medical condition – a parameter confounded by the lack of consensus over what age counts as "old" in the context of prison. In the federal system, which is depicted in *Orange is the New Black*, early releases for medical and compassionate reasons are one of the few "escape hatches" from a determinate sentencing system with no provision for parole says Jamie Fellner, author of the Human Rights Watch report, *Old Behind Bars: The Aging Prison Population in the United States* (2010). The exceptions have been narrowly tailored by the United States Sentencing Commission to apply only to inmates suffering from terminal illnesses or unable to provide self-care in prison. The Bureau of Prisons do not consider the Sentencing Commission guidelines binding, as evident from the outcomes. The federal prison population grew from 95,034 in 1994 to 218,170 in 2011, but the number of motions for sentence reduction filed by the Bureau of Prisons increased merely from 23 to 30. For those who benefit from these policies – and even with the advent of medical coverage from the day of release under the Affordable Care Act – the isolation and fragility of many elderly and infirm inmates mean that release with no re-entry provisions is compassionate only in name.

Jimmy's release galvanizes Sister Ingalls and reawakens her spirit of political protest. A group of younger inmates begin a hunger strike to protest against various conditions. She is initially reluctant to participate, saying, "That's all behind me. I'm old, I have low blood sugar. I was hoping that prison would give me the chance to find the time for solemn contemplation". Sister Ingalls is then accused by the younger inmates of being "a pussy." Later, when the warden visits the inmates to discuss their demands, she addresses him directly:

> I have an issue. What are you going to do about the quality of senior care in this institution? The elderly are the fastest growing population in prison, and they have special needs. So-called "compassionate release" in lieu of care is completely unacceptable. You can't dump sick old ladies on the street. It's unconscionable, inhumane, and... illegal. You must meet your obligations.

In this statement, Sister Ingalls offers mainstream viewers a quick primer on the challenges faced by inmates. While she does not explain which "special needs" she refers to, her protest speech encapsulates a variety of issues that prison scholarship addresses. She draws attention to an issue highlighted by criminologist Azrini Wahidin in her interviews with aging female inmates – age is important in the institutional context. It is aging in incarceration that gives rise to "the feeling of a discrepancy between ascribed age and the subjective experience of age. This is because the aging prisoners are at the mercy of how others see them (the Foucaultian 'gaze')" (2004, p. 54). Until imprisonment women could view aging as a period of possibilities – gardening, cooking, playing piano, and the new adventures of grandparenthood. In the context of prison old primarily implies "not young," and hence, culturally different and set apart by a set of needs and experiences that the majority of the prison population is unlikely to share.

In her study, Wahidin's interviewees identify various ways in which their age is used to stereotype them: they are perceived as "daft," spoken about in derogatory terms in their presence, and monitored for responsibility and use of language more than the younger inmates. They resent the fact that the few educational opportunities available are heavily feminized and menial, catering to a younger, less educated population, and of ignorance and neglect concerning their particular needs. One of Wahidin's interviewees expresses dismay at the discontinuation of her menopause medication. Indeed, these concerns reflect a considerable gap in prison health care. My survey of prison medical literature reveals virtually no scholarship on menopause. The only mention of the problem appears in a correctional nursing manual by Catherine Schoenly and Lorry Knox, in which a blog by a prison nurse mentions the fact that prison conditions, by nature, aggravate menopause, as the lack of air conditioning, ventilation and sunshine contribute to symptoms such as hot flashes and Vitamin D deficiencies.

It is fairly evident that Sister Ingalls' protest is driven by witnessing these, and other, iniquities and violations. When a younger inmate, who is happy to have Sister Ingalls on board for the hunger strike, teases her, "it's because I called you a pussy, isn't it?" Sister Ingalls replies: "It's for Jimmy." Later, prison authorities manage to break the will of the hunger strikers with pizza. Sister Ingalls remains the lone, principled, hunger striker – even in the face of the threat of medical segregation. As she is wheeled away in a wheelchair, she gives the peace sign to a gauntlet of applauding and supportive inmates.

In a plot turn that echoes the end of the Pelican Bay prison hunger strike in California, the medical authorities threaten to force-feed Sister Ingalls. In an effort to prevent this barbarous proceeding, she screams, "I'm awake, I'm awake, I'm awake!" As she refuses food and the medical authorities approach her, she frantically cries out "Do not feed me! I did not give my permission. This is not right! It's not fair! Please! Please!" The screen goes dark and the viewers are deprived the actual force-feeding process. This avoidance stops short of visiting Sister Ingalls – one of the more privileged, eloquent, and assertive inmates – in her liminal place between person and animal, subject and object, inmate and patient.

Nonetheless, the end of the scene leaves this storyline at a tense moment. The seriousness of the situation is then somewhat alleviated by later comical scenes, in which Sister Ingalls and a fellow inmate, Red, bond and joke in their hospital beds, and in a further scene in which Ingalls ends her hunger strike but is mortified at the thought of this decision reaching her many supporters outside the gates. The return to humor, arguably necessary in a television series aimed at entertaining as well as educating, turns Sister Ingalls into an eloquent and principled – albeit not entirely selfless – interlocutor for a class of voiceless inmates.

Similar contradictions emerge in another examination of the liminal space in the storyline following Rosa Cisneros, a Latina inmate diagnosed with terminal cancer. The first season of *OITNB* mostly depicts Rosa's pain and exhaustion as she is shuttled back and forth to her chemotherapy treatment. In the second season, we are introduced to Rosa's background story: a young, vibrant and impulsive woman convicted of a series of daring bank robberies. This image is contrasted to her frail, aging present self, which the viewers attribute to her chemotherapy treatments.

Handcuffed and watched by a prison correctional officer, Rosa befriends a fellow patient, a teenager who assumes her drab apparel is "just old lady chemo clothes." The lines between age, sickness, and imprisonment are blurred, pointing to the fact that any and all of these categories intersect to challenge Rosa's humanity. Rosa's struggle against this marginalization sees her confront these challenges and assert her humanity, even though these efforts are unsuccessful. In one scene, she is called to Lieutenant Healy's office to discuss her future. The conversation wryly illustrates the unbridgeable power gap between the two:

HEALY: The doctor recommends a bilateral salpingo-oophorectomy.
ROSA: Who doesn't love a surgery with "ooph" in it?
HEALY: Yeah, well, uh… the, uh, DOC has set certain limits on invasive… it's
    not gonna happen.
    [Rosa sighs]
    You're not out of options. We'll stick with the chemo.

ROSA: "We?" You got cancer in your ovaries, too?

HEALY: I'm your counselor. I'm here to help you with this.

ROSA: There is no "through this." I'm gonna die.

HEALY: Hey. Come on, now. You could live for years.

ROSA: That's a fucking lie.

HEALY: Language!

> [cut to Rosa's wry, dismayed expression]

> Look, I know this is difficult for you. My cousin had lung cancer, it didn't look good for him, but he stuck with the chemo and now he's back fixing roofs in Oneonta.

ROSA: Lucky duck, your cousin. Me? Dead duck.

HEALY: You have to try to remain positive. No one knows the future.

ROSA: Doctors know the future. They think I need the surgery.

HEALY: I wish I could help you.

ROSA: But it's out of your hands. It's always out of your hands. You're all the same... useless.

Rosa's wry replies reveal both the futility of arguing with Healy and the fundamental inhumanity in his hopeful approach toward her condition, comparing her to his cousin. Her dread and hopelessness echo findings by Dayron Deaton and colleagues, who conducted a death anxiety survey among female inmates over the age of 50 in five Southern states. Their results reveal a substantial degree of death anxiety, correlated with physical and mental health measures. The qualitative findings, based on the inmates' personal reports, reveal that their concerns about dying in prison were often influenced by the perceived lack of adequate health care and the indifference of prison staff and other instances of penal harm.

The way in which death anxiety and other feelings of powerlessness are exacerbated is highlighted in a subsequent scene, which sees Rosa at her oncologist's office. She is accompanied by a prison correctional officer who is standing behind her.

ONCOLOGIST: Miss Cisneros, Hello. [to the correctional officer:] There's a chair outside in the hallway, if you'd like to wait there.

GUARD: I gotta stay. It's policy.

ONCOLOGIST: I understand, of course... but I would appreciate a few moments alone with my patient.

GUARD: I'm just doing my job.

ROSA: It's alright, Doc. I'm used to it.

ONCOLOGIST: Fine. [pause] Miss Cisneros, we've received your results.

ROSA: I'm dying, I know.

ONCOLOGIST: Well... yes, that's true. But...

ROSA: Look, Doc. I don't need any bullshit about percentages or millimeters or stages. Do me a favor and talk to me like you would if... I was a person you loved.

> [pause]

ONCOLOGIST: The chemo is not working. The cancer is aggressive.
ROSA: How long I got?
ONCOLOGIST: Three to six weeks, I'd say.
ROSA: Thank you.

This exchange sees Rosa accepting the liminal place she occupies at the clinic, in her status between inmate and patient. She is the one who diffuses the conflict between the oncologist and the correctional officer about the correctional officer's presence in the room. But at the same time, she insists on being treated with humanity and dignity by the oncologist. Her words echo the words of an interviewee who told researchers Sheila Enders, Debora Paterniti and Frederick Meyers that she would like to tell her doctors:

> I have a terminal illness. I just wish you could step into my head for a minute to see what I'm feeling. Then you could understand the helplessness I feel, but you don't understand. I feel like, don't just look at my number, look at my face. I have a spirit. You have a spirit. I feel, you feel.
>
> *(2005)*

In making Rosa both helpless and an eloquent self-advocate, the series hints at the problem less eloquent inmates face in making health care decisions. Enders and her colleagues who facilitated focus groups of inmates at the California Central Women's Facility, found that the inmates felt they lacked knowledge of medical conditions, body parts, and medical terms, and found the language barriers and patronizing interactions difficult to bridge, thus, hindering self-advocacy. They identified deficiencies in translating medical jargon, seeking input from patients, and offering them resources.

Rosa's liminal place is challenged again in the van that transports her back to prison. A fellow inmate, Morello, drives the van, and the correctional officer freely speaks of Rosa's condition in Murillo and Rosa's presence:

GUARD: She's done. Done, done.
[pause]
Only has a few more weeks. That's what the doc said. Man... it's real fucked up to die in prison. I mean, it's fucked up to die, period, but... this is fucked up.
[Guard sings *Breakfast in Tiffany's* along with the radio.]

This scene highlights the inherent problems in planning end-of-life care for inmates. For many inmates their incarceration is the first time in which they have consistent access to health care, and yet the prison setting impedes treatment. The limited extent to which prisons finance health care, and the inherent power imbalances, further impair a secure and trusted relationship between the inmate and caregivers, especially in the context of end-of-life care. Correctional agencies' limited financing of experimental care "simplifies the transition from disease-directed therapy to palliative care", assert John Linder and Frederick Myers (2007, p. 897). While it is highly doubtful that Rosa perceives her situation as "simplified", she is clearly disempowered in the situation.

The series again steps away from the liminal place by creating a plot device to empower Rosa to end her life on her terms, on an empowered, positive note. After the correctional officer leaves the gate, Morello deliberately leaves the keys in the van, saying to Rosa:

MORELLO: Fuck it. Don't die in here, Miss Rosa. Do it your way.
ROSA: What do I do?
MORELLO: Go fast.

Rosa turns the ignition key and drives the van away, fleeing the prison at a great speed (and, incidentally, almost crashing into Sister Ingalls' hunger strike supporter posse). Along the way she sees a fellow inmate, Dee, who had been consistently rude to her. Rosa changes channels in the van radio, eventually finding the song *Don't Fear the Reaper*. She smiles and drums on the wheel. When she spots Dee, she veers off the road, hitting Dee and killing her. Rosa [after hitting Dee] states: "Always so rude, that one."

Conclusion

The series then treats us to a blissful end. As Rosa blissfully drives the van away, she is visually transformed from her ill, aging physical self to her younger, bank robber self, and her smile widens to a loud rendition of *Don't Fear the Reaper*. This ending to the second season of *OITNB* enables us to remember Rosa on a triumphant, powerful note of free agency. But while as a narrative device it is laudable and empowering, it also obscures the realities of death in prison. Studies of prison health care and gerontology point to the fact that prison patients are hindered, due to the power imbalances inherent to their situation, from effectively advocating for themselves. A number of scholars highlight the low health literacy among their interviewees and their difficulties in self-advocacy given the impaired communication between them and their caregivers.

The stories of Rosa and Sister Ingalls are important because they confront viewers with inmates at their most basic, fragile, and deserving place: that of an animal trapped in a cage, a helpless ward of the state, deserving of basic health needs. This paradigm is contrasted with the prison paradigm, which perceives the care of inmates through the prism of cost savings and bureaucratic management. But the artistic choice to tell these stories through eloquent, empowered inter-locutors, and to stop the narrative frame short of the liminal place, might hinder the audience from fully acknowledging the more silent, and more futile, struggle of people deprived of anything beyond their identities as aging, frail subjects, in which they fight back with the only thing they have left – their bodies, their age, and their fragility.

References

Agamben, G. (1998). *Homo Sacer: Sovereign Power and Bare Life*. Palo Alto: Stanford University Press.

Ahalt, C., Trestman, R., Rich, J. D., Greifinger, R. B., & Williams, B. A. (2013). Paying the price: the pressing need for quality, cost, and outcomes data to improve correctional health care for older prisoners. *Journal of American Geriatric Society*, 61(11), 2013–2019.

Buchanan, K. S. (2007). It could happen to 'you': Pay-to stay jail upgrades. *Michigan Law Review First Impressions*, 106, 60–67.

Deaton, D., Aday, R. & Wahidin, A. (2009). The effect of health and penal harm on aging female prisoners' views of dying in prison. *Omega: Journal of Death and Dying*, 60(1), 51–70.

Enders, S. R., Paterniti, D. A., & Meyers, F. (2005). An approach to develop effective care decision making for women in prison. *Journal of Palliative Medicine*, 8(2), 432–439.

Feeley, M. & Simon, J. (1992). The new penology: Notes on the emerging strategy of corrections and its implications. *Criminology*, 30, 449–474.

Fellner, J. (2010). *Old behind Bars: The Aging Prison Population in the United States*. Human Rights Watch. Retrieved from https://www.hrw.org/sites/default/files/reports/usprisons0112webwcover_0.pdf

Goffman, E. (1961). *Asylums: Essays on the Social Situation of Mental Patients and other Inmates*. New York: Anchor Books/Doubleday.

Kim, K. & Peterson, B. (2014). Aging behind bars: Trends and implications of graying prisoners in the federal prison system. *Urban Institute*. Retrieved from http://www.urban.org/sites/default/files/alfresco/publication-pdfs/413222-Aging-Behind-Bars-Trends-and-Implications-of-Graying-Prisoners-in-the-Federal-Prison-System.PDF

Linder, J. F. & Meyers, F. J. (2007). Palliative care for prison inmates: "Don't let me die in prison." *Journal of the American Medical Association*, 298(8), 894–901.

Simon, J. (2007). *Governing through Crime: How the War on Crime transformed American Democracy and Created a Culture of Fear*. New York: Oxford University Press.

Simon, J. (2014). *Mass Incarceration on Trial: A Remarkable Court Decision and the Future of Prisons in America*. New York and London: The Free Press.

Wacquant, L. (2009). *Punishing the Poor: The Neoliberal Government of Social Insecurity*. Durham and London: Duke University Press.

Wahidin, A. (2004). *Older Women in the Criminal Justice System: Running out of Time*. London: Jessica Kingsley Publishers.

Weisberg, R. (2007). Pay-to-stay in California jails and the value of systemic self-embarassment. *Michigan Law Review First Impressions*, 106, 55–59.

Williams, M. E. & Vann Rikard, R. (2014). Marginality or neglect: An exploratory study of policies and programs for aging female inmates. *Women & Criminal Justice*, 15(3/4), 121–141.

17

BROCCOLI, LOVE AND THE HOLY TOAST

Cultural Depictions of Religion in *Orange is the New Black*

Terri Toles Patkin

Introduction: Religion and Prisons

From the very first scene, where Piper Chapman is introduced as a "blonde, shiksa, WASP" – the trifecta of White privilege – and joins her Jewish fiancé Larry for a pig roast on the night before her incarceration, religion provides a rhythmic undercurrent to the events in *Orange is the New Black* (*OITNB*) that punctuates the more overt representations of race, class, and gender throughout the series. The prison population at Litchfield Penitentiary appears as a multicultural soup of religious diversity: from an incarcerated nun, to a yoga teacher spouting Buddhist aphorisms, to Pennsatucky's subversion of mainstream Christianity for personal gain, to demands for the more appetizing kosher meals, to faith healing, to an Amish girl who discovered drugs during her rumspringa, to Santería, to the Cult of Norma, the story of Litchfield prison is framed by the pillars of religious belief, or at least popular stereotypes of many faith traditions. The prison presents as a paradise of multiculturalism; the chapel is shared among religious denominations, and it is also used for secular gatherings. At the same time, religion, like the mythical chicken believed to be roaming the prison grounds (*The Chickening*), is presented as an illusion serving to give one's life meaning.

Incarceration and reform have long gone hand-in hand, and Litchfield's fictional world more or less mirrors the religious diversity of America's nonfictional prison population. More than two million people are incarcerated in American prisons and jails, and they are disproportionately people of color and poor. According to *Statista*, in 2011 just over half (50.6%) of American prison inmates identified as Protestant, and 14.5% as Catholic. Muslims accounted for 9.4%, "no religious preference" for 10.6%, Jewish for 1.7%, and Mormon for 0.8%. Unknown was selected for 5% of inmates, and other religions (including Orthodox

Christian, Buddhist, Hindu, Pagan/Earth-based, Native American spirituality and "other") came in at 7.4%. That more or less mirrors the overall religious affiliation of Americans as reported by the Pew Research Center (2015), which reported the following numbers in 2015: Protestant 49.8%, Catholic 20.8%, Muslim 0.9%, Jewish 1.9%, Mormon 1.6%, and Other 6.1%. Unaffiliated (including agnostic and atheist) come in at 22.8%.

The television series is, of course, based on the actual imprisonment of Piper Kerman, and she herself makes multiple references to religion in her memoir, *Orange is the New Black: My Year in a Women's Prison.* Piper's friend says she is "working like a Hebrew slave" to produce Piper's surprise birthday banquet, Piper describes her solicitous friends trying to feed her as being "like having half a dozen Jewish mothers," and her weekly radio listening as a "Sabbath ritual," and she sometimes labels people by religion ("a cheerful Christian"). It is hard to imagine that Kerman's actual prison community was filled with characters who embodied the overblown stereotypes of television's Litchfield to quite such an extent, however.

The tension between materiality and spirituality is interpreted via interpersonal relationships in the closed community. A prison is, of course, a prime example of what sociologist Erving Goffman dubbed a total institution, those segregated and isolated establishments that function as quasi-independent social systems. Religion is part of the outside world, and may represent one of the few connections a prisoner can maintain with that world while incarcerated. It is also one of the few aspects of prison life where the prisoner has agency and (at least to a degree) autonomy. One may choose to participate in religious observance, or one may decline to do so. As Joshua Dubler puts it in his book about religious life at a maximum security prison, *Down in the Chapel,* "First come the steel and concrete, then authority structures, regulations, and only then the prisoners' religious ideas and practices" (p. 271).

Broccoli: Material Manifestations of Spirituality

The tension between body, mind, and spirit pervades the practice of religion in prison, and food takes on a symbolic significance that exceeds even its importance in the outside world. Kerman points out that in her experience "institutional food required a Zen outlook." Food as metaphor permeates prison culture in *OITNB*: holiday meals are special, whether turkey on Thanksgiving (accompanied by the recitation of grace before the meal unlike most other days) or decorated cookies for Valentine's Day. Food is love (Sam Healy is given gifts of food by both Red and his estranged mail-order bride), food is reward (the winner of the pool betting on when Maria's baby will be born gets a Twix, Healy offers donuts to the inmates elected to the WAC), food is connection ("I threw my pie for you!" Crazy Eyes wails at Piper, Red hosts dinner parties for her friends).

Most of all, food represents power in *OITNB*, as first Red, then Gloria, then Red again, uses her position as head of the kitchen to consolidate her power base. Red starves out Piper (and Alex, when she offers Piper food), the Latinas over-salt the trays of the African-American inmates following a dispute over access to clean showers, Piper's panty business operates on a ramen spice packet economy. When Leanne and Angie want to protest, they initiate a hunger strike, and the unappetizing boil-in-bag meals introduced in Season 3 as the prison is taken over by a private management firm lead to about a third of the inmates requesting kosher food trays.

The Religious Land Use and Institutionalized Persons Act of 2000 mandates that a person holding a "sincere belief" requiring kosher or halal food must be accommodated as part of their religious observance. Actual prison inmates requesting kosher meals are closely scrutinized; if found eating any unsanctioned products from the cafeteria or commissary, their kosher request is immediately revoked, and it is difficult for a formerly non-kosher inmate to switch to a kosher meal plan, as it is more expensive. Nationwide, about 2% of the prison population in 35 states receive the special meals, which cost almost twice as much as regular prison fare, In fact, some states and institutions simply serve religious inmates a vegan diet because they cannot afford the special meals. The process for determining whether the religious request is "sincere" is at best ambiguous and fraught with difficulty.

The rise in kosher meal requests at Litchfield results in a rabbi being brought in to determine whether the prisoners keeping kosher are really Jewish, over administrator Caputo's, warning that this could lead to a lawsuit (*Where My Dreidel At*). Every stereotype of Judaism is trotted out during these interviews as the prisoners strive for approval: calling one's mother often, loving a bargain, having a big bat mitzvah, Woody Allen movies (Taystee conflates *Annie Hall* and *Yentl* in a creative rewrite of her life story), unpronounceable holidays, controlling the media, but it really comes down to the food, as one inmate muses that now kosher means so much more to her than "really, really good hot dogs." The only inmate to "pass" for Jewish is Sister Ingalls, who quotes Old Testament scripture. Disappointed, Cindy plans to "convert for real" in order to get the better food. Ironically, her plan to game the system changes as she begins to identify as Jewish for real: in learning the rules for being Jewish, she comes to accept them.

In prison, one learns to follow the rules – written and unwritten – because the consequences of not doing so are painful. The counts and inspections reek of Old Testament regulations, for which there may be some immediate meaning, but which ultimately are performed because the powers that be declare that it shall be so. The surveillance of the prison organizes life there, except that the panopticon, at least at Litchfield, is flawed. There are secret meetings, assignations, and attacks; the number of hidden illicit items is astonishing. The performance of religious piety by a prisoner is often presumed to be just that, a performance. Insincerity of belief is assumed to be inherent in the prisoner's state of being as "bad person," as when two African-American inmates acknowledge that they know little about Kwanzaa but joke that they should demand time off to celebrate the holiday (*Tall Men With Feelings*). Even Sister's journey to becoming a nun was largely influenced by the camaraderie of joining with others in protest.

The gods/guards (correctional officers) are arbitrary in *OITNB*. If the correctional officer assigned to the van wants to be driven out of bounds to pick up his paycheck at a donut shop, or visit a park, he can make the assigned inmate driver do that. If he wants to rape that inmate, he can do so unless she can trick him. Indeed, there are even sacrifices to the gods – gifts to Healy and others for everyday luxuries (these can be physical or emotional). If Blanca is forced to stand on a table, her ordeal can be compared to the passion of the Christ, as her resistance becomes symbolic of the hope for redemption among the entire prison population.

Love: Going to the Chapel and...

Prison – and correctional officers – can control your body but not your mind or spirit. Because of the way the rules work, religion is often the stated cause for group interaction; the chapel is a center for social (and sexual) life in the fictional prison. Faith provides strength in the midst of powerlessness, agency in the midst of control, privilege in the midst of deprivation. Non-religious faith also permeates the world of the prison: both correctional officers and prisoners express faith in cultural myths (meritocracy, true love, the happy family, being true to oneself). There is an openness and fluidity in the vernacular beliefs of the inmates that is rarely matched by institutional religion in the outside world, and which reflects the sustained hope that there is a better life to be found, if only the right pathway could be discovered. Cindy's embrace of Judaism reveals a naïve optimism in the power of self-determination. The prison chapel is the setting for many of the most important scenes (the cafeteria is the other), but more sex happens in the chapel. Sex – and attempted death – also happens in the library, interestingly both places for inmates to explore a world beyond daily material existence. Celibacy exists only in the imagined prison; even Sister talks about being aroused by a particularly sexy statue of Jesus, and we learn that her sojourn in Nicaragua was inspired as much by the handsome freedom fighter Carlos as it was by moral objectives (*We Have Manners, We're Polite*).

Religion is a way of establishing community, and ritual illuminates the nature of social relations among group members. Institutional ceremonies, such as the Mother's Day Carnival or Christmas celebrations, may offer staff and inmates an unusual opportunity to mix and may be accompanied by a temporary lowering of social barriers. The balance between sacred and secular in religious practice in prison illustrates the dialectical tension between spontaneity and structure, between symbolic and instrumental action, between implicit and explicit. "The fact that I'd become used to life in prison shocked my friends and family, but no one on the outside can really appreciate the galvanizing effect of all the regimented rituals, whether official or informal," Piper Kerman muses (2011, p. 155). Ritual offers catharsis and control to participants: when Taystee holds a funeral for the books destroyed due to a bedbug epidemic, complete with eulogies for "those titles that we lost" and sprinkling of ashes under the trees (*Empathy is a Boner Killer*), it provides an emotional outlet for the prisoners who mourn one of the only sources of independent action available to them (the decision of which book to read). Indeed, increased religious observance is sometimes seen near an inmate's release, perhaps evidence of growing anxiety about the transition.

For example, Pennsatucky's brand of Christianity is based in immediate gratification: Jesus (or at least the donors to the evangelical legal fund) will save her, whether that means her immortal soul or her bid for election to the prison committee (*WAC Pack*). Her uneducated but enthusiastic embrace of her "Third Amendment right" causes her to attempt to hang a giant cross in the chapel, causing the ceiling to collapse (*The Chickening*). She becomes so irritating that the other inmates, led by Piper, prank her into believing that she is a successful faith healer, resulting in her admission to the psych ward and a serious confrontation with Piper. Pennsatucky's redemption comes at the cost of her faith, but it is accompanied by rewards, as she is given better health care (and new teeth) and a change in job. The character's evolution from Pennsatucky (who identifies strongly with Jesus and anticipates the rapture) to Doggett (struggling with her Christian identity) to Tiffany (who admits to faking her religious belief to get funds) reflects our growing appreciation for her as a complex individual, and our support is encouraged to grow the farther she retreats from her naïve religious practice.

The language of religion peppers conversations: when Piper unexpectedly returns from a sojourn in Chicago, other inmates murmur "She is risen," and her success at obtaining a leave of absence to attend her grandmother's funeral leads to comments about "miracles" and the "end of days." (Someone as self-absorbed as the entitled Piper might well view herself as messianic; the surprise is that others appear to share that vision.) Yoga Jones often uses the mandala metaphor, urging the women to make something as beautiful as possible from their prison experience and then walk away from it. (Except that, unlike the monks, they have no choice in participation and no agency to decide when they are done and to walk away.)

The seriousness of pregnancy and especially childbirth can be read through the lens of religion. The separation of baby from mother – emotionally wrenching – and baby as savior calls to mind Christian tropes. Inmates count the days until they can be reunited with their children and family visiting days form a central rhythm of prison life. Daya's prison nativity points to the belief in family: her mother would rather have the baby raised by her drug-dealing cheating husband than give it an affluent home with an adoptive parent. According to the website thenamemeaning.com, the name "Dayanara" means "husband slayer; destroyer," and *OITNB*'s Dayanara does become the anti-Virgin Mary whose pregnancy leads not to redemption but to ruin for all involved.

When Cindy converts to Judaism, having studied and prepared for her *beit din*, the rabbi is partially convinced by Cindy's sincerity but largely by the game of "Jewish geography" played by Jewish inmate Ginsburg (who has been teaching Cindy), in which it turns out that she was a college friend of the rabbi's cousin. Cindy notes that being Jewish differs from her upbringing where she was raised in a strict church, where she had to believe and follow the rules or she would go to hell. But for Jews, she says, "As far as God is concerned, it's your job to keep asking questions and to keep learning and to keep arguing. It's like a verb, it's like you *do* God. And it's a lot of work" (*Trust No Bitch*). The presentation of her conversion is clearly more simplistic than it would be in the real world.

The cultural trope that religion in prison is either a con – a tactic to acquire more privileges – or a superficial panacea not really understood by the devout runs throughout the *OITNB* series. Pennsatucky's conversion comes not in church but as she enters a courtroom filled with supporters; for her, the belief in evangelical Christianity is a very personal path to emotional self-esteem. The real Piper is skeptical of religion in prison, noting that "a lot of pilgrims in prison seem to be making it up as they go along." When Piper refuses to be baptized in the laundry room sink by Pennsatucky, saying that she cannot pretend to believe in something she does not, her passionate monologue sums up the show's philosophy (*Tall Men with Feelings*):

> I believe in science. I believe in evolution. I believe in Nate Silver and Neil deGrasse Tyson, and Christopher Hitchens. Although I do admit he could be a kind of an asshole. I cannot get behind some supreme being who weighs in on the Tony Awards while a million people get whacked with machetes. I don't believe a billion Indians are going to hell. I don't think we get cancer to learn life lessons, and I don't believe that people die young because God needs another angel. I think it's just bullshit, and on some level, I think we all know that, I mean, don't you?... Look I understand that religion makes it easier to deal with all of the random shitty things that happen to us. And I wish I could get on that ride, I'm sure I would be happier. But I can't. Feelings aren't enough. I need it to be real.

Feelings may not be enough for Piper, but ultimately, connection grows from relationship, not from rules. When Tricia dies, Piper tries to organize a formal memorial service, only to discover that the true memorial is a vernacular gathering of inmates who come to clean out her bunk and express condolences (*Tall Men With Feelings*). When inmates gather to mourn the loss of one of the "family" through death, release from prison, or transfer to another facility, it parallels the

Jewish practice of sitting shiva as others stop by with condolences and gifts of food. The differentiation between a rules-orientation and a relational-orientation explains much about life in prison, and religious life in particular. Rule-oriented social actors – often those with higher social status – interpret activities, and particularly disputes, in terms of principles that apply regardless of social status. Society becomes a network of contractual opportunities. A relational orientation, typical of those with lower social status, frames the world in relational terms. Individuals who lack autonomy associate rewards and punishments with their network of social relationships; the individual becomes a passive recipient of either good or bad fortune (see Conley & O'Barr, 1990). Obviously, inmates are in prison because they have broken some sort of societal rule, but often relationships have played a role in this: Taystee commits crimes because of her dependence on Vee, Piper became involved in the drug trade due to her relationship with Alex, Tiffany shoots the abortion clinic worker because she is offended by a remark.

As Piper changes in response to her incarceration, so do we. Where once we sympathized with her ties to the outside world, now we are proud of her as she becomes hardened, navigating the underworld, running her illicit prison panty business and trusting no bitch. We too have moved from a rules to a relational perspective.

The Holy Toast: The Inmates of Chelm

Despite First Amendment protection of religious exercise, in reality prison officials tend to give more support to mainstream, familiar practices than new religious traditions, such as the Cult of Norma. Norma's group provides a fast-forward parallel to the evolution of organized religious institutions, moving from spontaneous generation to heresy and schism to an authoritarian structure within the course of days rather than hundreds of years. The group borrows elements of many religious traditions as Norma re-enacts her life with Guru Mac. Leanne articulates the group's belief system even as she excludes and even bullies anyone who disagrees with her (*Where My Dreidal At*):

> We believe in kindness and acceptance. And finding the peace within that can then radiate out into the world and create change. And through silent meditation we address the roar of pain and loneliness and tame it. And through reflection we can see nothingness. And in nothingness we find clarity. We have faith.

The juxtaposition of Norma's group, culminating in the veneration of Toast Norma (a piece of toast with an image of Norma allegedly burned into it), with the manipulation of the kosher meal system provides a mounting groundswell of anti-religious sentiment as it veers into the realm of absurdity, culminating with

Angie consuming the bread in an effort to find communion with the special powers imparted by Toast Norma. Absurdity pushes stereotypes to the extreme.

Religious stereotypes abound in *OITNB*. Jews are great lawyers and good with money, Muslims are jihadists with bombs, Christians are inflexible hypocrites. Hidden lines divide one from the other until some outside force – like standing up against Captain of the Guard Piscatella's inadvertent replication of the Zimbardo prison experiment – forces them to stand together (*The Animals*). Some of this no doubt is caused by the need for comedic writing: what's funnier than a nun who stuffs a cell phone up her vagina to ensure the safety of her transgender friend in solitary confinement?

Perhaps Kohan is imitating Norman Lear's prejudice-reduction attempt with the bigoted Archie Bunker character who managed to embrace every prejudice and stereotype in existence while still remaining a lovable curmudgeon? Just as most people who tuned in to *All in the Family* did so to ridicule Archie, a minority of the audience found that Archie's views legitimated their own prejudice. Still others experienced an evolution in their own attitudes after watching, and ultimately the show accelerated the already-existing decline in racial prejudice during the 1970s. But Lear's portrayal of the lone bigot – always gently challenged by his wife and daughter or not-so-gently confronted by his son-in-law – exemplified racism as an individual attitude, and therefore a character flaw akin to a bad habit and something that might be changed. Kohan's stereotyped portrayals, whether they skewer race, sex, class, religion, or other aspects of social identity, demonstrate the systemic nature of prejudice. While individuals at Litchfield may utter slurs while targeting specific others, the undercurrent of stereotyping and bias is institutional and foundational to identity. Where we could easily dismiss Archie as an embarrassing outlier for his views, Kohan asks us to do the much harder work of stepping outside our own cultural framework and challenge the web of sociological forces that connect and detach us from one another. We are given so many biases to confront that the task becomes overwhelming. Do we begin with countering sexism? Racial bias? Religious practice? Social class? Capitalism itself?

What Jenji Kohan has written is a new Chelm story. In Chelm, the traditional Jewish folktale town, the population consists of stock types, noodleheads, who cannot seem to do anything right. Nothing truly evil happens, although there are plenty of problems that emerge. The Chelmfolk give complicated solutions to simple problems and simple solutions to complicated ones; they illustrate the absurdity of life. The schlimazel (a person with perennially bad luck, a victim of circumstance) and the schlemiel (one who participates in his own destruction, whose luck diminishes in direct proportion to his own efforts) are both well-worn tropes in Jewish literature, perhaps extending even to Biblical and Talmudic sources. Victimhood may be a prerequisite of the schlemiel's condition, but the schlemiel himself is unaware of the impending disaster until it occurs... unlike others, who have long anticipated his doom, and in the end, the schlemiel may even transform defeat into victory. Stories of towns filled with foolish people are not strictly Jewish; similar tales featuring Christian fools dating from the late 1500s have been found. Like the fools of Chelm, they too are so certain of their wisdom that they never permit common sense to interfere with their plans.

Certainly, bad things happen to the good people of Litchfield (and sometimes even to the bad people, too). But the tale skates along the surface, romanticizing prison life while pretending to pull back the curtain on the grim reality of incarceration. In much the same way that the residents of Chelm only realized there was a crisis in the village when they learned the word "crisis," so too do the residents of Litchfield struggle to come to grips with purgatory, redemption, hope, love, and death. And it is not only the inmates who are foolish. In one episode, *Low Self Esteem City*, a Latino man complains to Gloria that lighting the candle to St. Peter that she sold him didn't get him the job he wanted, and she responds, pragmatically, "You filled out another application and actually gave it to the employer, right?" "That wasn't in the instructions," he grumbles.

OITNB, like the foibles of the Chelmites, sometimes hits uncomfortably close to home, and its message occasionally needs to be softened by humor in order for the show to remain a digestible form of entertainment, especially as the series progresses and the comedic aspects become hidden under ever darker story arcs. Perhaps that is why awards shows keep moving it from comedy to drama and back again as we try to untangle the meaning of the message. At the end of Season 3 (with its insistent focus on religious themes), the prisoners are cavorting in the lake after a worker accidentally leaves a gap in the fence. No one attempts a real escape; simply enjoying those few minutes of freedom seems to be enough, whether it is Cindy using the lake as a mikvah to finalize her conversion or the healing power of the water to renew friendships and mend old wounds. Like Moses, the inmates can see the Promised Land on the other side of this metaphorical River Jordan (*Trust No Bitch*), but like Taystee, they cannot conceive of leaving the structure provided by Litchfield (*Fool Me Once*).

Certainly, the fictional Litchfield is based on the real Danbury that Kerman describes. The demands of television as a medium leave us with a significantly less nuanced portrait of the women and men in Piper's life, and the visual medium simultaneously is free to explore aspects of prison life not articulated by Kerman and is forced to use the visual tropes common to visual signification. Like the new inmate who marvels at how clean and pleasant Litchfield is, since there has been no screaming in the few minutes since she arrived and there is no blood on the walls, so too does Kohan for the most part provide a sanitized and romanticized vision of the prison experience. Even though audience members do not generally perceive media presentations as serious sources of information about issues such as crime and imprisonment, the (distorted) images presented do in fact contribute to the construction of social reality. Bill Yousman's study, *Prime Time Prisons on U.S. TV*, demonstrates the ways in which media presentations of prisons frame our perceptions by selecting and excluding certain content as well as emphasizing or de-emphasizing aspects of that content. We have developed a cultural narrative about prison as the number of persons incarcerated skyrocketed during the late 20th century, while crime actually decreased. *OITNB* does well in bringing up topics often absent in prison programming, such as poor health care, limited educational opportunities, abuse by the staff, bad nutrition, the challenges of post-release adjustment, inadequate correctional officer training, and the like. It also does a pretty good job in reflecting the types of offenses for which prisoners are incarcerated (largely drug-related and nonviolent offenses), and it introduces television audiences to many women whose beauty falls outside conventional television programming.

As in some other prison programs, the prison setting in *OITNB* is less important than the portrayal of the relationships, positive and negative, among the inmates, visitors, and staff. At the same time, those relationships are almost wholly shaped by the environment. Kohan's presentation of Jewish stereotypes in Season 3, for example, could be seen as comedic, offensive, educational, or dangerous reinforcement of already held biases, by different viewers. Comedic prison programming may not only misinform audiences about the reality of prison life, it can also contribute to a sense of complacency and slow prison reform efforts. *OITNB* depicts racial and ethnic tension in the prison as akin to middle school cliquishness, and suggests that these barriers can be broken through sincerity or shared interests (such as potential profit stemming from participating in Piper's panty business); it is *Mean Girls* goes to prison. And of course religion is connected with ethnicity. It forms a secondary form of community. Norma's "quiet energy" is very calming and, says Angie, "She's white, so I trust her magic more than the Spanish kind" (*Empathy is a Boner Killer*). Similarly, Taystee says to Cindy in the midst of an argument, "You've got to stop using slavery every time you want to justify some foolish shit," and Cindy replies "I'm just using it as a placeholder until I become Jewish and I can pin it on Hitler" (*Don't Make me Come Back There*). The intersectionality of race and religion comes into sharp focus when Judy King, the celebrity chef inmate whose story calls Martha Stewart to mind, ends her counterfeit relationship with Cindy not because Cindy is Black but because she is Jewish.

Islam was significant in its absence during the first three seasons (Janae Watson's strict Muslim father was the only mention), but in Season 4, a hijab-wearing character is introduced, and is placed in the bunk with Cindy mere hours following her "official" immersion in the lake-mikvah during the breakout. Cindy, never before having exhibited any evidence of racism or anti-Islam sentiment, sarcastically greets the newcomer with "Shalom," and the new inmate's response of "Salaam aleikem" sets the stage for a strained relationship that could be read as a (flawed) analogue to the Israeli–Palestinian situation. When Cindy confronts her new bunkmate, Alison, who is Muslim, about using space in their cubicle, the conversation incorporates both their Black and religious identities (*Power Suit*):

CINDY: You and Tova [her new Hebrew name] got beef.
ALISON: That's not your name. Black people been naming their kids some crazy
    shit but that's not on any list, unless the V is a 5 or something.
CINDY: It's Hebrew.
ALISON: Please, you ain't no Jew.
CINDY: You wanna say that again bitch? Like you were born in Karachi.

But intersectionality is what ultimately salvages the relationship between Alison
the Muslim and Cindy the Jew: they discover that their shared Black experience
(symbolized by their common belief in the Tupac death conspiracy) bridges the
gap (*Piece of Sh★t*). But absence is as important as presence. Even the introduction
of Alison Abdullah as a new inmate about whom we know little other than that
she wears a hijab (in which she stashes an illegal cell phone), offers little insight;
we never see her actually praying or practicing her religion. Her main purpose
appears to be a counter to Cindy's startling new dislike for Muslims, something
she mysteriously must have acquired during her conversion. When a bedbug
infestation causes the prison to burn mattresses and library books, the one book
they were afraid to burn was a Quran (*Bed Bugs and Beyond*). Similarly, the
Buddhist monks on bicycles with twinkling lights who convey Poussey to her
destination turn out to be simply part of an improv troupe, and even they cannot
find anyone to portray an Imam (*Toast Can't Never Be Bread Again*). Given that
almost 10% of inmates in actual prisons practice Islam, the symbolic annihilation
of Islam in *OITNB* cannot be ignored, and Kohan's motives for doing so may be
questioned.

Anti-religious sentiment abounds in the show, but within limits. Christians,
especially the fundamentalist evangelical variety, come in for lots of criticism.
Jews are lampooned. Catholicism, personified by the hypocritical Sister Ingalls, is
disparaged as dysfunctional. Cults of personality are a safe target. The Amish are
gently mocked. Wiccans come off better than other new religious traditions, and
Buddhists, Hindus, Jainists, Taoists and the like get little attention. Atheists
abound, but most of Litchfield's inmates are simply indifferent to religion most
of the time. If anything, the message is that religious practice is fine – in mod-
eration. Just as the rules for decorating the chapel specify: no religious symbol is
allowed that can't be removed (*The Chickening*). A death calls for gospel music,
regardless of identity (*Toast Can't Never Be Bread Again*). Sister Ingalls even tears
a page from her Bible to send a note to Sophia Burset in the SHU (*Bunny,
Skull, Bunny, Skull*).

A secular ethical code pervades the prison, however. In her book, Piper
Kerman discusses the code of mutual support with examples of using her new
electrical shop skills to fix other inmates' appliances or "paying it forward" by
providing new inmates with toiletries and shower shoes just as she had been
helped by others. When Big Boo, an atheist, tries to scam Pennsatucky's church
with a phony story of her having seen the light and turning away from her

lesbian sins, she finds that she is unable to compromise her hard-won identity in the end (*Finger in the Dyke*). Alex Vause leaves notes with the name of the correctional officer she killed and buried in the garden, saying that as bad as he was, his family should be able to mourn him (*Toast Can't Never Be Bread Again*). Even if an individual is not religious per se, there is a belief in mythic arcs.

Religion demarcates and delineates – darkness from light, good from evil, heaven from hell – in much the same way that prison demarcates and delineates the lived experience of both the inmates and the staff. Faith in the midst of powerlessness gives agency in the midst of control. But the message of *OITNB* is not one where faith – or even good works – leads to salvation, but rather one of spontaneous and whimsical randomness, much like the world of *Alice in Wonderland*. *OITNB*'s post-religious sensibility situates religious practice within the intersectional connections of race, class and gender; like Litchfield's mythical chicken, each individual must decide whether faith is an illusion or something to give meaning to life.

References

Conley, J. M., & O'Barr, W. M. (1990). *Rules versus Relationships: The Ethnography of Legal Discourse.* Chicago: University of Chicago Press.

Dubler, J. (2013). *Down in the Chapel: Religious Life in an American Prison.* New York: Farrar Straus and Giroux.

Goffman, E. (1961). *Asylums.* Garden City, NY: Anchor Books.

Kerman, P. (2011). *Orange is the New Black: My Year in a Women's Prison.* New York: Spiegel and Grau.

Pew Research Center. (2015, May 12). America's changing religious landscape. Pew Forum. Retrieved from http://www.pewforum.org/2015/05/12/americas-changing-religious-landscape/

Statista. (2011). Mean religious affiliation of inmates in U.S. prisons, as reported by prison chaplains in 2011. Retrieved from http://www.statista.com/statistics/234653/religious-affiliation-of-us-prisoners/

Yousman, B. (2009). *Prime Time Prisons on U.S. TV: Representation of Incarceration.* New York: Peter Lang.

INDEX